www.wadsworth.com

wadsworth.com is the World Wide Web site for Wadsworth and is your direct source to dozens of online resources.

At *wadsworth.com* you can find out about supplements, demonstration software, and student resources. You can also send email to many of our authors and preview new publications and exciting new technologies.

wadsworth.com
Changing the way the world learns®

United States Public Policy

A BUDGETARY APPROACH

Dianne Rahm
University of Texas, San Antonio

THOMSON
™
WADSWORTH

Australia · Canada · Mexico · Singapore · Spain · United Kingdom · United States

THOMSON
™
WADSWORTH

Publisher: Clark Baxter
Executive Editor: David Tatom
Development Editor: Sybil Sosin
Assistant Editor: Heather Hogan
Editorial Assistant: Dianna Long
Technology Project Manager: Mary Ho
Marketing Manager: Janise Fry
Marketing Assistant: Mary Ho
Advertising Project Manager:
   Nathaniel Bergson-Michelson

Project Manager, Editorial Production:
   Matt Ballantyne
Print/Media Buyer: Doreen Suruki
Permissions Editor: Sarah Harkrader
Production Service: Vicki Moran
Copy Editor: Sybil Sosin
Illustrator: Lotus Art
Cover Designer: Ross Carron
Compositor: Better Graphics, Inc.
Text and Cover Printer: Webcom, Limited

For more information about our products,
contact us at:
**Thomson Learning Academic
Resource Center
1-800-423-0563**
For permission to use material from this
text, contact us by:
Phone: 1-800-730-2214
Fax: 1-800-730-2215
Web: http://www.thomsonrights.com

Library of Congress Control Number:
2003105624

ISBN 0-534-63607-1

Wadsworth/Thomson Learning
10 Davis Drive
Belmont, CA 94002-3098
USA

Asia
Thomson Learning
5 Shenton Way #01-01
UIC Building
Singapore 068808

Australia/New Zealand
Thomson Learning
102 Dodds Street
Southbank, Victoria 3006
Australia

Canada
Nelson
1120 Birchmount Road
Toronto, Ontario M1K 5G4
Canada

Europe/Middle East/Africa
Thomson Learning
High Holborn House
50/51 Bedford Row
London WC1R 4LR
United Kingdom

Latin America
Thomson Learning
Seneca, 53
Colonia Polanco
11560 Mexico D.F.
Mexico

Spain/Portugal
Paraninfo
Calle/Magallanes, 25
28015 Madrid, Spain

To Anastasia

Brief Contents

Contents

Illustrations

Preface

There are a number of useful ways to approach the study of contemporary public policy. This book uses the budget as the primary lens through which to view it. While it is true that many issues of critical importance to public policy are not those on which we spend vast sums of money, there is much to be learned by looking at the way we do spend our money. Decisions about how much to spend, on what, and who has the authority to spend it speak volumes about our values, goals, and priorities.

Looking at budget numbers provides a useful context for understanding a key aspect of contemporary public policy, but numbers do not tell the whole story. To understand today's public policy, students need two companion frameworks. The first is an understanding of the institutions and actors that engage in policymaking at the federal, state, and local levels. The second is the perspective that history brings to understanding how we got to where we are and what problems we faced along the way.

The first three chapters of *United States Public Policy: A Budgetary Approach* lay the foundation for understanding the general context of public policy. Chapter 1, Public Policy Institutions and Actors, focuses on the executive, legislature, bureaucracy, and courts. Chapter 1 emphasizes the characteristics of these institutions that determine their capacity, including such indicators as budget, number of staff members, and scope of operations. This chapter introduces the role of the states, and all subsequent chapters frame the policy discussion in terms of federalism and intergovernmental relations. Chapter 1 also introduces the role of interest groups and other actors in the policy process.

Chapter 2, Policymaking Processes, details the policymaking process from the perspectives of the executive, legislature, bureaucracy, and courts. The section on the executive looks at the role of the president or governor as the manager of the executive branch and at the administrative powers that enable policymaking. Also highlighted is the ability of the executive to set the legislative agenda so that policy matters of interest are, hopefully, addressed. In the section on the legislature, the policy cycle is discussed. For the bureaucracy, the emphasis is on rule making. The section on the courts focuses on the effect of court decisions and judicial activism on public policymaking. Chapter 2 also discusses the role of the states, both in terms of implementing policies made at the national level and independently making policy in some critical areas.

Chapter 3, Paying for Programs, provides information on federal, state, local, and private-sector (regulatory compliance) spending. The chapter provides information on the major areas in which our society spends resources on public policy.

The next seven chapters describe the policies. The chapters are arranged in the order of decreasing governmental expenditure. Chapter 4 (Income Security Policy), Chapter 5 (Health Care Policy), Chapter 6 (Protection Policy), Chapter 7 (Education Policy), and Chapter 8 (Transportation Policy) all provide detailed descriptions of these policy areas. Keeping within the budgetary framework, each of the substantive policy chapters begins with a graphic that shows the relative devotion of federal and state dollars to the policy issue along with discussion of how many federal dollars flow to the states to support state implementation of federal policy. Chapter 9, Environmental Policy, is included under the budgetary rationale because of the large regulatory compliance expense imposed on industry, communities, and individuals. Chapter 10, Nonmonetary Policy Areas, departs from the basic framework to discuss policy areas of great importance that do not consume large sums of public or private dollars.

Each chapter begins with historical information that places policy in the context of United States tradition and past action. Each then describes the current organization and operation of programs implementing this policy area, and each ends with a discussion of the conflicts, concerns, and value and opinion differences that surround the policy area. The themes set out in Chapters 1 through 3—the shared roles of the presidency, Congress, federal bureaucracy, federal courts, and states in policymaking—are carried through the substantive chapters. The chapters include figures and tables that help explain or display the points made by the text.

At the end of each chapter is an annotated listing of Web sites that provide additional information about the topic of the chapter. The majority are government Web pages because the contents are likely to be accurate and the addresses are less likely to change than are those of nongovernment sites. In addition, each chapter ends with discussion questions and dedicated Web questions that an instructor may assign. Chapters also include a list of the key terms that are set in bold type within the text.

I wish to thank the thoughtful reviewers who provided very useful comments after reading the manuscript—Theodore J. Davis, Jr., University of Delaware; W. D. Kay, Northeastern University; and Kevin B. Smith, University of Nebraska. I also want to thank Leah Curran, Doreen Swetkis, and Tamara Sulak for their assistance with graphics, Web sites, and editing. I extend my gratitude to Dick Welna and Sybil Sosin for their encouragement, patience, and responsiveness. Any errors remaining within the text are mine alone.

Introduction

"FOLLOW THE MONEY"[1]

In 1940 in an article in the *American Political Science Review*, political scientist V. O. Key asked a question that has continued to challenge scholars to this day. The question was simple: "On what basis shall it be decided to allocate x dollars to activity A instead of activity B?"[2]

This question draws attention to public expenditures for public programs (which Key calls activities). How much should the government spend? On what? How do we decide on our nation's goals and priorities? Key's question also makes us think about how we raise the revenue to fund the programs. Who should pay for them? Who should be taxed, and at what level? Are we getting our money's worth? What level of government (federal, state, or local) most efficiently and effectively delivers programs? To what extent should we try to achieve national goals by requiring private citizens or private-sector companies to follow regulations (and assume the associated costs) that produce desired policy outcomes?

This book uses Key's question as the focal point of the study of American public policy. Many of the details of the answer to the question can be found in the budget. Budgets show how much money is available to be spent (revenues) and on what programs or policies the money is spent (expenditures). All levels of government maintain budgets. The federal budget reports annual federal revenues and expenditures, while state and local budgets reveal the same information at the state and local levels. State and local financial statements also list the money they receive from the federal government to operate certain programs or perform certain functions.

In many ways a budget is a fundamental policy document. Since it lists the financial obligations of the government, it tells us a great deal about the government's public policy priorities and goals. Budgets show what we are willing to pay for and what we are not willing to pay for. They reveal a great deal of information about how we want programs to run and who we want to pay for them.[3]

Budgets are also central policy documents from the revenue side. Even if there is general political agreement about the correctness of government action, there is always a question about how much to spend. Those who wish to spend money on programs are faced with the task of raising the money. Since most of the government's activities are financed through taxation, there is almost always a desire to provide the program at the lowest possible cost. Most public programs are expensive, and the price tags make us ask questions about the most appropriate use of funds.

Money spent on one program, by definition, cannot be spent on another. When we decide to allocate funds to one program rather than another, we create winners and losers. Understanding the pattern of budgetary support for a policy issue provides considerable insight into who might gain and who stands to lose.

Public programs, once established, generate many supporters (and perhaps detractors). By examining why one activity or set of influential actors commanded greater levels of financial support, we can explain a great deal about the public policy process. Established programs are rarely changed and new policy initiatives are rarely introduced without careful attention to existing program structures and implementation frameworks. The pattern of budgetary support over time reveals much about powerful interests and actors who might resist changing levels of program support. Attempts to modify long-standing programs or to introduce new programs that will shift funds can generate considerable friction. Reallocation of program funding says much about the ability of contending groups to muster and sustain adequate political support.[4]

SOCIAL VALUES AND PREFERENCES

An assumption implicit in the use of budgets as policy documents is that social values and preferences are revealed by the use of public funds. What public policies should the government pursue? What programs ought the government to fund? Responses to these questions disclose societal preferences. Ideology, as it is applied to public policy, implies a set of principles or values that underlie policy decisions. Ideology can be thought of as philosophy toward government as well as a set of beliefs, ideas, or thoughts regarding the appropriate role of government in society. People with different ideologies often disagree about the policies the country should follow. The controversies that swirl around decisions to fund certain programs or policies reveal the ideology underlying the viewpoints.

Some people prefer a smaller, less active government, while others prefer a more expansive and engaged government. Some think that government should play a role in both fiscal and social arenas, while others prefer the government to limit its actions in the social sphere. These values are the starting point for debate about public policy. Political philosophy guides decisions about the appropriate extent of public involvement in any particular set of policy issues. Ideology is closely linked to a preference for the type of programs the government should support.

Americans draw different conclusions when it comes to determining the appropriate role of government. While there are many different political ideologies, two—conservatism and liberalism—are dominant in the United States. Political parties, politicians, and voters often identify with one or the other position. Republicans tend to be ideological conservatives; Democrats to be ideological liberals. Within each of these main ideological groups, adherents differ in terms of how far left (liberal) and how far right (conservative) their views are.

Given the wide differences within these groups, what can be said about the social values and preferences of conservatives and liberals? Conservatives are more likely than liberals to stress reliance on individuals and families over reliance on government. Conservatives are typically opposed to a large role for government (especially the federal government) in American life. On the other hand, conservatives are willing to allow the use of government to control social behavior that they consider immoral or inappropriate. Government control of drug use and vice is considered acceptable by conservatives. Many conservatives would like to see the role of government expanded to include the prohibition of abortion. Typically, when conservatives are interested in putting government programs in place, they are more likely to favor implementation by state or local governments rather than the federal government. The exception may be in the arena of national and homeland defense. The terrorist attacks in New York and Washington, D.C., on September 11, 2001, generated a demand for the federal government to play a wider role in preventing terrorism and maintaining the security of the nation, which many conservatives support. Conservatives are willing to accept unequal social and economic circumstances as long as they were arrived at with equality of opportunity in place. Differences in income, for instance, are acceptable to conservatives as long as each person had an equal chance to acquire a high income. Conservatives believe that the appropriate role for government is to make sure that opportunity is available to all, but that each individual is personally responsible for her or his own success.

Liberals typically support a wide role for the government, in particular for the federal government, since it is the only nationwide organization with the capacity to deal with perennial problems such as poverty, racism, and inequality. Liberals are apt to see government in general and the federal government in particular as responsible for providing for the overall economic and social welfare (well-being) of all individuals living in the United States. Liberals tend to view the government as the defender of the individual. Liberals are interested in equality of outcome in addition to equality of opportunity. Liberals believe that there are widespread inequities in society and that some people are less able to take advantage of opportunities than others. Liberals generally believe the government ought to play a role in promoting greater equality of outcome.

The differences between conservatives and liberals result in disagreements when it comes to public policymaking. In some cases, a policy desired by liberals might be viewed by conservatives as a matter of personal responsibility and not a subject for any public action. In other cases, values may underlie the design of programs and policies, effectively limiting program size and scope. Since liberals and conservatives hold such radically different views of the correct role of government, these ideologies have a direct effect on which public policies and programs they will support.

The traditional American dislike for taxation is a major factor in determining which public policies we undertake. Revenue generation is also ideologically charged. Conservative Republicans, for instance, chastise "tax and spend" Democrats, arguing that money is better left in the pockets of citizens who can invest it or spend it to meet their needs, rather than have the federal government decide what those needs are. Democrats counter by complaining about Republican willingness to provide tax cuts to the wealthy rather than providing for the needy poor. The debate underlying support for supply-side economics or demand-side economics (Keysian fiscal policy) is revealed by the revenue side of a budgetary analysis (supply-side and demand-side economics are discussed in Chapter 3).

THE SETTING OF POLICYMAKING

Funding decisions occur under the shadow of changing national and international political, demographic, and economic realities. In times of national emergency or war, defense programs demand priority, which can result either in increased overall expenditure or in the reduction of non-defense-related programs. For example, the terrorist attacks on the World Trade Center and the Pentagon on September 11, 2001, followed by the mailing of several anthrax-contaminated letters, alerted government managers of the need to rapidly divert resources to homeland security. Federal, state, and local governments began to reallocate or increase funding of programs critical to domestic security. Sorting out the correct balance between increased security and the civil liberties of Americans has had dramatic effects on American public policy.

Over the last few decades, a major international economic transition toward a more integrated world economy has been in process. The growth of multinational corporations, the expansion of free-trade zones such as NAFTA

(North American Free Trade Agreement), and the negotiation of worldwide trade agreements through international organizations such as the World Trade Organization (WTO) have substantially altered the basic U.S. economic framework. The increasingly globalized economy has highlighted the differences between the developing and the developed nations. Income gaps between rich and poor nations increasingly factor into domestic policy debates. American public policy functions under the influence of and in response to the globalization trend.

Profound changes in the American workforce have occurred in reaction to economic globalization. Movement toward a high-tech, science- and technology-based economy and away from the industrial base has created a demand for a better, specially educated workforce. People with the requisite skills benefit from the changing economy, but the others fall behind. Despite overall national economic growth, many Americans have not shared in the bounty. Even during good economic times, many lack access to health care and other fundamental needs of life. When economic downturns hit the economy, the poor bear a heavier burden. Bridging the gap between Americans able to thrive in the changing economy and those left behind by it is a critical issue for domestic public policy. Should the government intervene on the behalf of workers in this shifting economic landscape, and what role should it play?[5] Deciding how much to spend to help displaced workers and on what programs to spend it challenges policymakers.

Changes in the international political and economic order are not the only overarching factors that affect the cost of and need for domestic public programs. Another critical factor is demographic change. The United States is an aging society. Programs such as Social Security and Medicare function on the basis of intergenerational transfers of funds. The younger workers pay into the programs, while the older beneficiaries draw the funds out. As long as the number of workers and beneficiaries is roughly equal, this system works well. Changing demographic trends, however, threaten its fiscal health. As society ages, there will be too many beneficiaries and not enough workers to keep the programs financially solvent. The expected benefits may not be there when we need them the most.[6]

Demographic trends play out in other policy areas as well. Education is particularly hard hit. The elderly and people still in their prime whose children are grown are less willing to support tax levies that benefit schools. This results in declining schools and eventually in an untrained workforce. Finding ways to ensure adequate school funding is a challenge. High levels of immigration may reverse some of these trends insofar as the immigrants are young workers. If they work for only a few years before receiving benefits, however, immigration trends could exacerbate these problems.

A trend of considerable consequence over the last two decades of the twentieth century was the demand for the reduction in the size and power of the federal government and the devolution of power to states and localities. No one person popularized this movement more than President Ronald Reagan, who, as leader of the Republican Party from 1980 to 1988, fully elaborated the call for devolution and a smaller federal government. It would be incorrect to suggest, however, that this belief was or is held only by conservative Republicans. Jimmy Carter, the liberal Democrat who preceded Ronald Reagan as president, also believed that the federal government was too big, and centrist Democrat Bill Clinton also pushed for a smaller federal government, as did his predecessor, George H. W. Bush.

The downsizing of the federal government that did occur in the 1980s and 1990s created challenges for states and localities. Reducing the size of the federal government is not the same thing as reducing the size of government. Indeed, if the functions of government are not reduced, reducing the size of the federal government merely passes those functions along to the states and localities. Transferring the functions without adequate sums of money to perform them generates the separate problem of unfunded mandates. If the states and localities lack the organizational capacity to undertake the functions, either they will not be performed or the unit of government receiving the task will have to grow.[7] As states were given greater responsibility for a variety of programs in the 1980s and 1990s, they too had a tendency to shift the responsibility to even lower levels of government.[8]

Calls for smaller federal government also came from George W. Bush early in his presidency, but the September 11 terrorist attacks resulted in a moratorium on calls for government downsizing. The attacks focused the nation's attention on the need for the federal government to deal with the crisis of terrorism. In the aftermath, Congress voted to federalize airport security and George W. Bush expanded the federal government by creating a new Department of Homeland Security. The failure of the intelligence community to detect the terrorist threat resulted in intense scrutiny on the FBI and the CIA. Local and state governments began to think carefully about improving their local public health units and protecting vital infrastructure against attack. The Department of Homeland Security was charged with finding ways to ensure that local, state, and federal governments had the capacity to deal with a world that seemed infinitely more dangerous.

Finally, the setting of American public policy is shaped by precedent. Policy is not made in a vacuum. The existing framework and structure has an enormous effect on future policy. Models of policy action that flow from the past and from the status quo are typically carefully examined before we accept a rival approach to a policy issue. Because of this propensity to what some have called incrementalism, one of the most powerful dynamics affecting future public policymaking is the "way we did it before." A well-worn joke describes the importance of this factor. A woman who is showing her son how to prepare a ham for roasting in the oven cuts off the end of the ham and throws it away. When her son asks her why she threw the end of the ham away, she replies that is how her mother taught her to cook ham. The son then asks his grandmother, who answers that it is the way her mother taught her to cook ham. So the boy asks his great-grandmother "Why do you throw the end of the ham away?" She tells him, "That's because that old brown pot I have is too small to fit a whole ham!" The way we did it before has an enormous influence on the way we do it now and the way we will do it in the future, even if we no longer understand why we decided to do it that way in the first place.

OVERVIEW OF THE BOOK

This book approaches public policy from a budgetary perspective. The chapters emphasize how much we spend, what we spend it on, and who influences the spending. This perspective draws from the context of the large trends that influence decision making in the policy issue area. Special attention is paid to the influential actors, policy framework, and implementation structure already in place to deal with particular policy issues. The tensions that result from changing circumstances that cause policymakers to reform current programs or launch entirely new initiatives are discussed.

The book begins with three chapters that lay the foundation for understanding the general context of public policy. Chapter 1, Public Policy Institutions and Actors, begins with the executive branch, the legislature, the bureaucracy, and the courts. The chapter emphasizes the characteristics of these institutions that determine their institutional capacity (budget, number of staff, and scope of operations). It introduces the role of the states, since all subsequent chapters frame the policy discussion in terms of federalism and intergovernmental relations (IGR). Chapter 1 also introduces the role of interest groups and influential actors in the policy process.

Chapter 2, Policymaking Processes, provides an overview of the variety of theoretical approaches to understanding policymaking and details the policymaking process from the perspectives of the executive, the legislature, the bureaucracy, and the courts. The chapter includes a discussion on how the president goes about influencing the national agenda. It addresses the policy cycle, the role of rule making and regulation, and the role of courts in policymaking, focusing particularly on court decisions that have had enormous policy effects. The chapter also discusses the role of the states, particularly their role in implementing policies made at the national level.

Chapter 3, Paying for Programs, begins with a general discussion of economic policy and provides an overview of fiscal and monetary policy as well as some details about the supply-side and demand-side approaches. Chapter 3 also presents information on federal, state, local, and private-sector spending (in terms of regulatory compliance). It discusses the major policy areas that consume the largest amount of federal and state public expenditures.

The next six chapters discuss the specific policies that together constitute the bulk of public policy expenditure. Chapter 4 (Income Security Policy), Chapter 5 (Health Care Policy), Chapter 6 (Protection Policy), Chapter 7 (Education Policy), Chapter 8 (Transportation Policy), and Chapter 9 (Environmental Policy) provide detailed descriptions of these policy areas. These topics were selected because they are the largest areas of spending in American public policy. The chapters seek not only to describe current policy but also treat the context of policymaking in order to explain the current programs. Each chapter explores the tradition of policymaking for the particular issue, the current state of policymaking, and the tensions that create pressure for policy change. Each discusses the conflicts and concerns or differences in values and opinions that surround the policy area.

One can think of a budget as a general map of public policy. Examining how much we spend and on what activities will not fully reveal all of American public policy, but it takes us a long way toward such an understanding. Once we grasp the large picture, we can expand our understanding by looking at important but less expensive policies. Chapter 10, Nonmonetary Policy Areas, provides an overview of some of these.

Public policy is constantly changing, and new events date material written just weeks earlier. To help remedy this problem, each chapter includes URLs for World Wide Web sites that provide useful additional information. Each site is described so that students will get a sense of what they will find there. Taking advantage of material posted on the Internet will bring daily currency to the material in the text. Each chapter also includes a list of the key terms introduced in the chapter, general discussion questions, and Web exercises.

NOTES

1. Deep Throat's advice to *Washington Post* journalist Bob Woodward during his and Carl Bernstein's investigation of President Nixon's possible involvement in the Watergate break-in and cover-up.

2. V.O. Key, Jr., "The Lack of Budgetary Theory," *American Political Science Review,* 34, December 1940.

3. Aaron Wildavsky, *The Politics of the Budgetary Process* (Boston: Little, Brown and Company, 1964).

4. Randall B. Ripley, Grace A. Franklin, William M. Holmes, and William B. Moreland, *Structure, Environment, and Policy Actions: Exploring a Model of Policy-Making* (Beverly Hills, CA: Sage Publications, 1973).

5. Marshall McLuhan and Quentin Fiore, *War and Peace in the Global Village* (New York: Touchstone, 1968).

6. Clarke E. Cochran, Lawrence C. Mayer, T. R. Carr, and N. Joseph Cayer, *American Public Policy: An Introduction,* 6th ed. (Boston: St. Martin's, 1999).

7. Richard Stillman II, *The American Bureaucracy: The Core of Modern Government,* 2nd ed. (Chicago: Nelson-Hall Publishers, 1996).

8. Laurence J. O'Toole, Jr., "American Intergovernmental Relations: An Overview," in *American Intergovernmental Relations,* ed. Laurence J. O'Toole, Jr. (Washington, DC: CQ Press, 2000), 1–31.

1

Public Policy Institutions and Actors

On Friday, January 11, 2002, the Energy Department cleared the way for the construction of a large, centralized underground storage facility to hold the nation's nuclear waste. According to Energy Secretary Spencer Abraham, the government had concluded that it was safe to store tons of nuclear waste in a facility planned to be built in Yucca Mountain, ninety miles northwest of Las Vegas, Nevada. This announcement culminated a protracted program history dating back to the 1950s. Since the beginning of the atomic age, the United States had tried to figure out what to do with the toxic waste from nuclear reactors. Nearly half a century later, the Energy Department finally decided that the proposed repository at the Yucca Mountain site was a scientifically sound way to dispose of the nation's spent fuel and recommended that the president authorize construction.

The Energy Department announcement was immediately challenged. Nevada officials and environmentalists protested that there was overwhelming scientific evidence that the groundwater under the mountain would become contaminated. They also argued that the Energy Department had ignored the risks of transporting the waste, which was currently being held in temporary cooling ponds at operating nuclear power plants, through forty-three states to Nevada. Numerous lawsuits were filed in the courts. President George W. Bush signaled that he would approve the project, and Nevada Governor Kenny Guinn announced his opposition. When the state of Nevada rejected the plan,

Congress was put in the position of having to override the state's veto. Then Senate majority leader Thomas Daschle vowed to block the Yucca Mountain project.

The dispute is about more than the siting of a nuclear facility in the American desert. Rather, the decision about Yucca Mountain is an episode in the ongoing policy debate over the use of nuclear power in the United States. Developed in the aftermath of World War II, the nuclear industry grew until an accident occurred at Three Mile Island, Pennsylvania, in the 1970s. After that, no new nuclear power plant was commissioned in the United States. Prior to the Three Mile Island accident, however, more than a hundred nuclear reactors had been built, and they continue in operation. These plants currently store all the spent fuel that they have generated since they began operations, and they continue to generate additional waste.

The forces that favor the use of nuclear power not only need to convince the American public that nuclear energy is safe, but they also need to solve the problem of disposal of nuclear waste. The concept of building a national repository to safely house all the nation's waste was developed in the 1980s. Although Congress authorized the scientific selection of a site, politics drove the process, and in 1987 Congress ruled out nine other potential sites and settled on the desert in Nevada. Nevada residents believe they have been singled out because they lack political influence in Washington.

The Bush administration supports the project as a means of expanding the use of nuclear power in the United States. After the terrorist attacks on New York and Washington, D.C., on September 11, 2001, the administration and the nuclear industry made a case for the urgent construction of the Yucca Mountain facility because of the risk they say is associated with keeping the waste in cooling ponds near nuclear reactors. These locations are far more vulnerable to terrorist attack, they argue, than Yucca Mountain would be.

The story of Yucca Mountain reveals mind-bogglingly slow, expensive, and irrational policymaking. Fifty years and $6.8 billion dollars later, there is still no resolution to the issue of nuclear power use or a place for the safe permanent storage of nuclear waste. Is the Yucca Mountain story typical of public policymaking in America, or is it an oddity? Before we can answer that question, we have to answer a few others. Just what is public policy? Who makes public policy? This second question can be divided into two smaller questions. What government institutions are involved in policymaking? Who has the power to influence those institutions? The answers to these simple questions provide a good starting point for the investigation of U.S. public policy.

WHAT IS PUBLIC POLICY?

There are many definitions of public policy. Most include some recognition that public policy in some manner involves government. For our purposes, **public policy** can be defined as a course of action followed by government in response to an issue of public concern. Governmental courses of action include actions taken by the president, laws passed by Congress, regulations posted by government agencies, and court decrees. Adherence to these governmental decisions is not optional. Public policy is backed by the coercive power of the state. Failure to comply with laws, rules, or court decrees can result in incarceration, fines, or both.[1]

When government decides to act, the result is most often the establishment of a public program that spends government revenues to achieve a desired outcome. Government revenues are most often generated by income tax, although sometimes funds for public programs are raised through user fees or special taxes. For example, when the government decides to build a new weapons system, the funding comes from general taxation. When the government decided to provide a national repository for spent nuclear fuel, a special tax was placed on the nuclear power industry to raise money. National parks, which operate on sums paid by the people visiting them, are an example of programs funded by user fees.

Public policies can also be put in place by government regulation. In this case the government determines the desired outcome and passes a law requiring companies to implement and pay for their own programs to achieve the sought-after results. For example, when the Clean Air Act was amended in 1990, it required the Environmental Protection Agency (EPA) to regulate a large number of chemicals and other pollutants that had previously been uncontrolled. After passage of the act, private industry was held responsible for putting programs in place to eliminate the offending pollutants. Thus, public policy was enacted, but the required outcome (cleaner air) was to be paid for by the private sector.

Public policies can also be mandated by the courts. In 1954 in the famous case of *Brown* v. *Board of Education*, the U.S. Supreme Court ruled that segregated educational facilities were a violation of the Constitution. After the decision, it fell to all other levels of government to implement and pay costs associated with the desegregation of schools. Likewise, when the courts ruled that the overcrowding of prisons violated the rights of prisoners, states were required either to release prisoners or to assume the cost of expanding their corrections facilities.

Not all issues of concern to some portion of the public are acted upon by the government. The government may decide to do nothing about a particular issue because most people consider it to be a private, rather than public, matter. Public policy, then, also consists of what governments fail to do in response to an issue of public concern.[2]

FEDERAL PUBLIC POLICY INSTITUTIONS

The **legislature, executive, bureaucracy,** and **judiciary** are the formal institutions through which public policy is made on the national level. Articles I, II, and III of the Constitution are devoted to the design and function of the legislature, the executive, and the courts, respectively. The bureaucracy, which has expanded enormously since the establishment of the United States, is not given much attention in the Constitution. Despite this, the bureaucracy is a major actor in public policymaking.

The Founders of the Republic were careful to disperse power across government organizations so as to ensure that no one unit of government would have dominance. The notion of one part of government "checking" the other, which is commonly known as **checks and balances,** was a fundamental part of the design.[3] The Founders had an enormous fear of tyranny, and they sought to distribute power so that no one organization could control the entire government. Commonly referred to as the **separation of powers,** the distribution of authority across the executive, the legislative, and the judiciary seeks to ensure that no single institution will be able to dominate federal governance.

At the top of the organizational chart depicted in Figure 1.1 is the Constitution. This indicates that the United States is ruled by a system of laws and procedures agreed upon by the governed. The first three words in the Preamble to the Constitution, "We the People," denote the source of authority of the laws.

Figure 1.1 shows the three branches of government—the legislative, the executive, and the judiciary. The figure and Figure 1.2 also provide considerable detail about the bureaucracy, which consists of fifteen cabinet departments as well as a host of agencies, commissions, and boards. These bureaus are part of the executive branch. As the solid line on the chart suggests, all the organizations that comprise the bureaucracy are under the authority of the president of the United States. The sections that follow look briefly at each of these parts of the federal government. The discussion emphasizes how each institution is organized, indicates its size and scope, and suggests its key public policy roles.

Congress

At the federal level the legislative function is vested in **Congress,** which consists of two elected bodies: the House of Representatives and the Senate. The **House of Representatives** is comprised of 435 members of Congress elected for two-year terms. The states have varying numbers of congressional representatives based upon their population. Every ten years, a census counts the nation's population, and the new figures are used to reapportion the House of Representatives. The process of reapportionment adjusts the congressional districts so that the 435 House seats best represent the population of the country. Heavily populated states, like New York and California, have a greater number of Representatives than do states with modest populations, such as Wyoming. The **Senate** is comprised of 100 senators, 2 from each state, elected for terms of six years.

Congress has several key public policy roles. Its first major role is that it passes the laws that establish the programs that constitute much of American public policy. Congress has the **power of the purse,** or the authority to raise money through taxation and to spend it through appropriation.[4] In other words, Congress both establishes (or authorizes) programs to exist and appropriates

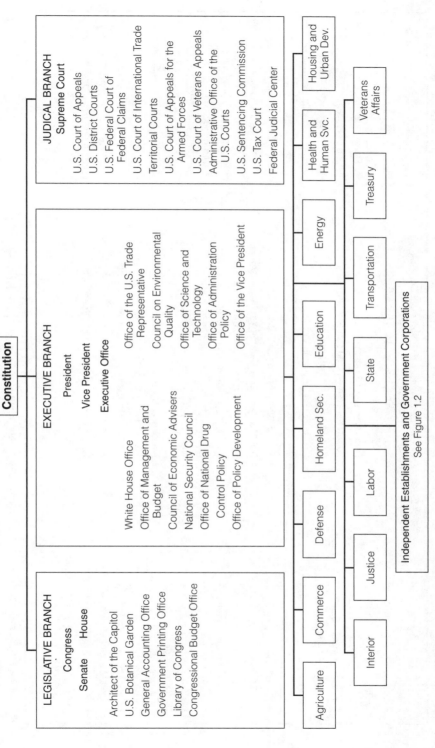

FIGURE 1.1 Organizational Chart of U.S. Government

SOURCE: Adapted from National Archives and Records Administration, *The United States Government Manual—2001/2002.* http://www.access.gpo.gov/nara/browse-gm-01.html, p. 22.

Independent Establishments and Government Corporations

African Development Foundation
Central Intelligence Agency
Commodity Futures Trading Commission
Consumer Product Safety Commission
Corporation for National Service
Defense Nuclear Facilities Safety Board
Environmental Protection Agency
Equal Employment Opportunity Commission
Export-Import Bank of the U.S.
Farm Credit Administration
Federal Communications Commission
Federal Deposit Insurance Corporation
Federal Election Commission
Federal Emergency Management Agency
Federal Housing Finance Board
Federal Labor Relations Authority
Federal Maritime Commission
National Mediation and Conciliation Service

Federal Mine Safety and Health Review Commission
Federal Reserve System
Federal Retirement Thrift Investment Board
Federal Trade Commission
General Services Administration
Inter-American Foundation
Merit Systems Protection Board
National Aeronautics and Space Administration
National Archives and Records Administration
National Capital Planning Commission
National Credit Union Administration
National Foundation on the Arts and the Humanities
National Labor Relations Board
National Mediation Board
National Railroad Passenger Corp. (Amtrak)
National Science Foundation
National Transportation Safety Board

Nuclear Regulatory Commission
Occupational Safety and Health Review Commission
Office of Government Ethics
Office of Personnel Management
Office of Special Counsel
Panama Canal Commission
Peace Corp.
Pension Benefit Guaranty Corporation
Postal Rate Commission
Railroad Retirement Board
Securities and Exchange Com.
Selective Service System
Small Business Administration
Social Security Administration
Tennessee Valley Authority
Trade and Development Agency
U.S. International Development Cooperation Agency
U.S. International Trade Com.
U.S. Postal Service

FIGURE 1.2 Organizational Chart of U.S. Government: Independent Establishments and Government Corporations

SOURCE: National Archives and Records Administration, *The United States Government Manual—2001/2002.* http://www.access.gpo.gov/nara/browse-gm-01.html, p. 22.

the money to run them.[5] A second and essential power of Congress is **oversight.** Congress has the authority to supervise the administration of programs that it has established to determine how well they are doing. Congress exercises this oversight by holding hearings, conducting investigations, visiting agencies, and consulting with the public and constituents about government programs and issues of concern.[6]

At a fundamental level, Congress is organized by political party. In the U.S. two-party system, this typically means Republicans and Democrats. Voters decide whether they prefer the Republican or Democratic candidate for each seat that is up for election. The party that wins the majority of the seats in each house of Congress becomes the majority party of that house. For instance, if the Democrats hold the greatest number of seats in the House of Representatives, they are the majority party in the House of Representatives. This means that the Speaker of the House would be the ranking Democrat, and all committees would be chaired and dominated by Democrats. Likewise, the Senate is run by the leadership of the party that wins the majority of Senate seats, and all committees are chaired and dominated by members of the majority party. One party, say the Democrats, might win the majority in the House of Representatives, while the other party, say the Republicans, might win the majority in the Senate, or one party might win both houses of Congress.

To do its work, Congress organizes itself into a series of **committees** and **subcommittees,** each with specific expertise. It is not possible for members of Congress to be experts on all matters. The division of Congress into committees and subcommittees allows members to focus their attention on a relatively small number of issues. This form of institutional design has several immediate consequences. First, the procedural rules followed by Congress make it difficult for legislation to be voted upon by either the House or the Senate without first being positively voted out of the committee with jurisdiction.[7] Second, Congress relies heavily on committee expertise. Most members of Congress defer to the opinions of their colleagues who serve as committee members and follow their lead in voting.[8] These two factors render committees very powerful.

The organization of Congress into committees and their power over policy goes back to the early Republic, when ad hoc, select, or special committees were established from time to time to deal with matters of concern. Permanent **standing committees** organized to deal with specific recurring matters of interest soon became a feature of congressional institutional design. Committees are typically organized to receive proposals for legislation and to produce bills ready to be voted upon. **Committee jurisdiction** is usually based upon the subject matter of legislation. Today the jurisdiction of standing committees (with the exception of the House Rules Committee and the House and Senate Appropriations Committees) parallels the major agencies in the executive bureaucracy.[9] These committees and subcommittees hold hearings and conduct investigations of programs in the parallel executive agency.

Tables 1.1 and 1.2 show the standing committees in the 106th Senate and House of Representatives (1999–2000). The Senate standing committees were

Agriculture, Appropriations, Armed Services, Banking, Commerce, Science and Energy, Energy and Natural Resources, Environment and Public Works, Finance, Foreign Relations, Government Affairs, Health, Education, Labor and Pensions, Indian Affairs, Judiciary, Small Business, Finance, and Rules and Administration. In the House, the standing committees were Agriculture, Appropriations, Armed Services, Banking and Financial Services, Budget, Commerce, Education and Workforce, Government Reform, House Administration, International Relations, Judiciary, Resources, Rules, Science, Small Business, Standards of Official Conduct, Transportation and Infrastructure, Veteran's Affairs, Ways and Means, and the Permanent Select Committee on Intelligence.

Committees are divided into subcommittees, each of which is given jurisdiction over specific matters. For instance, the House Committee on Commerce of the 106th Congress was subdivided into the subcommittees on Telecommunications, Trade and Consumer Protection, Finance and Hazardous Materials, Health and Environment, Energy and Power, and Oversight and Investigations. The jurisdiction of the Subcommittee on Finance and Hazardous Materials was "Securities, exchanges, and finance; solid waste, hazardous waste and toxic substances, including Superfund and RCRA (excluding mining, oil, gas, and coal combustion waste); noise pollution control; insurance, except health insurance; and regulation of travel, tourism, and time."[10] The subcommittee was charged with oversight for these areas.

Political parties play a critical role here. A member of the majority party chairs each committee or subcommittee. Members are assigned to committees by their party's leadership in the House and Senate, and they generally are given the assignments they request. Typically, members of Congress seek to be on the most prestigious committees and those that directly affect their constituencies. Prestige is determined largely by the extent of power of the committee. Committees of high prestige in the House are Appropriations, Budget, Commerce, Rules, and Ways and Means. Prestigious committees in the Senate include Appropriations, Armed Services, Budget, Finance, and Foreign Relations.[11]

A large number of staff members are assigned to committees and subcommittees to assist members of Congress with their legislative work. Time pressures and the ever-increasing complexity of policy issues force members of Congress to rely heavily on staff for advice and guidance. Tables 1.1 and 1.2 show the number of members and staff on the various committees. In the 106th Congress, there were 840 staff positions for Senate committees and subcommittees and 1,105 for House committees and subcommittees.[12] As these numbers suggest, committee work is substantial, and members of Congress require much assistance in the form of paid professional staff. The legislative branch of government also employs a large workforce to assist with the administrative, policy, management, and secretarial aspects of its work. In 1998 the legislative branch employed 31,000 civilian employees and met a payroll of $1.5 billion.[13]

Table 1.1 Committee and Subcommittee Membership and Staffing of the 106th Senate

Senate Committee	Rep.	Dem.	Total Members	Rep. Staff	Dem. Staff	Total Staff	Sub-committees
Agriculture[1]	10	8	18	20	6	26	4
Appropriations	15	13	28	11	5	16	13
Subcommittees	—	—	—	47	26	73	—
Armed Services[1]	11	9	20	34	12	46	6
Banking	11	9	20	30	10	40	5
Subcommittees	—	—	—	7	0	7	—
Budget	12	10	22	28	12	40	0
Commerce, Science & Energy	11	9	20	9	22	31	7
Subcommittees	—	—	—	19	0	19	—
Energy & Natural Resources	11	9	20	19	9	28	4
Subcommittees	—	—	—	10	9	19	—
Environment & Public Works[1]	10	8	18	25	7	32	4
Finance[1]	11	9	20	24	17	41	5
Foreign Relations[1]	10	8	18	31	15	46	7
Government Affairs	9	7	16	29	13	42	3
Subcommittees	—	—	—	28	13	41	—
Health, Ed., Labor & Pensions	10	8	18	28	16	44	4
Subcommittees	—	—	—	17	9	26	—
Indian Affairs	8	6	14	13	6	19	0
Judiciary	10	8	18	32	8	40	7
Subcommittees	—	—	—	24	22	46	—
Rules & Administration	9	7	16	13	5	18	0
Small Business	10	8	18	13	5	18	0
Veteran's Affairs	7	5	12	11	7	18	0
Select Committee on Ethics[2]	3	3	6	—	—	11	0
Select Committee on Intelligence[2]	9	8	17	—	—	28	0
Special Committee on Aging	11	9	20	8	5	13	0
Special Committee on Year 2000	5	4	9	—	—	12	0
Total	**203**	**165**	**368**	**530**	**259**	**840**	**69**

[1]Subcommittees operate from the offices of the full committees.

[2]Political affiliation of staff members not identified.

SOURCE: United States Congress, Senate, *Committee and Subcommittee Membership* (106th Congress). http://www.senate.gov/legislative/legis_act_committee_membership.html.

Table 1.2 Committee and Subcommittee Membership and Staffing of the 106th House of Representatives

Committee	Rep.	Dem.	Ind.	Total Members	Rep. Staff	Dem. Staff	Total Staff	Sub-committees
Agriculture	27	24	0	51	28	13	41	4
Subcommittees	—	—	—	—	6	4	10	—
Appropriations	34	27	0	61	16	12	28	13
Subcommittees	—	—	—	—	66	0	66	—
Armed Services[1,2]	32	28	0	60	—	—	52	7
Banking & Financial Services	32	27	1	60	18	7	25	5
Subcommittees	—	—	—	—	23	6	29	—
Budget	24	19	0	43	28	14	42	0
Commerce[1]	29	24	0	53	65	23	88	5
Education & Workforce[1]	27	22	0	49	56	21	77	5
Government Reform	24	19	1	44	29	29	58	8
Subcommittees	—	—	—	—	48	0	48	—
House Administration	6	3	0	9	20	13	33	0
International Relations	26	23	0	49	32	14	46	5
Subcommittees	—	—	—	—	15	5	20	—
Judiciary	21	16	0	37	29	17	46	5
Subcommittees	—	—	—	—	20	1	21	—
Resources	28	24	0	52	22	14	36	5
Subcommittees	—	—	—	—	22	0	22	—
Rules	9	4	0	13	20	10	30	2
Subcommittees	—	—	—	—	2	2	4	—
Science	25	22	0	47	18	7	25	4
Subcommittees	—	—	—	—	19	7	26	—
Small Business	19	17	0	36	15	5	20	6
Subcommittees	—	—	—	—	5	0	5	—
Standards of Official Conduct[2]	5	5	0	10	—	—	12	0
Transportation & Infrastructure	41	34	0	75	20	6	26	7
Subcommittees	—	—	—	—	29	22	51	—
Veteran's Affairs	17	14	0	31	10	2	12	3
Subcommittees	—	—	—	—	10	8	18	—
Ways & Means	23	16	0	39	22	10	32	5
Subcommittees	—	—	—	—	25	7	32	—
Permanent Select Committee on Intelligence	9	7	0	16	17	7	24	2
Total	**458**	**375**	**2**	**835**	**755**	**286**	**1105**	**91**

[1]Subcommittees operate from the office of the full committee.

[2]Political affiliation of staff members not identified.

SOURCE: *Congressional Yellow Book, Fall 1999 Leadership Directory*, 25, no. 3 (New York: Leadership Directories, Inc., 1999).

The Presidency

On the national level the **president** is the leader of the executive branch. Elected for a maximum of two four-year terms, the president plays a number of roles in making public policy. First, the president is the **commander in chief** and the lead actor when it comes to establishing American foreign policy. Second, the president has what President Theodore Roosevelt called the "bully pulpit," the ability to set the legislative agenda by persuading Congress to pass legislation the administration desires. This power is substantial. One of the most important ways the president communicates what the administration wants accomplished in the course of the year is by presenting Congress with a draft **presidential budget** for annual governmental spending. Third, the president has the power to **veto** legislation passed by Congress. Finally, the president is the managerial head of the executive branch of government, with extensive power over the operation of the bureaucracy.

The public policy powers of the executive rest largely on the ability of the president to set the legislative agenda.[14] This mainly occurs at the beginning of a new administration, when the incoming president announces the major administrative policy initiatives. Most presidents also avail themselves of an annual opportunity to influence the legislative agenda. Article II, Section 3 of the Constitution states that the president "shall from time to time give to the Congress information on the State of the Union and recommend to their consideration such measures" judged "necessary and expedient." The **State of the Union address** is typically given by modern presidents with great fanfare as they ceremoniously enter the halls of Congress and present their priorities for legislative action.[15] While the State of Union address may not always be a succinct list of presidential desires, it does provide the administration with an opportunity to inform Congress of preferred policy directions.[16]

The president plays a key role in setting the tone for the country's economic policy. The levels of taxation and spending are key to everything else that government does, and it is the president who elaborates a vision for how to manage the economy. One of the most significant ways in which the administration does this is by presenting Congress with a budget request, to be approved by Congress, for each fiscal year.

As managerial head of the executive branch of government, the president has two key policy roles. Since 1921 agency budget requests have been reviewed and approved by the **Office of Management and Budget (OMB)** before being sent to Congress. This gives the president extensive power over the planned activities of the bureaucracy. A president who frowns on a particular agency or a programmatic emphasis can simply cut or refuse the budget request.[17] Second, presidents have the power to appoint the senior bureaucrats who head the government's bureaus for the duration of the administration. In making these choices, presidents have some control over the direction bureaucracy will follow.[18]

The organization of the White House and its staff are important to an understanding of public policy. Before the 1920s presidents relied heavily on their cabinet secretaries for policy advice. By 1939, however, managing the presidency had become far too complex, and three permanent managerial changes were instituted. The first was the creation of the Executive Office of the President (EOP) as the official staff arm of the presidency. The second was that the Office of Management and Budget (called the Bureau of Budget until 1970) was moved from the Treasury Department into the EOP. Finally, the White House Office (WHO) was created within the EOP to serve as a smaller, more direct staff office to provide presidents with immediate advice and information.[19]

Even with these changes, presidents struggle with the managerial task of supervising so many people. The total number of executive staffers has varied from time to time. During World War II, President Franklin D. Roosevelt (FDR) ran the war effort out of the White House; as a consequence, the number of executive staffers grew to nearly two hundred thousand. After the war, the number dropped rapidly. For most of Harry Truman's, Dwight Eisenhower's, and John Kennedy's administrations, the executive staff averaged about two thousand employees. Under the Great Society programs of Lyndon Johnson's administration, the staff averaged about four thousand, and it grew during the Richard Nixon years to more than five thousand. Gerald Ford cut the number back substantially, to less than two thousand, and subsequent presidents have maintained that level. Ronald Reagan's administration had an executive staff of about fifteen hundred. The George H. W. Bush administration employed an executive staff of about seventeen hundred, which William Clinton reduced to about fifteen hundred.[20] The large size of the White House staff suggests a certain amount of organizational complexity. Greater size brings communications challenges and the real possibility of the emergence of competing policy goals from among the many subunits.

The Bureaucracy

Unlike the other institutions of government that comprise our national system, the bureaucracy is not fully specified in the Constitution. While the executive, legislative, and judiciary each have a full article of the Constitution devoted to them, the bureaucracy is mentioned only in passing. For instance, under a listing of powers granted to Congress in Section 8 of Article I, the Constitution references certain functions of government such as providing for an army and navy, coining money, creating standards for weights and measures, establishing post offices, and protecting the rights of inventors. These functions have become institutionalized in, respectively, the Department of Defense, the Department of Treasury, the National Institutes for Standards and Technology (formerly the Bureau of Weights and Standards), the U.S. Postal Service, and the Office of Patents and Trademarks. The function of performing a census of the population every ten years (and thus the foundation for the U.S. Census Bureau) is also specified in the Constitution (Article I, Section 2).

The bureaucracy has expanded enormously over time. As Congress passed laws to regulate areas that the Constitution specified as within its domain of authority, many government programs were established. The first major growth spurt came during the Great Depression in programs instituted during the administration of Franklin D. Roosevelt. In the early 1930s Congress approved a large number of new programs as part of what came to be called the New Deal. These initiatives provided for the stabilization of the banking industry (the Emergency Banking Act), work and shelter for the destitute and unem-ployed (the Civilian Conservation Corps), regulation of agricultural prices and production (the Agricultural Adjustment Act), grants to the states so that they could help the poor (the Federal Emergency Relief Act), a major economic development program in the hard-hit southeast (the Tennessee Valley Authority), the regulation of the securities industry (the Federal Truth in Securities Act), a national system of state-run public employment offices (the Wagner-Peyser Act), financial protection for homeowners (the Home Owners' Loan Act), and a major industrial policy effort to stabilize industry (the National Industrial Recovery Act).[21] Each created or expanded government bureaus to oversee and manage a host of new programs. The Roosevelt admin-istration also created what is today the largest single federal program, Social Security.

The bureaucracy reached another point of great expansion in the 1960s with the establishment of President Lyndon Johnson's Great Society programs. Among these were several large health and poverty programs, including Medicare, Medicaid, and food stamps. Each necessitated the creation of large bureaus. By the late 1980s the executive branch of government employed about 3 million civilians, most of whom worked in bureaucratic positions over-seeing and running government programs.[22] By 1990 the federal workforce had grown to 3.2 million, but the trend of expansion reversed after 1990 in response to widely accepted political goals to reduce the size of the federal government. As of 2000, however, the executive branch still employed 2.8 mil-lion people in its departments, agencies, boards, and commissions.[23] With the emphasis on homeland security in the aftermath of the 2001 terrorist attacks, the federal government once again began growing. The Justice Department, intelligence agencies, and the military expanded, and the federalization of airport security alone added thousands of new employees to the federal workforce.

A better sense of the size of the federal bureaucracy can be had by comparing it to American corporations. In 1999 the largest single private-sector employer in the United States was Wal-Mart, which employed 910,000 workers. To Wal-Mart's employees, we could add the workers of General Motors (594,000), Ford (363,000), General Electric (293,000), IBM (291,000), and Boeing (210,700), and we still would not match the size of the federal bureaucracy.[24]

The bureaucracy is generally thought of as having a key role in public pol-icymaking. Its main function is to implement the policies called for by con-gressional legislation, which typically involves provision of services through government programs as well as the establishment and enforcement of rules and regulations. The rulemaking and enforcement authority granted to agen-cies by Congress is a powerful policy role. Moreover, Congress frequently writes vague legislation, which vastly increases the extent of administrative discretion exercised by bureaucrats. Congressional instructions to bureaucratic organizations are frequently no more detailed than "to establish regulations suitable and necessary for carrying this law into effect; which regulations shall be binding."[25]

The Courts

The federal courts play a significant role in public policymaking in several ways. Their case-by-case decisions set precedents for later cases. In public policy this role is important because interest groups bring "test" cases to court so that the court's decision will set a precedent for future decisions by other judges. Second, the courts interpret the intent of congressional language in legislation. Third, while not specifically stated in the Constitution, judicial power over policymaking has been vastly enhanced by the successful attempt on the part of the courts to review acts of other branches of government and invalidate those they view as unconstitutional. This is referred to as the power of **judicial review.** Not only do courts invalidate legislation passed by Congress, but they also hear appeals on decisions made by regulatory agencies (concerning both individual cases and general regulations).[26]

The prominent public policy role of the courts has a long history in the United States. They have traditionally acted as a referee between contending actors disagreeing over controversial issues. Frequently, the contention has involved highly visible policy outcomes. Before the Civil War, for instance, the courts were involved in disputes over the appropriate role of the federal government, states rights, and slavery. In the Progressive Era, the courts mediated the growing problems of urbanization and industrialization, often acting to protect property rights. With the passage of large volumes of Depression era legislation, the courts eventually moved from protecting property to protecting civil rights. In *Brown* v. *Board of Education* in 1954 they began an extensive public policy role in civil rights, which would continue and expand.[27] Indeed, the agenda of the Supreme Court after *Brown* shifted away from a focus on economics to more clearly address the issues of social and moral policy.

The federal court system is composed of several types of specialty courts (such as tax courts and international trade courts) and three types of general courts. These general courts, which do most of the work of the system, are district courts, courts of appeals, and the Supreme Court.

For most cases, the point of entry into the federal judicial system is the **district court.** Most cases go no farther, and these are the main courts of the federal system. There are ninety-four federal district courts, one in each judicial district. Each state has at least one judicial district, and some states have several. Cases in a district court are tried by a single judge, with or without a jury. Decisions can be appealed to the federal courts of appeals. The **courts of appeals** are organized based upon twelve circuits. Cases are decided by panels of three judges. The highest court is the **Supreme Court.** Its size, determined by Congress, has been set at nine since 1869.[28]

The court system has grown substantially over time. In 1925 there were fewer than two hundred federal judges. By 1995 there were more than eight hundred. Similarly, in 1925 the entire federal court system employed just over twelve hundred people, including judges, magistrates, law clerks, secretaries, and probation officers. By 1995 more than twenty-six thousand people worked in the federal court system.[29]

The workload of the courts is substantial. For fiscal year 1995, more than 283,000 cases were filed in the federal district courts, about 16 percent of which were criminal cases and 84 percent civil cases. Of those, about 47,000 made their way to the courts of appeals. The Supreme Court decides which cases merit its attention. As a consequence, far fewer cases are heard. In 1994 the Court heard only 94 cases.[30]

THE ROLE OF THE STATES

Not all areas of public concern fall to the federal level of government for programmatic action. State and local governments have primary authority for large areas of public policy, including elementary and secondary education, public health and safety, disaster emergency response, and provision of such services as highway maintenance, libraries, water and sewer utilities, and public hospitals. The states share power with the federal government in many areas of public policy, including environmental protection, social welfare, economic development, and job training.

The division of power between federal and state governments was established by the Constitution. The federal government was given the powers enumerated in the first three articles of the Constitution. The Tenth Amendment reserves all powers not clearly delegated to the federal government (or prohibited to the states) for the states. This division of power is often referred to as **federalism,** and the interactions between the different levels of government are referred to as **intergovernmental relations (IGR).**

The states draw their authority from their citizens, who draft and approve the state constitutions. A state constitution establishes the executive, legislative, judicial, and bureaucratic framework for the state. Local governments within the states include municipal governments, counties, townships, school districts, and special districts (for example, flood control districts).[31] In addition, there are a host of interstate compacts that deal with problems that cross state lines.[32] In areas of current policy in which both the state and federal governments have power, such as taxation, federal law is superior when there is a conflict between it and state law. In other words, a state law may not overturn or lessen the effect of a federal law.[33]

Federal power grew over time. The Fourteenth Amendment made the federal government the guarantor of individual rights, thus expanding its role. In addition, the commerce clause (Article I, Section 8, clause 3) came to be interpreted more broadly, and the federal government used the idea of regulating commerce between the states as an opportunity to regulate industries such as transportation, food, and drugs. To raise the money to support these new federal efforts, the Sixteenth Amendment created a national income tax.

Troubled times also increased the power of the federal government. FDR's grants-in-aid to state and local governments helped them finance Depression era programs designed at the federal level but implemented in the states. The 1960s brought another wave of increased federal support to state and local governments. To implement policies desired by the federal government that were controversial in many states, the federal government created a series of federal–local partnerships that often bypassed state governments entirely. Federal money was carefully allocated in the form of categorical grants, whereby the state or local government applying for the funding was carefully monitored by a federal agency.[34]

This process of transferring federal revenues to states and localities in the form of grants to be spent on specific programs is a key feature of public policy. The federal government partners with other levels of government by providing full or partial funding for programs implemented and managed on the lower level. Many human service, agricultural, transportation, education, training, and environmental programs receive some, if not all, of their funding from the federal government.

If there has been a general trend in intergovernmental relations over the last several decades, it has been the restructuring of intergovernmental relationships to emphasize state and local control.[35] President Richard Nixon's **revenue sharing** program began the process by making federal money available to states and localities without extensive federal controls over their use. President Ronald Reagan had an even greater effect with his policy of **New Federalism,** which provided even greater policy flexibility and control to the states. The steady ascendancy to the presidency of former state governors (including Arkansas Governor William Clinton and Texas Governor George W. Bush) has ensured that the states receive a hearing at the highest level of the federal government.

The Supreme Court has taken a special interest in the role of the states over the last decade. For instance, the Brady Handgun Violence Prevention Act of 1994, which required local law enforcement officers to implement federal gun control background checks, was successfully challenged in the Court. The Court held that requiring local officials to conduct federal background checks was a violation of the Tenth Amendment (*Printz* v. *United States,* 1997).

Public policy in the last several decades has been affected by the trend of federal government downsizing. The efforts to reduce the size of the federal government have been accompanied by a movement toward **devolution,** the transfer of federal functions to the state or local level. As the federal presence has grown smaller, the role of the states and localities has become more important.

OTHER PUBLIC POLICY ACTORS

There are a large number of other potential actors in public policymaking. Besides judges, members of Congress, the president, and the vast staffs that attend to them, there are political parties, policy advocates and interest groups, the media, and members of the public and the business community who are interested in particular issues and policy outcomes.

Political Parties

Political parties play an important role in policymaking. Their chief influence is on the ideology regarding which policies should be promoted and which should not. **Party platforms,** or official statements of party opinion on particular issues, are determined by delegates at party conventions. Platforms are sometimes thought to be no more than rhetorical statements of the party's values. However, they are frequently illustrative of the true values and social preferences of influential party members.

Parties play two roles—one in the electorate and the other in the government.[36] In the electorate, parties vie for dominance among voters. In the United States, third parties have been rare and short-lived, and the battle is primarily between Republicans and Democrats. The parties fight to get greater percentages of the electorate to support and vote for their candidates. In government, the battle has to do with the control of the presidency, majority control of each house of Congress, and the size of the majority party's margin in each house of Congress. The degree of control reveals how confident a party might be of moving its agenda forward.

Interest Groups

The First Amendment states, "Congress shall make no law . . . abridging the freedom of speech, or of the press; or the right of the people peaceably to assemble, and to petition the Government for a redress of grievances." Numerous policy advocacy or **interest groups** take this right very seriously. These groups vary widely in ideology and the means they undertake to achieve desired policy outcomes. Some are tightly associated with particular industries or trade associations. Others form around shared ideology or values. Groups such as the National Rifle Association, the Sierra Club, Mothers Against Drunk Driving, the Chemical Manufacturers Association, the League of Women Voters, Planned Parenthood, the Cato Institute, the Heritage Foundation, and Earthfirst! differ greatly; yet they share the common goal of wanting to influence policy outcomes.

Most interest groups restrict their activities to peaceful participation in the democratic process. Interest groups use petition drives to influence public opinion and thus win the attention of members of Congress. They produce and distribute literature that explains their positions on policy issues. They may raise enough money to hire professional lobbyists or use volunteers to **lobby** members of Congress and staff. By knocking on doors and talking with staff and members of Congress, they attempt to communicate their views and desires. Through lobbying activities, interest groups provide the information that they consider essential to understanding a policy issue. Interest groups ask the general public to write, call, or send e-mail to their representatives. Interest groups often appear at public hearings and enter formal comments about proposed policies. They may raise funds and give the money to political candidates running for reelection.[37]

Some interest groups and policy advocates engage in public protests and civil disobedience to try to influence the policy debate. The civil rights marches of the 1960s and the anti–Vietnam war protests of the 1960s and 1970s were very successful in influencing public opinion and policymakers. The more recent Million Mom March in Washington, D.C., for gun control and the public protest against the World Trade Organization in Seattle in 2001 are recent examples of this type of civic activism. Members of environmental interest groups have chained themselves to trees to keep them from being cut down. Some militant groups have engaged in violent guerilla tactics, including driving long nails into trees so as to cause a chain saw to recoil and kill its operator, in order to save trees from loggers.

The business community can be particularly effective in influencing public policy, particularly at the state and local levels. Communities, states, and the country as a whole are sensitive to the need for jobs. Government actions that might adversely affect job creation or retention are likely to cause concern. The business community also has financial resources from which to draw in its attempts to weigh in on policy approaches.

The Media

The First Amendment's protections of freedom of speech and the press created an environment for the development of a number of well-established written and broadcast **media** in the United States. The media have a long reach, and nearly all Americans have access to some of them. They affect policy debates by providing space and time to discuss policy issues, and they can give an issue high salience by providing this forum.[38]

The media used to be dominated by a tiny elite. Three major broadcast channels (ABC, NBC, and CBS) and a handful of influential national newspapers, journals, and news services (the *New York Times,* the *Wall Street Journal,* the *Washington Post, Time, Newsweek, U.S. News and World Report,* and the Associated Press) took precedence in informing debate. Their dominance has been challenged by the rise of cable broadcast news providers such as CNN and stations that deliver direct coverage of national policy events without journalistic commentary such as C-SPAN. The greatest threat to the preeminence of the elite, though, has been the emergence of news providers using the Internet as a means of delivery. The unique nature of the Internet as a non–peer-reviewed source has made it difficult to guarantee the accuracy of reports, but its effect should not be underestimated.

Public Opinion

Not all members of the community are involved in policy debates. Many people are not even interested. Those who do have an interest, however, can influence policy outcomes in a variety of ways. As voters, they can alert their representatives about their views on policy issues. They can donate money to causes that interest them and to politicians who support those causes. They can participate in public forums and express their viewpoints by writing letters to newspapers and other public sources. In the era of the Internet, members of the public have access to a host of chat rooms and listservs where they can air their views.

Common measures of general public opinion include surveys of trust in government, ratings of presidential job handling, ratings about the most serious problems facing the nation, consumer confidence in the economic future of the country, and general public concern over specific policy issues. Overall, public opinion has an influence on governance in that the common measures say something about how the people feel about their leaders. Public attitudes can affect the choices the leaders make.

SUMMARY

This chapter focused on three related questions: What is public policy? What government institutions are involved in policymaking? Who has the power to influence those institutions? We defined public policy as a course of action by government in response to an issue of public concern. Sometimes government decision makers see an issue as a private matter or as better handled by the private sector. In this case, there will be no government action, and public policy consists of what government fails to do in response to an issue.

The legislative branch, the executive branch, the bureaucracy, and the judiciary each has a special role in the policymaking process. The legislature writes the laws and is responsible for overseeing implementation. The division of Congress into committees and the general reliance on committee reports places decision-making power in the hands of a relatively small number of members of Congress. The president sets the legislative agenda by persuading Congress to pass legislation that the administration desires. The president is the managerial head of the executive branch of government, with extensive power over the operation of the bureaucracy. The courts influence public policy when they render judgments on individual cases as well as on appeals over bureaucratic rules. The bureaucracy is charged with implementing public policy. When the extent of administrative discretion is significant, the bureaucracy exercises enormous influence in not only the implementation of policy but in its formation as well.

Many actors are involved in public policy. These include all the people working in the executive, legislative, and judicial branches, including judges, members of Congress, the president, and their staffs. State and local governments play a critical role. The general trend over the last several decades has been the restructuring of intergovernmental relationships to emphasize state and local control. A large and varied group of special interests influence public policy. Interest groups differ in ideology and the means they undertake to influence policy outcomes. The media affect policy debates by providing a forum for policy debate. Finally the attentive public plays a role in public policymaking by voting and voicing opinion.

KEY TERMS

bureaucracy

checks and balances

commander in chief

committee

committee jurisdiction

Congress

courts of appeals

devolution

district court

executive

federalism

House of
Representatives

interest group

intergovernmental relations (IGR)

judicial review

judiciary

legislature

lobby

media

New Federalism

Office of Management
and Budget (OMB)

oversight

party platform

power of the purse

president

presidential budget

public policy

revenue sharing

Senate

separation of powers

standing committees

State of the Union
address

subcommittee

Supreme Court

veto

WEB SITES

The Constitution

http://www.house.gov/Constitution/Constitution.html
This U.S. House of Representatives Web page contains a copy of the Constitution with footnotes that explain which sections of the original text have been superceded by amendments. The text of the Constitution is suitable for downloading or printing.

http://www.law.emory.edu/FEDERAL/usconst.html
This is an easy-to-navigate site that allows the user to select articles and sections of the Constitution by clicking on a simple table of contents.

http://www.nara.gov/exhall/charters/constitution/constitution.html
This National Archives and Records Administration site contains hyperlinks to the biographies of delegates to the Constitutional Convention. The site also underscores sections of the original Constitution that have been superceded and links them to the amendments that overrode them.

The Legislature

http://www.house.gov
The official home page of the United States House of Representatives makes it easier for citizens to communicate with their elected officials. By clicking on *Write Your Representative*, you can identify and send an e-mail message to your representative. Other interesting highlights include tracking legislation currently being considered by the House through *The Legislative Process*, and a link to Thomas, the Library of Congress service through which you can search for legislation by bill number, topic, or title. The site also contains links to the rules of the House and the U.S. Code.

http://www.senate.gov
The official home page of the Senate lets you access your senators' home pages and send them e-mail, as well as track current legislation as it moves through the Senate. A major highlight is the U.S. Capitol Virtual Tour (http://www.senate.gov/visiting/index.html), found by clicking on *Visiting the Senate* at the top of the page and then clicking on *Visiting without leaving home*.

The President and the Bureaucracy

http://www.whitehouse.gov
This is the official Internet address of the White House and the executive branch of the government. Here you can take a tour of the White House and write to the president, vice president, cabinet, or White House offices and agencies. Highlights from this home page include the following.

http://www.whitehouse.gov/WH/glimpse/tour/html/index.html
A virtual tour of the White House, including photos of furniture, artwork, and china.

http://www.whitehouse.gov/WH/Cabinet/html/cabinet_links.html
An index page with links to the agencies in the president's cabinet. Currently, there are fourteen departments in the cabinet.

http://www.whitehouse.gov/WH/EOP/html/EOP_org.html
Provides information on presidential initiatives, such as the national AIDS policy, and links to the Executive Office of the President and agencies.

http://www.whitehouse.gov/WH/Independent_Agencies/html/independent_links.html
An index page with active links to the official home pages of federal agencies and commissions. If you do not find a particular bureaucratic organization, look under a larger department. For example, the Bureau of Prisons is found under the Department of Justice, which is a department in the cabinet.

The Courts

http://www.uscourts.gov/outreach
By clicking on *Understanding the Federal Courts,* you can access a PDF file that outlines the federal court system, including the U.S. Constitution, the

structure of the courts, jurisdiction, and the judicial process. Adobe Acrobat Reader, a free software application, is required to view PDF files.

The States

http://www.state.**.us
Replace the two asterisks with the two-letter postal abbreviation of the state you are looking for in order to access its official home page. For example, to access the state of Ohio home page, type *http://www.state.oh.us/*. Some states have moved their Internet home pages to different addresses, but this URL provides easy access to most official state sites.

Other Actors

http://opensecrets.org
Because so many entities fall into the category of other actors, it is difficult to find an "official" comprehensive and up-to-date list of these groups. One good source of information is the Center for Responsive Politics. From this page, you can access information on political action committees (PACs) and lobby groups.

The Media

http://www.cspan.org
The official Internet address of cable television channel C-SPAN. This site has live feeds from the floors of Congress, as well as taped events. C-SPAN is one of several media outlets on the Internet in which you can find information on public policy.

http://www.pbs.org/neighborhood/news
Provides access to political programs and news pieces that were recently aired on the Public Broadcasting System.

DISCUSSION QUESTIONS

1. Define and discuss the term *public policy*.
2. Name and discuss the roles of the branches of government that make public policy.
3. What are the functions of congressional committees and subcommittees?
4. Look at Figure 1.1, and discuss the entity at the top of the organizational structure.

WEB QUESTIONS

1. Find a copy of the U.S. Constitution at http://www.house.gov/Constitution/Constitution.html. Why was the Constitution established, as stated in the Preamble?

2. Go to http://www.house.gov/. Identify your representative and list his or her contact information and committee memberships.

3. A good source of information on other actors in the public policy arena is the Center for Responsive Politics, at http://opensecrets.org. From this page, access information on political action committees (PACs) and lobby groups. What five industries contribute the most to political campaigns?

4. Go to http://www.house.gov and click the link to Thomas. Use Thomas to track a bill through the Senate or the House. List the bill number, the member of Congress who introduced it, and why it was introduced.

5. Compare two state Web sites. How easy was each to navigate? Could you easily access the state constitutions? Was there more tourist information than government information? How easy was it to find a way to contact state government officials?

6. Go to one of the official home pages of a bureaucratic agency (a cabinet department or an independent agency), and discuss how many different places the public can access the agency. For example, does the agency's site provide names, e-mail addresses, phone numbers, mailing addresses, and the like of key people in the agency, or is there just one person or place to contact? Does the site have a separate link to a public forum? Does the agency indicate when it will be holding public meetings?

NOTES

1. Clarke E. Cochran, Lawrence C. Mayer, T. R. Carr, and N. Joseph Cayer, *American Public Policy: An Introduction* (Boston: St. Martin's, 1999).

2. Thomas R. Dye, *Understanding Public Policy,* 8th ed. (Englewood Cliffs, NJ: Prentice-Hall, 1995).

3. Alexander Hamilton, John Jay, and James Madison, *The Federalist: A Commentary on the Constitution of the United States* (New York: Modern Library, 1937).

4. Jack E. Holmes, Michael J. Englehardt, Robert E. Elder, Jr., James M. Zoetewey, and David K. Ryden, *American Government: Essentials and Perspectives,* 3rd ed. (New York: McGraw-Hill, 1998).

5. Allen Schick, *Congress and Money: Budgeting, Spending and Taxing* (Washington, DC: The Urban Institute, 1980).

6. Theodore J. Lowi and Benjamin Ginsberg, *American Government: Freedom and Power,* 5th ed. (New York: W.W. Norton & Company, 1998).

7. Charles E. Lindbloom, *The Policy Making Process* (Englewood Cliffs, NJ: Prentice-Hall, 1968).

8. Steven Kelman, *Making Public Policy: A Hopeful View of American Government* (New York: Basic Books, 1987).

9. Lowi and Ginsberg, *American Government.*

10. Welcome to the House Committee on Commerce: 106th Congress. http://comnotes.house.gov/cchear/hearings106.nsf/main.

11. Holmes et al., *American Government.*

12. United States Congress, Senate, *Committee and Subcommittee Membership* (106th Congress). http://www.senate.gov/legislative/legis_act_committee_member-ship.html. Also see Leadership Directories, Inc., *Congressional Yellow Book, Fall 1999 Leadership Directory,* 25, No. 3 (New York: Leadership Directories, Inc., 1999) and United States Congress, Senate, *Committee and Subcommittee Membership* (106th

Congress). http://www.senate.gov/legislative/legis_act_committee_membership.html (12/1/00).

13. U.S. Census Bureau, *Statistical Abstract of the United States: 1999,* 119th ed. (Washington, DC: U.S. Government Printing Office, 1999).

14. Lance T. LeLoup and Steven A. Shull, *Congress and the President: The Policy Connection* (Belmont, CA: Wadsworth, 1993).

15. Paul C. Light, *The President's Agenda: Domestic Policy Choice from Kennedy to Clinton,* 3rd ed. (Baltimore: Johns Hopkins University Press, 1999).

16. John W. Kingdon, *Agendas, Alternatives and Public Policies,* 2nd ed. (New York: Addison-Wesley, 1995).

17. Kelman, *Making Public Policy.*

18. Cornell G. Hooton, *Executive Governance: Presidential Administrations and Policy Change in the Federal Bureaucracy* (London: M.E. Sharpe, 1997).

19. Lyn Ragsdale, *Vital Statistics on the Presidency: Washington to Clinton* (Washington, DC: Congressional Quarterly, 1998).

20. Ibid.

21. David Brian Robertson and Dennis R. Judd, *The Development of American Public Policy: The Structure of Policy Restraint* (Glenview, IL: Scott, Foresman and Company, 1989).

22. U.S. Census Bureau, *Statistical Abstract, 1999.*

23. U.S. Census Bureau, *Statistical Abstract of the United States, 2001,* 121st ed. (Washington, DC: U.S. Government Printing Office, 2001).

24. *Corporate Yellow Book,* 15, no. 4 (1999).

25. Cornelius M. Kerwin, *Rulemaking: How Government Agencies Write Law and Make Policy,* 2nd ed. (Washington, DC: CQ Press, 1999).

26. Christopher E. Smith, *Courts and Public Policy* (Chicago: Nelson-Hall Publishers, 1993).

27. Martin Shapiro, "The United States," in *The Global Expansion of Judicial Power,* ed. C. Neal Tate and Torbjorn Vallinder (New York: New York University Press, 1995), 43–49.

28. Lawrence Baum, *American Courts: Process and Policy,* 2nd ed. (Boston: Houghton Mifflin, 1990).

29. Richard A. Posner, *The Federal Courts: Challenge and Reform* (Cambridge: Harvard University Press, 1996).

30. Robert A. Carp and Ronald Stidham, *Judicial Process in America,* 4th ed. (Washington, DC: CQ Press, 1998).

31. Alfred De Grazia, *The American Way of Government* (New York: John Wiley & Sons, 1957).

32. David C. Saffell, *State and Local Government: Politics and Public Policies,* 5th ed. (New York: McGraw-Hill, 1993).

33. De Grazia, *American Way of Government.*

34. Cochran et al., *American Public Policy.*

35. Charles O. Jones, *An Introduction to the Study of Public Policy,* 3rd ed. (Monterey, CA: Brooks/Cole, 1984).

36. Randall B. Ripley, "Policy-Making: A Conceptual Scheme," in *Policy-Making in the Federal Executive Branch,* ed. Randall B. Ripley and Grace A. Franklin (London: Collier Macmillan Publishers, 1975), 1–20.

37. Jones, *Introduction to the Study of Public Policy.*

38. Dye, *Understanding Public Policy.*

2

Policymaking Processes

A budgetary approach to the study of public policy allows us to explore overarching policy preferences, goals, and priorities. Studying policy through the lens of the budget focuses attention on outcomes. An understanding of policy also requires some sense of the processes involved in policymaking. This chapter looks at these processes. At the federal level, there are four distinct processes to consider. Each is associated with the institution that is the driving force behind the policymaking.

Much public policy is the result of laws passed by Congress. Congress often leaves much of the detail work of policy implementation to the federal bureaucracy when the legislation directs the bureaucracy to make any regulations necessary for carrying out the law. Congress often passes laws at the request of the president. Indeed, a critical role of the executive is setting the congressional agenda. Finally, the federal courts are involved in policymaking by rendering case-by-case judgments, interpreting congressional intent, exercising judicial review, and hearing complaints regarding bureaucratic regulations.

State public policy processes mirror federal-level practice. A state legislature passes laws that create policy for the state, and the state bureaucracy acts in much the same way as the federal bureaucracy to implement the laws. State courts intervene when cases are brought forward questioning state law or policy implementation. The U.S. system of federalism also gives the states a special role in policymaking. States are often called upon by the federal government to implement, within their own borders, public policy programs that have been passed by the federal government. This chapter first looks at federal policy-making processes and then turns to a discussion of the separate role of the states.

Many theories seek to explain the policymaking process. These theories can be grouped into three main clusters. First, there are several theories that focus on agenda setting, or answering the question, What policy actions does government consider? Second, there are theories that attempt to explain the decision-making process in policymaking, How do we decide what we should do? Finally, there are theories that try to explain policymaking from the framework of policy types. Each of these groups of theories is discussed in this chapter.

PRESIDENTIAL POLICYMAKING

Presidents play a pivotal role in foreign policymaking. Both as commander in chief and as the principal diplomatic negotiator, a president can take the lead in determining the path the nation will follow internationally. At the most fundamental level, a president may engage American troops in combat. The president may seek a formal declaration of war from Congress. As the figure the world looks to for the "American" position on events, presidents have enormous power. Indeed, since the Second World War, the American president has been known as the "leader of the free world." Presidents sign treaties that indicate the willingness of the nation to comply with international agreements. Presidents, of course, must submit treaties to the Senate for ratification, but presidents may heavily lobby for Senate support. A president may also announce the intention of the government to withdraw from a treaty.

Presidents also play a critical role in domestic policymaking. Along with the constitutional power of the veto, presidents have other ways to influence the agenda of Congress. Presidents tell Congress what legislation they would like passed. While presidents have no power to write legislation themselves, they are well equipped to use the media and other popular forms of communication to demand specific actions from Congress. The extent to which presidents are successful depends on their ability to persuade. If a president can rally public support for a proposal or action, Congress is likely to go along. Presidents also take advantage of the State of the Union address to directly tell Congress what they would like to see passed and to set some priorities for desired legislation.

The role presidents play in the **budgetary process** gives them great power to steer public policy. The annual budgetary process begins with the preparation of the president's budget and its submission to Congress. This budget details the president's priorities by telling Congress what the administration wants to spend money on and how much. It is sent to Congress for discussion, change, and approval early in each legislative session. The whole cycle is lengthy, consuming the better part of several years.

While the Constitution does not require the president to make recommendations concerning the revenues and expenditures of government, since

1921 the presidential budget has been one of the most important presidential policy tools. By estimating revenues, expenditures, borrowing, and debt for the next fiscal year, the president's budget reveals the administration's legislative and policy wishes consistent with monetary requests. Because the budget details borrowing and debt levels, it discloses much about the president's management of the economy. The budget also provides information on the performance of the economy over time as well as the actual expenditures of government agencies and programs.[1]

CONGRESSIONAL POLICYMAKING

Public policy scholars typically focus on legislative policymaking. This process has a series of key stages, which are depicted in Table 2.1 and described below.[2]

Problem Perception/Definition

The process begins when the issue is first perceived as a general social concern. The central question asked at this stage is, What is the problem? The way the issue is perceived and defined will have much to do with policy formulation. Problem perception and definition are clearly affected by the number of people who consider the issue a problem and how well organized they are. The people who consider an issue to be of primary importance may be too few in

Table 2.1 The Policy Process Model

Problem Perception/definition
Agenda Setting
Formulation
Budgeting
Implementation
Evaluation/adjustment/termination

A Policy Process Model*

- Perception/definition — What Is the Problem?
- Agenda Setting — How Is Agenda Status Achieved?
- Formulation — What Is the Proposed Solution?
  Who Supports It and How Is Support Maintained?
- Budgeting — How Much Money Is Provided? Is It Enough?
- Implementation — Who Administers the Program?
  Do They Command Support?
- Evaluation/adjustment/termination — What Changes
  Need to Be Implemented?

* Adapted from Jones, Charles O., *An Introduction to the Study of Public Policy*, Brooks/Cole: Monterey, CA, 1984.

number or too poorly organized to command the attention of actors within government who have the power to change public policy.[3]

For example, let's say that over the course of a few weeks gasoline prices rose drastically and the price increase was severe enough to get everyone's attention. What is the problem? Are the oil companies gouging the public by unreasonably charging excessive rates? Is there a fuel shortage due to the limited number of refineries that can make gas in compliance with the Environmental Protection Agency's (EPA) clean air standards? The way the problem is perceived will affect the type of policy formulated to address it. If it is a case of corporate greed, the Federal Trade Commission can be called in to investigate. If EPA standards are to blame, perhaps policy formulation will deal with reversing clean air standards. The perception and definition of the problem will drive the solution.

Issue perception is the beginning of the policy process and in many respects sets the stage for the rest of the process. If, for instance, the issue of homelessness is perceived as a problem of a lack of affordable housing, the solution will involve policy to increase the number of low-cost housing units. On the other hand, if those who seek a solution to the issue of homelessness define the problem as lack of treatment facilities for the mentally ill, who then wander the streets without a place to call home, the solution will involve a policy to provide more hospital beds in mental health facilities.

It is possible for a problem to be a matter of social concern and yet be perceived in a way that prohibits government action. In the U.S. system, when problems are viewed as private rather than public, government intervention typically does not occur. For instance, some observers could consider homelessness to be a matter of personal choice, of decisions by some people to live as hobos. Given that definition, little public policy response is needed.

The way we perceive issues can change over time. For a very long time, providing financial aid (welfare) to poor families was perceived of as an appropriate and necessary federal government role. That perception changed drastically in the mid-1990s, resulting in the passage of the Personal Responsibility and Work Opportunity Reconciliation Act. That law dramatically reduced the role of the federal government as a financial provider for the poor.[4] Our perception of immigration has also changed several times since this nation was founded. At times immigrants were seen as very desirable, and immigration laws were open and inviting. At other times immigrants have been viewed with suspicion, and laws have been restrictive. Perception and definition change public policy.

Agenda Setting

What does "getting on the agenda" mean? The word *agenda* is often used in different ways. In terms of public policy, agenda status is obtained when influential actors inside government recognize a problem as something they want to pay serious attention to.[5]

Much has been written about the process of **agenda setting** and the conditions necessary for an issue to achieve agenda status. Crisis, for example, is often cited as a reason for the rapid achievement of agenda status.[6] The quick passage of Superfund legislation to clean up dangerous hazardous waste sites across the nation in the wake of the toxic chemical contamination of the Love Canal community in western New York is one example. The September 11, 2001, attacks on New York's World Trade Center and the Pentagon in our nation's capital riveted attention to the critical problem of terrorism. Having a focusing event, whether crisis or not, is extremely helpful in moving an issue to national agenda status.[7] Events can rapidly catapult an issue into the center of the national stage.

Agenda status is often achieved when those in powerful positions, especially the president, personally adopt an issue. Being on the president's "must list" can drive an issue forward for public action very rapidly.[8] President Dwight Eisenhower's "Atoms for Peace" speech launched the civilian nuclear power industry in the United States. In a similar manner, President John Kennedy's desire for American achievement in the space race culminated with the moon landing.

Agenda status is easier to gain when policy experts think they have a solution to a pressing issue. With a viable solution at hand, the political will often arises to do something about a problem. When known problems have no ready solution, however, it is unlikely that they will achieve agenda status.[9] Failure to get on the agenda does not mean that a problem goes away. Rather, the problem persists, but government will not do anything about it.

Policy Formulation

Policy formulation consists of plans made by legislators as they write laws to address policy problems. Congressional staff, lobbyists, consultants, and policy experts have considerable input into the substance of policy. At this stage of the policy process, they hammer out the general guidelines of how a particular policy problem will be addressed. Policy formulation is the stage at which decisions are made regarding a realistic solution to the perceived policy problem.[10]

Policy formulation flows from policy goals, which must be clearly elaborated for the formulation to be successful. Goals can be long range (the decade-long goal of landing on the moon) or short term (immediately reducing crime rates by putting more police on the streets). Formulation is intimately tied to policymakers' overall conception of policy outcomes. The fundamental questions at this stage of the policy process are, What kind of program is envisioned, and what type of results are expected?

Policy formulation gets at the large questions of program size and scope. There are a variety of possible formulations within one policy issue. In the area of health care policy, for instance, a narrow policy targeting only the elderly might be developed. This is what happened with Medicare. Presidents as far back as Franklin Delano Roosevelt sought to widen the formulation of health care policy to all U.S. residents, but a universal health care policy has not yet been successful in passing through Congress.

Budgeting

The framework for budgeting comes out of policy formulation. After the general size and scope of a program are decided, it is essential to determine how it will be funded. There are various alternatives and key questions to consider. Should the policy evenly distribute its outputs across all groups, or will there be redistribution of resources? Congress could decide that a general tax will fund a program for all Americans; for example, all taxpayers pay for and benefit from national defense. Conversely, Congress could decide to use tax money from one group to fund a program that will benefit another group. Policies that redistribute resources from one group to another include Social Security, welfare, and food stamps. Policymakers are keen observers of how proposed policies will affect their constituents.[11]

Another financing alternative is for Congress to impose a fee only on people who are directly linked to a program as recipients of program outputs or key players in the issue addressed by the policy. Paying for entry into a national park is an example of this type of financing. Only those enjoying the park are taxed, and only they receive the benefit of the government program. Another example of this type of financing is the special tax levied on the civilian nuclear power industry in exchange for the construction of a national repository to house the nuclear waste their facilities generate.

While not all policy requires funding, the amount of money devoted to a problem is an indicator of the relative importance of the policy. Often policies that have a moral component do not require large expenditures of public funds. For instance, efforts in support of "family values" are largely rhetorical, as opposed to substantive, yet few would deny the impact of this line of policy in recent years. Most important policy, however, requires the dedication of funds.

Congressional budgeting is an annual process. Each year, Congress adopts a **budget resolution** that specifies budget totals and priorities. Congress reviews the presidential budget request drawn from agency requests for funding and presidential priorities and compares it with the congressional budget resolution, makes decisions on what to fund and at what level, and appropriates monies for programs to spend during the next year. Prior to giving new programs money to spend, Congress authorizes them by legislation. This authorizing legislation specifies details about the organization and its duties.[12]

Only about one-third of the money appropriated each year by Congress is classified as discretionary spending. Programs within the Defense Department, the operating costs of most federal agencies, and many of the grants made each year to states and local governments involve discretionary spending. A vast portion of the annual budget is set aside for entitlement programs, like Social Security and Medicare, that are controlled by legislation that sets eligibility criteria and payment formulas. Congress is not permitted to fund these programs at levels that differ from those mandated by the law.[13]

Implementation

Implementation involves the day-to-day activities of the programs that Congress has authorized and given an annual appropriation. Congress leaves the implementation of public policies largely up to the agencies and departments that make up the bureaucracy. In some cases Congress will have given agency management strict and clear guidelines specifying exactly how the program is to be run. In most cases, however, Congress allows program administrators a wide range of discretion.[14]

Government programs can be implemented in two general ways. Either the agency itself can carry out the delivery of service necessary to put the law into effect, or the bureaucracy may oversee a private contractor that is hired to provide the service. Both approaches have a long history of use. The Departments of Defense and Energy, for instance, often hire private contractors to provide equipment and services. The military does not build its own planes, but instead buys them from defense contractors. Similarly, the Department of Energy hires management companies to run weapons complex facilities. The social service agencies have provided their own services for many years, but they too are relying more and more on private companies for service delivery.

Evaluation

After a program that carries out a public policy has been in place for a while, it is often subject to evaluation.[15] The evaluation takes the form of an internal or external review of program outcomes and processes to determine whether it is indeed in accord with congressional intent as expressed in the authorizing legislation. The Government Performance and Results Act of 1992 emphasized the need for agencies to develop measures to evaluate performance.[16] Congress has also insisted on periodic evaluation by writing "sunset" provisions into legislation. If an evaluation of a program shows that it is not working well, it may be subject to **modification** or even **termination.**

A program that was drastically modified because of general dissatisfaction with results and processes is welfare. Put in place as part of the New Deal legislation of the 1930s and expanded vastly during the Great Society period of the 1960s, the nation's welfare program gradually came to be viewed as a failure. After several unsuccessful reform attempts, the program was drastically modified with the passage of the Personal Responsibility and Work Opportunity Reconciliation Act of 1996. The act replaced the old Aid to Families with Dependent Children (AFDC) program with the new Temporary Assistance to Needy Families (TANF) program.[17]

Evaluation is frequently the weakest link in the policy process. It often is undertaken only because of well-publicized failure. For example, when the Enron Corporation declared bankruptcy in 2002, the scandal focused attention on the failure of the Security and Exchange Commission (SEC) to adequately oversee financial transactions. Within a month of the company's failure, Congress had convened eleven committee and subcommittee hearings to look into the problem. In a like manner, the flurry of committee investigations following the

2001 terrorist attacks on the World Trade Center and Pentagon exposed the scandalously poor state of public health agencies and their inability to respond to chemical or biological attacks. Other congressional inquiries explored the failure of the FBI and the CIA to prevent the attack. In both cases, public outrage led to a thorough evaluation of the policy in place at the time of the crisis and reassessment of its effectiveness.

BUREAUCRATIC POLICYMAKING

Agencies make policy when they implement programs authorized by Congress. Although Congress passes the laws and establishes the programs, Congress frequently provides the bureaucracy with great latitude regarding both the means and content of program implementation. Agencies are given the authority to make **rules** and regulations associated with carrying out the laws. This rule-making authority is significant in establishing the context of public policy.

Writing vague legislation and leaving the details of implementation to the executive branch has a long history. The earliest Congresses of the United States passed legislation giving the executive branch the authority to make regulations governing trade with Indian tribes. In 1816 Congress granted the Secretary of the Treasury the power to regulate the importation of goods into the United States. The legislation was extremely vague and said only that the secretary should "establish regulations suitable and necessary for carrying this law into effect; which regulations shall be binding."[18]

A more recent example is the instruction to the Environmental Protection Agency (EPA) in the Clean Water Act to make the nation's waters "fishable and swimable" while leaving it up to the EPA to determine what level of toxins would be permitted in the water.[19] When Congress created the Nuclear Regulatory Commission (NRC) through the Atomic Energy Reorganization Act of 1974, the NRC was instructed to regulate civilian nuclear power plants to guarantee safe operations.[20] The NRC has the authority to decide what levels of risk are allowed and to require private-sector firms to comply with their decisions.

Many agencies have been given regulatory authority by Congress. For instance, the Interstate Commerce Commission (ICC) regulates interstate commerce and business practices; the Securities and Exchange Commission (SEC) regulates securities and stock exchange activities; and the Food and Drug Administration (FDA) oversees the safety of foods and drugs.[21] The Environmental Protection Agency (EPA), the Bureau of Mines, the Bureau of Land Management, the Fish and Wildlife Service, and the Forest Service all play key roles in the regulation of the natural environment. The Federal Trade Commission regulates business mergers. The Occupational Safety and Health Administration (OSHA) sets working conditions. The Consumer Product Safety Commission regulates products to make sure they are safe. The Federal

Aviation Administration (FAA) controls air flight safety. The Federal Communications Commission (FCC) controls the airwaves. The list of agencies and their regulatory functions could go on and on.

The number of regulatory agencies grew vastly during the New Deal and again with the implementation of the Great Society programs in the 1960s. The largest growth took place in the 1970s with the passage of substantial legislation governing environmental quality as well as occupational safety and health.

The volume of rules made by regulatory agencies is substantial. In the two decades between 1977 and 1997, nearly 84,000 new regulations were put into effect. Thousands of new rules are written each year. In 1997 alone, over 4,500 new rules were implemented, and another 2,800 rules were in the process of being written.[22] The impact of these regulations on businesses and people's personal lives is substantial.

The process by which rules are made is specified in the Administrative Procedures Act of 1946 (APA). A regulatory agency must first publish a general notice of a proposed rule in the *Federal Register*, along with a statement of the time and place of public rule-making proceedings. Interested persons are given the right to participate in the rule-making process by submitting data, views, or arguments. After considering the comments submitted by concerned parties, the agency publishes a final rule in the *Federal Register*. The rule is also added to the Code of Federal Regulations (CFR), which is arranged into fifty "titles" by subject area. Title 21, for instance, covers Food and Drugs, while Title 26 is Internal Revenue and Title 40 is Protection of the Environment. Table 2.2 lists the fifty titles in the Code of Federal Regulations.

The large volume of rules and their impact on the personal and economic life of the country has resulted in attempts to control bureaucratic rule making. Presidents Jimmy Carter, Ronald Reagan, George H. W. Bush, and William Clinton each tried his hand at regulatory reform.[23] President Carter issued Executive Order 12044, which created a regulatory council that consisted of the heads of most regulatory agencies. The council was thought to help coordinate rule making across the different agencies so that conflicts on rules might be avoided. Along with the council, the Regulatory Analysis Review Group, headed by the Council of Economic Advisers, was created. This group looked at the economic impact of rules.

President Reagan continued most of Carter's reforms and added a few of his own. He issued Executive Order 12291, which put a sixty-day moratorium on new rules in place and required cost-benefit analyses of all upcoming major rules. Before a new rule could be put in effect, the issuing agency was required to show that its social benefits were greater than its cost. The Reagan order also required a review of all rules by the Office of Management and Budget.[24] The idea was to slow and reduce the number of regulations coming out of agencies. President George H. W. Bush continued the policies of the Reagan administration.

President Clinton also attempted to control the volume and impact of rules as part of his National Performance Review effort to improve the efficiency of government.[25] The Clinton administration emphasized such reforms as negotiated

Table 2.2 Titles in the Code of Federal Regulations

Title 1—General Provisions

Title 2—[reserved]

Title 3—The President

Title 4—Accounts

Title 5—Administrative Personnel

Title 6—[reserved]

Title 7—Agriculture

Title 8—Aliens and Nationality

Title 9—Animals and Animal Products

Title 10—Energy

Title 11—Federal Elections

Title 12—Banks and Banking

Title 13—Business Credit and Assistance

Title 14—Aeronautics and Space

Title 15—Commerce and Foreign Trade

Title 16—Commercial Practices

Title 17—Commodity and Securities Exchanges

Title 18—Conservation of Power and Water Resources

Title 19—Custom Duties

Title 20—Employees' Benefits

Title 21—Food and Drugs

Title 22—Foreign Relations

Title 23—Highways

Title 24—Housing and Urban Development

Title 25—Indians

Title 26—Internal Revenue

Title 27—Alcohol, Tobacco Products and Firearms

Title 28—Judicial Administration

Title 29—Labor

Title 30—Mineral Resources

Title 31—Money and Finance: Treasury

Title 32—National Defense

Title 33—Navigation and Navigable Waters

Title 34—Education

Title 35—Panama Canal

Title 36—Parks, Forests, and Public Property

Title 37—Patents, Trademarks, and Copyrights

Title 38—Pensions, Bonuses, and Veterans' Relief

Title 39—Postal Service

Title 40—Protection of the Environment

Title 41—Public Contracts and Property Management

Title 42—Public Health

Title 43—Public Lands: Interior

Title 44—Emergency Management and Assistance

Title 45—Public Welfare

Title 46—Shipping

Title 47—Telecommunications

Title 48—Federal Acquisition Regulations System

Title 49—Transportation

Title 50—Wildlife and Fisheries

SOURCE: Code of Federal Regulation.

rule making, whereby the sector to be regulated would have significant input into writing new rules.

None of these presidential efforts was successful in reducing the number of rules generated by the regulatory agencies. The average annual number of pages added to the Code of Federal Regulations increased with each president. During the Carter administration, 94,000 pages were added to the CFR each year. Under Reagan 110,000 pages were added annually. The Bush administration saw the addition of 126,000 pages per year. The Clinton administration added an average of 134,000 pages to the CFR each year.[26] Like his predecessors, George W. Bush has put out some early signals indicating a desire to curtail rule-making activities.

JUDICIAL POLICYMAKING

Through judicial decision making on individual cases or appeals regarding regulatory regulations, the courts play a critical public policy role. Court involvement in public policy is often termed **judicial activism** and is frequently thought of in a negative way. Many observers suggest that courts have no business in public policymaking, but the history of judicial involvement in the policy process has a long and well-established history in America.

In 1803 *Marbury* v. *Madison* established the principal of **judicial review.** In this decision the Supreme Court asserted its authority to review acts of other branches of government and to invalidate them if they were determined to be unconstitutional. The Court has used this authority to become the protector of individual rights. In the nineteenth century, the Court protected the economic rights of property owners, and conservative judicial decisions time and again overturned congressional attempts to legislate control over the economy or social welfare. In the twentieth century, the Court shifted its position and supported individual civil liberties, overturning government practices that maintained racial discrimination, restrained freedom of speech, and subjected prisoners to harsh conditions.[27] Few would deny that the Court made national public policy in 1954 with the *Brown* v. *Board of Education* decision to outlaw school segregation or in a later case that imposed busing as a remedy for the segregation of schools. In one of its more controversial decisions, the Court made public policy by protecting the right of privacy for women, thus legalizing abortion.

While the courts are very powerful in policymaking, two significant restrictions inhibit judicial action. The first is that the courts in large part do not set their own agendas. Courts can act only on cases that are brought to them. The Supreme Court has some control over its agenda in that it can refuse to hear a case, but the cases that get to the Court come from outside groups rather than being initiated by the Court itself. Policy advocates carefully select **test cases** to bring to court with the hope that the court will rule in their favor. Interest groups bringing such cases will often "shop" for the "right" court. This **venue shopping** is litigants' attempt to get a hearing in a sympathetic court. District courts typically hear a case first. Appeals may be made to a circuit court. Since there are only thirteen circuits in the United States, the opinions of the judges in each circuit are fairly well known. Policy advocates file the case in the district and circuit that will give them an advantage.

The second restriction on judicial authority is that the courts have no power over implementation. A court can render a judgment, but it relies on others to implement the decision. These others include the people who communicate the decision to other actors within the system and the people who implement the decision. For instance, when the Supreme Court ruled that school prayer was unconstitutional, that decision was communicated, largely by school boards, to principals and teachers. It was primarily individual teachers who were responsible for implementing the decision. In communities opposed to the ruling, the decision could simply be ignored. The only recourse for an individual wishing to see the decision implemented was to take the violators back to court—a lengthy and costly process.[28]

There is a considerable debate about the capacity of judges for effective policymaking. Some argue that the courts might be a viable place for policymaking because judges are relatively insulated from interest groups, political parties, and other direct political influences. Judges have a tradition of trying to be neutral when considering competing arguments. They also are able to tailor their policymaking to a particular situation, unlike legislatures, which pass sweeping legislation. The ability of judges to render these small decisions means that they can effectively address particular situations and craft policy solutions that account for subtle differences associated with an issue. The judicial process allows a high degree of participation by interested parties. *Amicus curiae* (friend of the court) briefs and reliance on the opinion of outside experts are common. This allows judges to view a problem from various perspectives. Finally, unlike the legislative process, which routinely fails to act on issues, courts must respond to problems brought before them. All these factors speak to the capacity of the courts to act as policymakers.[29]

Not all scholars see the courts' role in policymaking as positive,[30] and they identify many features of the courts that make them less than desirable institutions for policymaking. For instance, judges cannot select the areas of policy on which they must act, so if they are not experts in all areas of policy, they are likely to be poorly prepared to undertake policy decision making in any one area. Judges are also removed from public opinion and are unlikely to understand the possible consequences of their decisions. The ad hoc nature of judicial decision making results in policies that lack comprehensive focus. Unlike legislation, which is based on average cases or the norm, judicial decisions are based on extreme cases, which are the only ones that make it to the courts. This has a distorting influence on policymaking. Finally, litigation ends with one party winning and the other losing. This is probably not a good way to craft a policy solution. More could be gained through negotiation and compromise.[31]

Which argument makes more sense? Do courts have the capacity to make public policy? It is difficult to assess judicial capacity to make policy. What is clear, however, is that courts are intricately involved with the process and have in the past rendered some of the more controversial changes to U.S. public policy.

THE ROLE OF THE STATES

State public policy processes parallel those at the federal level. Each of the states has the same four primary institutions: the legislature, the executive, the bureaucracy, and the courts. Governors, like presidents, attempt to set the legislative agenda. State legislatures pass laws that create policies for the state and, like Congress, control the allocation of resources. Governors may recommend state budgets, but ultimately it is the legislature that finally passes the legislation. State bureaucracies act to implement the laws passed by the state legislature in much the same way as the federal bureaucracy implements federal laws. State courts intervene in the process when cases are brought forward questioning state law or policy implementation.

The U.S. system of federalism gives the states a special role to play in policymaking. States are often called upon by the federal government to implement, within their own borders, public policy programs that have been passed by the federal government. The states are further divided into units of local government, such as counties and municipalities, that work with the state government to implement federal policy. Counties and municipalities also often work directly with the federal government in the implementation of public policies. A good example of this is the federal Food Stamp program, which is implemented at the local level.

The ability of the federal government to influence policymaking at the state, county, and local levels stems in large part from a flow of funds from Washington. States and localities were estimated to have received more than $300 billion in **grants** from the federal government in 2001.[32] These grants provided funding to implement programs that the federal government desired. Ideally, all programs that the federal government requires states or localities to implement should be paid for with federal dollars; however, this frequently does not occur. When the federal government requires the states or localities to implement a federal program but does not provide the money to do so, this is termed an **unfunded mandate.** Unfunded mandates frequently are seen by state and local officials as unacceptable federal meddling without the provision of resources.

States have a fundamental policy responsibility as a direct result of the Tenth Amendment to the Constitution, which reserves the powers not delegated to the federal government (such as foreign policy) nor prohibited by the Constitution (printing money, for instance) to the states. So the states have primary responsibility and authority in a variety of public policy areas, including education, police and crime control, roads and infrastructure (except the interstate highway system), and disaster management. The federal government may get involved in some of these issues, but its role is limited.

POLICY THEORIES

A number of theories seek to explain the policymaking process. They can be grouped into three main areas. The first area looks at agenda setting, the second at decision making, and the third at policy types.

Agenda-Setting Theories

What issues get on the agendas of policymakers? Why do they get there while other issues do not? A rational approach to policymaking could view agenda setting as a process in which a problem is brought to government, the government fashions a solution, and the problem is addressed.[33] This policy model typically describes the stages of the process in a linear fashion, beginning with problem perception. An inherent assumption is that government responds to problems, and that the response comprises public policy.[34]

A contrasting model of agenda setting advanced by John Kingdon,[35] based on Cohen, March, and Olsen's Garbage Can Model,[36] describes a chaotic process. According to this model, government operates much like a garbage can into which participants dump a random assortment of problems and solutions as they are generated. In the can are solutions looking for problems to fix, issues looking for decision situations in which they might emerge, and decision makers looking for work.

The problem stream consists of various problems that capture the interest of people in and around government. The policy stream consists of a policy community of specialists (bureaucrats, academics, legislative staffers, planners and analysts in budget offices, interest groups, and researchers) who have favorite ideas they want to push forward. They float their ideas around the policy community, and some gather supporters. The political stream, which is comprised of swings in the national mood, public opinion, election results, partisan shifts in Congress, changes in administration, and pressure from interest groups, acts as an impetus or constraint. These three streams generally develop and operate independently of one another. Solutions are developed whether they respond to a problem or not. The political stream may change suddenly as a result of events (such as an economic recession or an international crisis). When the streams come together, however, a policy window opens for a short time; the agenda can be changed; and a policy issue can move higher on the policy agenda.

In explaining presidential agenda setting, yet another theoretical explanation has been offered. This is the theory of **legislative expense.**[37] Presidents have a limited amount of political capital to spend. In choosing among domestic policy alternatives, they have to consider how much congressional passage will cost them. Ensuring congressional passage of large-scale programs is difficult, so they demand more of a president's capital than do small programs. New programs are more costly than incremental changes to old programs. This theory suggests that presidents decide what they will put on their agendas based upon these considerations.

Anthony Downs proposed a theory of the **issue–attention cycle** to explain why the public's attention rarely stays focused on any one issue for any length of time. Downs suggests that crisis or discovery of problems may make the public aware of an issue and keen to do something about it. However, when the public fully realizes the cost of dealing with the issue, enthusiasm typically wanes.[38]

Decision-Making Theories

How do we decide which policies we should undertake? Who is influential in swaying decisions? Interest group activism is often discussed as critical to understanding policy decision making. Interest groups are thought to create **subgovernments,** or **iron triangles,** which are relationships between members of Congress, a bureaucracy, and an affected interest group. Once established, these subgovernments effectively see to it that all policy decisions are favorable to the involved parties. The classic case is the relationship of defense and foreign affairs committee members of Congress, the Department of Defense, and private-sector defense contractors.[39]

A closely related theory is **agency capture,**[40] the notion of a special interest group's dictating policy to a government regulatory or other agency.[41] For so-called **client agencies,** like the Department of Agriculture, that serve a particular clientele (farmers), the idea is that the client dictates how the government should act within the policy area affecting the client. While agency capture of a client agency may allow special interests to exert undue influence over policymaking, the capture of a regulatory agency is more serious. For instance, if the nuclear industry were to capture the Nuclear Regulatory Commission (NRC), the safety of nuclear reactors could come into question.[42]

Another theory of policy decision making involves the notion of which special interest groups have the ability to access and influence policymakers. This theory, elaborated by Charles Lindblom and Edward Woodhouse, centers on the inordinate ability of wealth to influence policymaking. In large part, proponents of this theory see the policymaking process as generally pluralistic. They argue that the system tends to permit members of diverse ethnic, racial, religious, and social groups to have access to policymakers. However, the theory suggests that there is a preference in the system whereby people with access to monetary resources (in particular, business interests) are more able to reach policymakers and are more likely to influence policy choices. They argue that funding is the fundamental source of inequality in democratic policymaking. According to this theory, the influence of wealth, from legal campaign contributions to the illegal explicit buying of political favors, explains much about the way policy decisions are made.[43]

Incrementalism is a theory of policy decision making rooted in budgetary considerations. In his 1964 book on the politics of the budgetary process, Aaron Wildavsky argues that budgeting is almost never undertaken in a comprehensive manner. Rather, the government typically uses the prior year's budget (and activities) as a baseline and makes small changes to a narrow range of items that command political attention.[44] While the government has experienced waves of reform that attempted to mandate annual comprehensive assessment of program outcomes, the incrementalism described by Wildavsky in the 1960s still describes government operations today. If the budget is considered a blueprint of government goals and social preferences, incrementalism is a reasonable explanation of policy behavior. Lindblom extends this line of reasoning to policymaking specifically. He argues that democracies almost always change their policies through small, incremental adjustments to already existing programs and policies.[45]

Policy Type Theories

Is public policy made in different ways based upon the policy type? What different kinds of policy are there? Theodore Lowi proposed that, since individual interrelations are to some measure established by expectations, and in politics expectations are determined by government outputs, political relations ought to be determined by the type of policy issue at stake. He argues that for every policy type, there will be a different set of political interrelations that structure policymaking. The three types of policy he identifies are distributive, redistributive, and regulatory. Each has a distinct policymaking process.[46]

Distributive policies evenly distribute government largess and are marked by consensual political processes. **Redistributive policies** take from one group and give to another. Their policymaking process emphasizes conflict between elite groups (typically, those who reap the benefits and those who shoulder the costs). **Regulatory policy** is used to regulate industry and other special interests in society; consequently, regulatory policymaking is dominated by bargaining among interest groups.[47]

SUMMARY

This chapter discussed the process of policymaking as it occurs in the executive, legislature, bureaucracy, and judiciary. On the federal level, the president is a key player in public policymaking both in foreign policy and in setting the domestic policy agenda. Most policy is made through legislation enacted by Congress. Congress often leaves much of the detail work of policy implementation to the bureaucracy when the legislation directs the bureaucracy to make regulations necessary for carrying it out. Finally, the courts are involved in policymaking by rendering case-by-case judgments as well as by hearing wider complaints regarding bureaucratic regulations.

The legislative policy process can be described as a series of steps or a cycle. These steps are problem definition and perception, agenda setting, policy formulation, budgeting, implementation, and evaluation. The process begins when the issue is first perceived as of general social concern. How an issue is perceived and defined has much to do with the policy formulation. Agenda status is obtained when influential actors inside government recognize a problem as something they want to pay serious attention to. Agenda status is often achieved when people in powerful positions, especially the president, personally adopt an issue. When policy entrepreneurs have a solution to a problem, the political will often arises to do something about it.

Policy formulation specifies the details of how a particular policy problem will be addressed, and the budgeting process allocates money to get the job done. Congress leaves the implementation of public policies largely up to the bureaucracy. In some cases Congress gives the bureaucracy strict and clear guidelines specifying exactly how to carry out the law. In most cases, however, Congress allows the bureaucracy a wide range of discretion in carrying out laws. After a program that carries out a public policy has been in place for a while, it is often subject to evaluation. If evaluation shows that it is not working well, it may be subject to modification or termination.

Bureaucratic agencies make policy when they implement programs authorized by Congress. Congress frequently gives agencies the authority to make rules and regulations associated with carrying out a law. This rule-making authority plays a significant role in establishing the context of public policy. The volume of rules made by regulatory agencies is substantial, and their impact on businesses and individuals is significant. The large volume of rules and their impact resulted in attempts to control bureaucratic rule making. In the final three decades of the twentieth century, Presidents Carter, Reagan, Bush, and Clinton tried to institute regulatory reform, but their efforts did not reduce the number of rules generated by the regulatory agencies.

Courts make public policy when they render decisions on individual cases or in appeals regarding regulatory regulations. The principal of judicial review, in which the Supreme Court reviews acts of other branches of government and invalidates those determined to be unconstitutional, gives the Court a great deal of power in policymaking. Two significant restrictions inhibit judicial actions. The first is that the courts do not set their own agendas, and the second is that they have no power over implementation. A court can render a judgment, but it relies on others to implement its decisions.

Federalism gives the states a distinctive role in policymaking. States are frequently the instrument of implementation of national policy within their jurisdiction. The ability of the national government to influence policymaking at the state, county, and local levels stems in large part from the transfer of funds from Washington to lower levels of government. The states also have an independent public policy process similar to that of the national government. Each state has independent legislative, executive, bureaucratic, and judicial functions that allow it to create and implement its own public policies.

Understanding how processes work is important. Understanding why they work that way involves the many theories explaining public policy. These theories can be grouped into three types: agenda setting, decision making, and policy types. This chapter addressed each.

KEY TERMS

agency capture	iron triangles	rules
agenda setting	issue-attention cycle	subgovernments
budgetary process	judicial activism	termination
budget resolution	judicial review	test cases
client agencies	legislative expense	unfunded mandates
distributive policies	modification	venue shopping
grants	redistributive policies	
incrementalism	regulatory policies	

WEB SITES

Congressional Policymaking

http://thomas.loc.gov
Thomas, the Library of Congress Web site, allows you to track any legislation through Congress. It shows the progress of resolutions as they make their way through committees to final votes.

http://thomas.loc.gov/home/hcomso.html
This site can be reached from Thomas and contains a list of all oversight hearings and committee meetings.

http://www.house.gov/house/Legproc.html
The official House of Representatives site called *The Legislative Process* allows you to follow a bill through the House.

http://www.house.gov/house/Tying_it_all.html
A House of Representatives site that explains how the legislative process works.

http://www.senate.gov/learning/index.cfm
This Senate site explains the legislative process from the Senate's point of view.

Bureaucratic Policymaking

http://www.access.gpo.gov/su_docs/aces/aces140.html
This site connects you to the *Federal Register* online, via the Government Printing Office and the National Archives and Records Administration, as well as the Code of Federal Regulations, the Weekly Compilation of Presidential Documents, all the public laws of the United States organized by Congress number, and public papers of the presidents of the United States. This is a very useful site for those wishing to do research or seeking detailed information. It is not the most user-friendly site, so beginners should beware.

http://www.whitehouse.gov/omb/index.html
The official home page of the Office of Management and Budget. This site contains links to the *OMB Federal Register*, showing proposed and final rules that have been submitted by OMB. It also contains links to a statement of administration policy that discloses presidential opinion on all resolutions making their way through Congress and to the budget of the United States.

http://www.whitehouse.gov/WH/html/handbook.html
The Gateway to Government from the White House home page. From here you can easily access all the cabinet-level departments (or go directly there via http://www.whitehouse.gov/WH/Cabinet/html/cabinet_links.html) as well as all the agencies not at the cabinet level (the direct address is http://www.whitehouse.gov/WH/Independent_Agencies/html/independent_links.html).

Judicial Policymaking

http://www.supremecourtus.gov/
The official site of the U.S. Supreme Court contains copies of decisions issued since 1991 as well as links to related sites, including the Administrative Office of the United States Courts, the Federal Judicial Center, the United States Sentencing Commission, the Department of Justice, the Office of the Solicitor General, the Supreme Court Historical Society, the National Center for State Courts, and the National Association of Attorneys General.

Intergovernmental Policymaking

http://www.firstgov.gov/
A helpful site that organizes access to most of the government. If you can't find what you are looking for elsewhere, try this site. It contains a state and local gateway from which you can get a host of information on the states.

http://www.piperinfo.com/state/index.cfm
A great site that allows access to all the state home pages as well as multistate sites such as the Appalachian Regional Commission, the Delaware River Basin Commission, the Great Lakes Commission, the Interstate Oil and Gas Compact Commission, the Multistate Tax Commission, the Ohio River Valley Water Sanitation Commission, the Ohio-Kentucky-Indiana Regional Council of Governments, the South Atlantic Fishery Management Council, and the Southern States Energy Board.

http://www.statelocal.gov/
This state and local gateway gives access to information by topic, such as administrative management, communities, commerce, disasters, emergencies, environment, families and children, housing, education, public safety, and workforce development. It also has hyperlinks to a number of useful associated sites, including the Council of State Governments, the International City Managers Association, the National Association of Counties, the National Conference of State Legislatures, the National Governors Association, the National League of Cities, and the United States Conference of Mayors. The site is a rich source of information on issues concerning state and local governments, including brownfields, performance measures, sustainable communities, and welfare reform.

DISCUSSION QUESTIONS

1. Name the four primary institutions of policymaking, and discuss their role in making public policy.
2. Name and discuss the six stages of the policy cycle.

3. How do the perception and definition of a social problem affect the solution?

4. List and explain two ways that an issue achieves agenda status.

5. Discuss the differences between evenly distributed, redistributive, and regulatory policies.

6. Discuss the difference between discretionary and nondiscretionary funding.

7. How does the U.S. system of federalism affect states' roles in public policymaking?

WEB QUESTIONS

1. Use Thomas to find a recently introduced piece of legislation, and describe its process through the legislative system.

2. Go to the budget of the United States, and find the amount spent on national defense last year.

3. What was the last decision of the U.S. Supreme Court?

NOTES

1. Allen Schick, *The Federal Budget: Politics, Policy, Process* (Washington, DC: Brookings, 1995).

2. Thomas R. Dye, *Understanding Public Policy*, 8th ed. (Englewood Cliffs, NJ: Prentice-Hall, 1995).

3. Charles O. Jones, *An Introduction to the Study of Public Policy*, 3rd ed. (Monterey, CA: Brooks/Cole Publishing Company, 1984).

4. Clarke E. Cochran, Lawrence C. Mayer, T. R. Carr, and N. Joseph Cayer, *American Public Policy: An Introduction*, 6th ed. (Boston: St. Martin's, 1999).

5. John W. Kingdon, *Agendas, Alternatives, and Public Policies*, 2nd ed. (New York: Longman, 1995).

6. Thomas A. Birkland, *After Disaster: Agenda Setting, Public Policy, and Focusing Events* (Washington, DC: Georgetown University Press, 1997).

7. Randall Ripley and Grace Franklin, *Congress, the Bureaucracy and Public Policy*, 3rd ed. (Homewood, IL.: Dorsey Press, 1984).

8. Paul C. Light, *The President's Agenda: Domestic Policy Choice from Kennedy to Clinton*, 3rd ed. (Baltimore: Johns Hopkins University Press, 1999).

9. Kingdon, *Agendas, Alternatives, and Public Policies.*

10. Mark E. Rushefsky, *Public Policy in the United States: Toward the Twenty-first Century* (Pacific Grove, CA: Brooks/Cole Publishing Company, 1990).

11. Theodore J. Lowi, "American Business, Public Policy, Case-Studies, and Political Theory," *World Politics*, 16 (4): 677–715.

12. Schick, *The Federal Budget.*

13. Aaron Wildavsky, *The New Politics of the Budgetary Process*, 2nd ed. (New York: HarperCollins, 1992).

14. Cornelius M. Kerwin, *Rulemaking: How Government Agencies Write Law and Make Policy*, 2nd ed. (Washington, DC: CQ Press, 1999).

15. Carol H. Weiss, *Evaluation: Methods for Studying Programs and Policies*, 2nd ed.

(Upper Saddle River, NJ: Prentice-Hall, 1998).

16. B. Guy Peters, *American Public Policy: Promise and Performance,* 4th ed. (Chatham, NJ: Chatham House Publishers, 1996).

17. Charles Murray, "What to Do About Welfare," in *Controversies in American Public Policy,* 2nd ed., ed. John A. Hird and Michael Reese (Boston: Bedford/St. Martin's, 1999), 8–22.

18. Quoted in Kerwin, *Rulemaking,* 8.

19. Walter Rosenbaum, *Environmental Politics and Policy* (Washington, DC: CQ Press, 1996).

20. Thomas A. Birkland, *After Disaster: Agenda Setting, Public Policy, and Focusing Events* (Washington, DC: Georgetown University Press, 1997).

21. Richard Stillman II, *The American Bureaucracy: The Core of Modern Government,* 2nd ed. (Chicago: Nelson-Hall Publishers, 1996).

22. Kerwin, *Rulemaking.*

23. James Fesler and Donald F. Kettl, *The Politics of the Administrative Process* (Chatham, NJ: Chatham House Publishers, 1991).

24. Rushefsky, *Public Policy in the United States.*

25. Kerwin, *Rulemaking.*

26. Ibid.

27. Christopher E. Smith, *Courts and Public Policy* (Chicago: Nelson-Hall Publishers, 1993).

28. Ibid.

29. Christopher E. Smith, *Courts, Politics, and the Judicial Process,* 2nd ed. (Chicago: Nelson-Hall Publishers, 1997).

30. Donald Horowitz, *The Courts and Social Policy* (Washington, DC: Brookings, 1977).

31. Smith, *Courts, Politics, and the Judicial Process.*

32. Laurence J. O'Toole, Jr., "American Intergovernmental Relations: An Overview," in *American Intergovernmental Relations,* ed. Laurence J. O'Toole, Jr. (Washington, DC: CQ Press, 2000), 1–31.

33. James P. Lester and Joseph Steward, Jr., *Public Policy: An Evolutionary Approach* (Minneapolis/St. Paul: West Publishing Company, 1996).

34. Jones, *Introduction to the Study of Public Policy.*

35. Kingdon, *Agendas, Alternatives, and Public Policies.*

36. Michael Cohen, James March, and Johan Olsen, "A Garbage Can Model of Organizational Choice," *Administrative Science Quarterly* (March 1972): 1–25.

37. Light, *The President's Agenda.*

38. Anthony Downs, "Up and Down with Ecology—The "Issue-Attention Cycle," in *Political Theory and Public Choice: The Selected Essays of Anthony Downs, Volume One,* ed. Anthony Downs (Cheltenham, UK: Edward Elgar, 1998), 100–112.

39. Randall B. Ripley and Grace A. Franklin, *Bureaucracy and Policy Implementation* (Homewood, IL: The Dorsey Press, 1982).

40. Eugene Bardach and Robert A. Kagan, *Going by the Book: The Problem of Regulatory Unreasonableness* (Philadelphia: Temple University Press, 1982).

41. Theodore J. Lowi, *The End of Liberalism: The Second Republic of the United States,* 2nd ed. (New York: W. W. Norton, 1979).

42. James Q. Wilson, *Bureaucracy: What Government Agencies Do and Why They Do It* (New York: Basic Books, 1989).

43. Charles E. Lindblom and Edward J. Woodhouse, *The Policy Making Process,* 3rd ed. (Englewood Cliffs, NJ: Prentice-Hall, 1993).

44. Aaron Wildavsky, *The Politics of the Budgetary Process* (Boston: Little, Brown and Company, 1964).

45. Charles E. Lindblom, "The Science of 'Muddling Through,'" *Public Administration Review,* 19 (Spring 1959): 79–88.

46. Lowi, "American Business."

47. Raymond A. Bauer and Kenneth J. Gergen, eds., *The Study of Policy Formation* (New York: The Free Press, 1968).

3

Paying for Programs

Government spending in the United States is substantial. One way to get a sense of the relative importance of government spending is to compare it to the whole of the U.S. economy. A common measure of the size of the economy is the **gross domestic product (GDP).** The GDP is the total value of goods and services produced in the economy. The GDP was $9.7 trillion in 2000, and it increased to nearly $10.2 trillion in 2001.[1] Figure 3.1 illustrates the relationship between the GDP and government spending. Total federal, state, and local government spending in 2000 was about 28 percent of the economy, with federal government spending accounting for about 18 percent of the GDP and state and local spending for about 10 percent. In 2000 the federal government spent nearly $1.8 trillion.

State and local governments are independent of the federal government. They have their own sources of funds (sales tax, property tax, and state income taxes). But Figure 3.1 also shows that some of the money used by states and localities for public programs is passed to them in the form of grants from the federal government. Of the nearly $1.2 trillion that state and local governments spent in 2000, $242 billion (21 percent) came from federal grants.[2]

Ninety percent of federal money comes from three major taxes: individual taxes, corporate taxes, and payroll taxes. In 2001, for example, individual income tax provided nearly half of the revenues of the federal government. Payroll taxes—primarily for Social Security and Medicare—accounted for the next 35 percent. Corporate income taxes made up a little more than 7 percent,

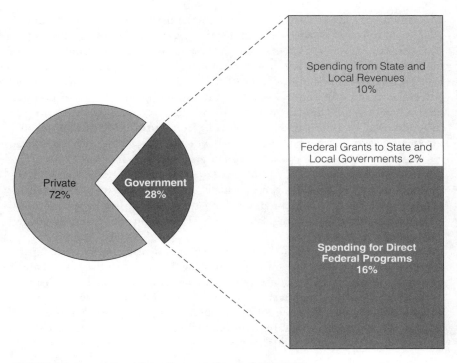

FIGURE 3.1 Government Spending as a Share of GDP, 2000

SOURCE: The Budget of the United States FY 2003, summary tables. [http://www.white-house.gov/omb/budget/index.html]

and excise and other small federal taxes and fees provided approximately 8 percent of federal revenues.[3]

When we establish programs to perform certain functions, we invest a substantial portion of our resources in those programs. While it is not true that only programs consuming large amounts of resources are important, how much a program costs does indicate something about the relative emphasis placed on it by the government. In this sense, it is useful to take a look at what we spend our money on and how much we spend.

Many citizens have a distorted sense of what the nation spends tax dollars on. For instance, a poll conducted in May 2000 showed that 47 percent of the American public thought that too much money was devoted to foreign aid.[4] In the budget, however, foreign aid is a very modest program by federal standards. Americans also show distrust for how their tax dollars are being spent. An April 2000 poll asked, "Out of every dollar the federal government collects in taxes, how many cents do you think are wasted?"[5] The average response was 46 cents. Most people feel that nearly half our tax dollars are being wasted! Government is frequently criticized for spending too much, for spending inefficiently, and for putting regulations in place whose costs far exceed the benefits.

Federal taxes are used to fund many government programs, but programs are funded in other ways as well. The federal government does not always pay all expenses involved in a program. In the case of partial federal funding, additional money can come from state governments, local governments, or private-sector actors. The states or localities can chip in some of their tax dollars, or the government might impose a special fee on a group of individuals or companies to pay the rest. The federal government can also require the states to pay for some or all of a program. Commonly called an **unfunded mandate,** this manner of paying for public programs is not popular among state and local governments. States and localities can, of course, decide to fund programs independently. They can also take advantage of matching federal dollars made available for specific program purposes. Finally, the private sector can be called upon to fund public policy programs. This typically happens when the government imposes rules and regulations on private companies that they are, by law, required to obey.

A variety of funding possibilities and the programs associated with them are discussed in this chapter. The purpose is to provide an idea of the general areas to which the United States devotes most of its public resources. Later chapters explore each area in more detail as well as other significant but less expensive public programs. The idea behind this chapter is to provide a quick overview of spending for public policy. In addition, the chapter frames budgetary decisions in the wider context of economic policy.

VALUES AND PROGRAM
FUNDING DECISIONS

Government is frequently criticized for spending too much or too little, for spending inefficiently, for spending on the "wrong" programs, and for putting confusing and pricey regulations in place.[6] How much to spend (or how much to mandate that the private sector spend) and on what programs are critical questions for public policy. They are value questions, and they are resolved in the political process.

A budget is a document that lists proposed expenditures for certain items and purposes. These items (salaries, vendor payments, equipment, supplies) and purposes (providing low-income housing, preventing terrorist attacks, guaranteeing airline safety) together form a basic plan of government action. Those who write the budget assume that there is a direct relationship between what is in the budget and what the government does. If requests for funds are granted and activities are carried out in an appropriate manner, it is reasonable to expect that the purposes stated in the budget document will be achieved. Funding decisions embodied in the budget, therefore, can be thought of as the connection between financial resources and policy objectives.[7] Annual agency appropriations and expenditures thus are a good measure of policy actions.[8]

Voters have something to say about how much they are willing to be taxed to fund particular programs. Voters also decide how much industry can be made to pay to comply with regulations, knowing that those costs frequently get passed along to consumers in increased prices. Their decisions most often take the form of supporting candidates and political parties that tend to align most closely with their values. The large political questions put before voters demand value decisions regarding the appropriate extent of government action. Should government set up and run many programs or just a few? Should industry pay large sums for environmental, health, and safety protection, or are businesses already controlled by too many regulations? Special interests also support candidates and parties sympathetic to their interests, often by making large monetary contributions. Special interests are a major force in getting candidates elected and in blocking (or assisting) legislation or regulations through the political process.

Decisions about public expenditure for programs or private-sector expenditure to achieve regulatory compliance rest first and foremost on the belief that the matter is one for public, not private, action. Some areas of public policy receive relatively low levels of direct or mandated funding because they are thought to be private, rather than public, issues. Energy policy, for instance, receives relatively little funding at the federal level in large part because we have decided to allow the market, with only a few constraints, to determine U.S. energy policy. There are also several areas of policy that are not on the government's agenda for action because we collectively believe that these issues are private issues better addressed by faith-based organizations or the family. Feeding the hungry and housing the homeless are increasingly being done by faith-based organizations within communities rather than by local governments. Helping individuals who have expended their five-year lifetime welfare benefit now falls to family members and faith-based organizations. More and more, teaching youth about sex and birth control is being removed from the schools and left to parents. Several states that consider sex education a private (family) rather than public (government) issue have refused to accept federal grants that require public school-based sex education.

The decision to fund one program before another or not to fund a program is a focal point of political contention. Presidents, members of Congress, bureaucrats, interest groups, political parties, and members of the attentive public struggle to have their preferences dominate the budgetary process. The winning and losing, the compromises and the bargains are at the core of both the U.S. political process and the policymaking process.[9]

ECONOMIC POLICY

The values discussed in the last section play out within the larger context of national economic policy. If we want to understand how decisions are made on specific policy areas or programs, it is necessary to frame those individual decisions in the larger context of the management of the economy. The management of the economy is often referred to as **economic policy.** The two basic tools used to direct the national economy are monetary policy and fiscal policy.

Monetary policy grew out of an act by Congress in 1913 that created the Federal Reserve system (the Fed). The Fed is the central bank of the United States. It has the authority to administer and regulate the nation's credit, money supply, and banking system. To accomplish this, the Fed raises or lowers interest rates, buys or sells U.S. Treasury securities, and exercises control over other aspects of the economy. The Fed is responsible for maintaining national economic growth, low inflation, and high employment. It also is supposed to ensure the stability and liquidity of the banking industry and other financial markets. The Fed supervises and regulates commercial banks to ensure safety and soundness. Finally, the Fed is responsible for the protection of consumers and communities through the regulation of consumer credit and community reinvestment and development.[10]

The Fed is independent of the Treasury Department but works closely with it so that there is no discrepancy between Fed policy and Treasury actions. The Fed is run by a seven-member board of governors appointed by the president and confirmed by the Senate. Board members are appointed for fourteen-year terms. The president appoints one of the members to be chairperson of the Fed, also with the advice and consent of the Senate. The Fed chairperson serves a four-year term, but may be reappointed. The Fed chairperson is required to testify before the House and Senate Banking Committees twice a year and often is asked to testify by other congressional committees. The Fed's Federal Open Market Committee (FOMC) meets every five to eight weeks to discuss possible increases or decreases in the interest rate.[11]

The second tool is **fiscal policy.** Fiscal policy, often called "tax and spend" policy, emerged during the Great Depression of the 1930s. Prior to the Depression, it was generally believed that the federal government ought to have a **balanced budget**—that is, that expenditure (spending) should not exceed revenue (taxing). Federal government borrowing did occasionally occur, especially in times of war, but the money would soon be repaid. With the persistence of the Depression, however, ideas began to shift. Franklin Delano Roosevelt's administration was desperate for new approaches to end the Depression, and the solution that emerged was supported by the work of economist John Maynard Keynes.

Keynesian economics suggested that it was appropriate in bad economic times for the government to spend to create demand and stimulate economic growth. The theory argued the government should spend in excess of revenues, thereby creating a **deficit.** In robust economic times, when the economy was in danger of growing too quickly and producing inflation, the government should reduce expenditures, creating a **surplus** and consequently lowering demand and slowing the economy. This surplus could be used to pay off any debt that had accumulated from the down cycles. Thus, according to the theory, the federal budget could become a tool to control the economy.

One of the problems associated with the implementation of Keynesian fiscal policy is that politically it is much easier for members of Congress to vote for increased spending that results in annual deficits than it is to vote to tighten the belt, balance the budget, or run a surplus. The political use of Keynesian fiscal policy led to years of deficit spending for reasons that had little to do with managing the economy.[12] Between the end of the Depression and 1994, annual budget deficits became chronic. The **national debt**—the cumulative annual deficits—soared.

The size of the national debt is of concern because the debt must be financed. Every year that the annual budget is in deficit, the government must borrow money to cover its costs. The money that is borrowed must be paid back with interest. In fiscal year (FY) 2001, 11 percent of the federal budget went to interest costs on the national debt. The national debt in 2002 was nearly $6 trillion. For each person living in the United States, the individual share of this debt is over $20,000. The national debt is continuing to increase on a daily basis. From 2001 to 2002 the national debt increased an average of $843 million a day.

Economists and policy analysts differ on how detrimental, if at all, the debt is. Some analysts suggest that interest payments on the debt rob the government of the flexibility to spend money on needed programs. They argue that spending 11 cents of every tax dollar on interest payments, as we did in 2001, is foolish. Other analysts suggest that if the debt is relatively small compared to the size of the overall economy, then it is not as much of a worry. They also suggest that if the debt is financed by Americans who buy U.S. savings bonds and other government securities, rather than by foreigners, the interest payments will stay in the United States and will benefit those Americans.

Despite the disagreement among economists and policy analysts regarding the extent of the problem, Congress has tried to deal with the ever-increasing debt since the 1970s. Just months before President Richard Nixon resigned as a result of the Watergate scandal, Congress passed the Congressional Budget Act of 1974. This act required Congress to adopt a budget resolution that set controls on the size of the deficit, total spending, and budget priorities. It did not require that the budget be balanced, but it did proceed on the expectation that deficits would be smaller if Congress had to vote explicitly on an allowable deficit. The reform was not effective, and between 1976 and 1985 the budget deficit averaged more than $110 billion each year, compared with $15 billion a year between 1966 and 1976.[13]

Beginning in the 1980s, in the midst of the political debate over the perennial budget deficits, traditional Keynesian fiscal policy was challenged by a newly emerging economic theory that came to be called **supply-side economics.** The supply-siders suggested that Keynes had it backward. The appropriate use of fiscal policy to stimulate the economy, they claimed, was to put measures in place that increased supply and to let the market take care of demand on its own. They argued that supply is most likely to increase with tax cuts targeted particularly at the wealthy, who will then invest their money in the economy and by so doing create jobs. The resulting **trickle-down effect,** theoretically, will make everyone better off.

Fiscal policy tends to follow partisan lines. Republicans typically favor supply-side economics, while Democrats favor Keynesian approaches. The first large-scale application of supply-side fiscal policy came during the presidency of Ronald

Reagan. Big tax cuts for the wealthy were put into place. At the same time, the Reagan administration ran enormous budget deficits that mirrored traditional Keynesian fiscal approaches. These deficits were caused, at least in part, by the largest peacetime buildup of the military in U.S. history.

The deficit crisis increased in the 1980s and early 1990s, when average annual deficits were running in excess of $200 billion. In 1985, to tackle this problem, Congress passed the Gramm-Rudman-Hollings Act, which called for the gradual reduction of deficits from 1986 to 1990 and the achievement of a balanced budget by 1991. Despite this, Congress exceeded the targets set by the act in each year from 1986 to 1990. In 1990 Congress passed the Budget Enforcement Act, which set up a new deficit control process by putting caps on discretionary spending and setting "pay-as-you-go" rules for any proposed new programs or proposed decreases in revenue so that new programs or tax decreases would not increase the deficit.[14]

Over the twelve years of the Reagan and George H. W. Bush administrations, the debt of the United States grew to four times its 1980 size. When Bill Clinton assumed the office of president, chronic annual deficits and the growth of the debt focused national attention on fixing the problem. During the last several years of the Clinton administration, it seemed that we had turned the corner. Several years of surpluses were used to pay down the debt.

The election of George W. Bush, who came to office with a supply-side campaign pledge of reducing taxes, resulted in the passage of an enormous tax cut targeted at the wealthy, coupled with the return of deficits. The return of deficits has been blamed on the tax cut, the onset of economic recession, the September 11, 2001, terrorist attacks, and the resulting war on terrorism. Regardless of the causes, President George W. Bush's first presidential budget, submitted to Congress in 2002, included a deficit of more than $100 billion. In August 2002 the Congressional Budget Office projected the continuation of annual deficits through 2006.[15]

FEDERAL SPENDING

Federal government money is the largest pool from which we draw to fund public programs. Federal spending for fiscal year 2001 was about $1.8 trillion dollars. That large sum probably needs to be put into some perspective. According to *Forbes* magazine, Bill Gates was the richest man in the world in 2000, with wealth amounting to $60 billion.[16] In one year the federal government spends thirty times Gates' total wealth. To spend $1.8 trillion over the course of one year, the government has to spend $4,931,506,849 each and every day.

How does the government spend all that money? To answer that question, a good starting place is to divide spending into two categories: mandatory and discretionary. **Mandatory expenditures** are those that the government has committed itself to year after year through its policy formulation. A mandatory program is created when Congress writes a law and specifies that the program is authorized for the current year and "each fiscal year thereafter."[17] A mandatory program is a permanent program. To reverse the authorization and change the status of the program to temporary, Congress would have to pass another law. Mandatory programs are often called **entitlement programs** because all people who meet the eligibility requirements specified in the law are entitled to the program's benefits.[18] Entitlements are often not funded for a specific amount; instead Congress typically uses such language as "there are authorized to be appropriated such sums as may be necessary to carry out the provisions" of the law.[19]

Discretionary expenditures are not specified by law in the same manner as mandatory programs; rather such programs are funded annually or for several years. Multiyear authorizations generally are for two to five years. The funding for discretionary programs may rise and fall or may completely disappear if Congress decides not to fund the programs any longer.

What does the federal government spend our money on? In FY 2001 56 percent of the federal budget was made up of mandatory programs. Interest payments on the national debt cost about another 11 percent—together comprising more than two-thirds of all federal spending. The remaining 33 percent went to discretionary programs. Figure 3.2 shows the major programs that comprise both the mandatory and discretionary portions of the budget. The main mandatory programs are Social Security, Medicare, other income-security entitlement programs, Medicaid, and other means-tested entitlement programs (such as the Food Stamp program).

Some have suggested that the most common activity of the federal government is to write checks. This may not be far from the truth. In 2001 the largest federal program, Social Security, accounted for almost one-quarter of all federal spending (see Figure 3.2 and Table 3.1). Social Security provides monthly payments to retired or disabled workers. Medicare, a program that provides health care coverage for elderly and disabled Americans, makes up nearly 12 percent of all federal spending. Qualification for these programs is based on age and, in the case of Social Security, on how much one paid into the program while employed.[20] Health expenditures other than Medicare comprised 9 percent of federal spending in 2001. The Medicaid program provides health care services for poor people and people with disabilities. Unlike Medicare, which is totally funded by the federal government, the states share the costs of the Medicaid program. Medicaid is a means-tested program; eligibility to receive benefits is determined by income (or means). Other means-tested entitlement programs provide benefits to people and families with incomes below certain minimum levels. The major means-tested income-security programs are the Food Stamp program, Supplemental Security Income, Child Nutrition, and the Earned Income Tax Credit.[21]

Table 3.1 also shows the projected growth of each of these programs through 2005. What actually gets spent in future years may not accurately match these projections. Nevertheless, the projections are useful to policymakers, for they make it possible to plan for anticipated expenditures. The large

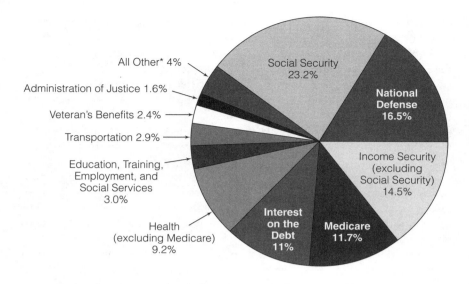

FIGURE 3.2 Federal Government Spending, FY 2001

* All Other category contains expenditures for agriculture, natural resources and the environment, science, space and technology, international affairs, general government, community and regional development, commerce and housing credit, and energy.

SOURCE: The Budget of the United States FY 2003, summary tables. [http://www.white-house.gov/omb/budget/index.html]

projected growth in Social Security, Medicare, and Medicaid, along with projected increases in national defense spending, show that the federal government will have to make difficult decisions in the near future: to decrease nonmilitary discretionary spending, to increase revenues by raising taxes, or to run large annual deficits.

STATE AND LOCAL SPENDING

State and local government spending patterns are different from the federal government patterns in important ways. The states spend considerably less than the federal government. Expenditures for all fifty states combined in FY 2001 came to a bit over $1 trillion. State and local governments get significant portions of their funding from other branches of government. The states receive just under one-quarter of their revenue from the federal government through federal grants-in-aid, and local governments receive about one-third of their revenue from either the federal or the state level.[22] State and local governments raise the rest of their revenues through taxation, but while the federal government heavily relies on personal income taxes for revenue, states have a greater dependence on sales taxes, and local governments depend primarily on property taxes. Most state and

Table 3.1 Federal Outlay Totals by Policy Function
(in billions of dollars)*

Policy Function	2001	2002	2003	2004	2005
Social Security	433.1	459.7	475.9	495.7	519.7
National Defense	308.5	348.0	379.0	393.8	413.5
Income Security (excluding Social Security)	269.8	310.7	319.7	325.0	334.3
Medicare	217.5	226.4	234.4	244.3	261.3
Interest on the Debt	206.2	178.4	180.7	188.8	190.2
Health (excluding Medicare)	172.6	195.2	231.9	258.8	277.8
Education, Training, Employment, and Social Services	57.3	71.7	79.0	81.0	82.7
Transportation	55.2	62.1	59.4	56.3	56.0
Veteran's Benefits	45.8	51.5	56.6	58.6	63.2
Administration of Justice	30.4	34.4	40.6	43.5	39.5
Natural Resources and the Environment	26.3	30.2	30.6	31.1	31.7
Agriculture	26.6	28.8	24.2	22.8	21.3
Science, Space, and Technology	19.9	21.8	22.2	22.8	23.5
International Affairs	16.6	23.5	22.5	22.8	23.3
General Government	15.2	18.3	17.6	19.6	18.6
Community and Regional Development	12.0	15.4	17.4	18.0	17.4
Commerce and Housing Credit	6.0	3.8	3.7	5.1	3.1
Energy	0.1	0.6	0.6	0.3	0.8
Total	**1,863.9**	**2,052.3**	**2,189.1**	**2,276.9**	**2,369.1**

* 2001 numbers are actual; numbers for all other years are estimates. Total does not include undistributed offsetting receipts.

SOURCE: The Budget of the United States FY 2003, summary tables. http://www.whitehouse.gov/omb/budget/index.html.

local governments are mandated by their constitutions or charters to run balanced budgets.

State and local governments have substantially different policy foci than the federal government and primarily concern themselves with education. Education funding comprises more than 33 percent of state spending and nearly 40 percent of local spending. It is important to distinguish between service delivery and service financing when considering the role of state and local governments. While states are the primary service deliverers of public higher education, they finance primary and secondary education by transferring funds to the local school districts that actually deliver the services.[23] Health and welfare issues are also of primary interest at the state level as a result of state contributions to Medicaid. Medicaid is the second largest component of state spending.[24] The states are also concerned with technology-related economic

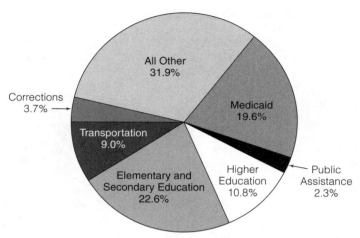

FIGURE 3.3 Total 50 State Expenditure by Function, FY 2001

SOURCE: National Association of State Budget Officers, State Expenditure Report 2001, 2002.

development initiatives, environmental programs, crime, and highway and transportation-related infrastructure spending.[25]

Figure 3.3 shows total state spending by policy area in 2001. Elementary and secondary education comprised nearly 23 percent of state spending, and Medicaid accounted for nearly 20 percent. Higher education spending ranked third, accounting for about 11 percent of state expenditures. Transportation consumed 9 percent of state resources; corrections another 4 percent; and cash assistance to the poor 2 percent.[26] The rest of what the states do is financed by the remaining third of their budgets. This includes such diverse functions as environmental protection, economic development, support for the arts, housing and infrastructure maintenance, interest payments for financed capital investments, and research and development.[27]

PRIVATE-SECTOR FUNDING

A large part of the cost of public policy is borne by the private sector. These costs are associated with government **regulations** that private-sector organizations are obligated to obey. Businesses must comply with a great variety of federal regulations. Companies are faced with the costs of licensing requirements, restrictions governing what they may produce and how they may produce it, controls on their financing, and paperwork trails and audit requirements for workers' health and safety, as well as compliance with government hiring and firing rules. Three general categories are social regulation, economic regulation, and process regulation.

Social regulations seek to benefit the public by prohibiting a firm from producing products in certain ways or with characteristics that are harmful to public health, safety, or the environment. These regulatory compliance costs are largely associated with federal environmental safety and health regulations issued by such agencies as the Environmental Protection Agency (EPA), the Occupational Safety and Health Administration (OSHA), the Food and Drug Administration (FDA), the Department of Transportation (DOT), and the Department of Energy (DOE). Examples include OSHA prohibitions on allowing more than one part per million of benzene in the workplace, DOE prohibition of the manufacture of refrigerators that are below prescribed energy efficiency standards, FDA-required food labels, and DOT's mandates of specific air bags in automobiles.[28]

Economic regulation is aimed at controlling the behavior of Wall Street, banks, and the business community. It prohibits firms from charging prices or making arrangements with other firms that might cause harm to the economy. Regulation in these areas typically falls to such commissions as the Security and Exchange Commission (SEC), the Federal Reserve, and the Department of Justice's Antitrust Division.[29] For example, banks are required to comply with regulations regarding both the availability of funds and the manner in which they make loans. Private companies are required to report profits and earning in accord with SEC reporting requirements. Corporate mergers and acquisitions are subject to approval by the Department of Justice.[30]

Process regulations impose administrative or paperwork requirements on companies. Examples include income tax paperwork requirements and the paperwork associated with hiring immigrants and certifying workers' legal residency. Social and economic regulations also involve a certain amount of paperwork.[31] Showing compliance with the Clean Air Act, for instance, requires businesses to keep records on smokestack emissions from their factories, and compliance requirements of the Clean Water Act require companies to document effluent emissions.[32]

While there is some disagreement about just how much regulatory compliance burdens the private sector, it is generally accepted that the expenditures are not trivial.[33] Both Congress and the president have tried to better understand regulatory costs and benefits. In 1999 Congress passed the Omnibus Consolidated and Emergency Supplemental Appropriations Act, which required an accounting statement on the costs and benefits of regulation. Executive Order 12866, Regulatory Planning and Review, issued by President Clinton in 1993, required agencies to measure the economic effects of their regulations. The Office of Management and Budget (OMB) reported these costs and benefits to Congress beginning in 1997.

According to OMB, in 1999 the annual costs of all social regulation amounted to between $146 billion and $229 billion. These costs were primarily associated with regulating the environment, transportation, and labor. Environmental regulation was the most costly, amounting to an estimated $96 to $170 billion. Transportation costs were estimated at between $15 and $18 billion, while regulations on labor amounted to approximately $18 to $19 billion.[34] Economic regulation was estimated by OMB to cost $71 billion in 1999, and process regulation, or the costs associated with paperwork imposed on the public, was estimated at $190 billion.[35] In addition to the costs imposed on the private sector, federal regulation also affects state and local governments. Between 1996 and 2000 compliance with just four new regulations issued by the federal government cost states and localities more than $100 million.[36]

Other estimates of the costs of regulation on the private sector are higher. Thomas Hopkins of the Rochester Institute of Technology estimated regulatory compliance costs to be as much as half as large as federal government taxation. For 1995, for instance, federal taxation was $1.5 trillion, and Hopkins estimates regulatory compliance costs to have been $668 billion.[37] Similarly, he suggested that regulatory costs for 1997 were $708 billion,[38] a sum considerably larger than OMB estimates.

The wide range in these cost estimates, particularly in costs associated with environmental protection, results from differences in what is counted as a cost and how it is counted. For instance, OMB bases cost estimates on environmental regulatory impact analyses for major rules, which use a varying set of baseline assumptions, differ in risk and valuation assumptions, and vary in the way they project interactions between different regulations.[39]

SUMMARY

The level at which we fund government programs is an excellent way to determine what our priorities are. When we look at the array of programs and the way they are funded, we get a sense of governmental goals and social preferences. Government funding of programs takes place in the wider environment of economic policy, which provides a framework for understanding the interplay of monetary and fiscal policy, debts, and deficits.

Government programs are funded in a variety of ways. The federal government may pay for all expenses involved in a program. The federal government may decide to fund only part of a program and to rely on state or local governments to complete necessary program funding. State and local governments may choose to spend their own money on public programs of their own design. Finally, rules and regulations issued by agencies call on private-sector actors to pay for policy initiatives.

Federal government spending can be divided into discretionary and nondiscretionary or mandatory spending. Nondiscretionary spending is dictated by laws entitling qualified recipients to receive certain government services. Discretionary spending is decided upon each year by Congress. Mandatory programs and interest payments on the national debt together comprise about two-thirds of the federal budget.

Social Security, the largest mandatory program, accounts for almost a quarter of all federal spending, followed by Medicare and Medicaid, which consume about 12 and 9 percent respectively of federal spending. The largest discretionary program is national defense, which accounts for about 16 percent of the federal budget. What is left over is what gets spent on everything else.

States and local governments focus their spending first on education and second on Medicaid. The states are also concerned with technology-related economic development initiatives, environmental programs, crime, and highway and transportation-related infrastructure spending.

Regulations issued by government agencies account for significant public policy expenditures that are absorbed by the private sector. Social regulations aim to protect the public by prohibiting firms from producing products in particular ways or with characteristics that are harmful to public health, safety, or the environment. Economic regulation tries to control the behavior of the banking and business community. It prohibits firms from charging prices or making arrangements with other firms that might harm the economy. Process regulations impose administrative or paperwork requirements on companies. The primary costs associated with process regulations are paperwork costs.

The choice of how much to spend and on what is a value question that is resolved in the political process. Once we decide that a policy matter belongs in the public domain, it is up to the political process to determine the size and scope of government intervention. We do not always rely on the public sector to deal with all possible policy functions. Indeed, we leave many policy issues to the market for resolution.

KEY TERMS

balanced budget

deficit

discretionary expenditures

economic policy

economic regulation

entitlement programs

fiscal policy

gross domestic product (GDP)

Keynesian economics

mandatory expenditures

monetary policy

national debt

process regulation

regulations

social regulation

supply-side economics

surplus

trickle-down effect

unfunded mandate

WEB SITES

The Federal Budget

http://www.access.gpo.gov/usbudget
This Office of Management and Budget site is a central location from which to begin the investigation of federal budgets. It contains the current budget as well as historical documents that can be browsed on line or downloaded in PDF format. This site also contains many supplemental documents that may be of use in understanding the budgeting process.

http://brillig.com/debt_clock
The U.S. National Debt Clock. This site shows the current national debt and provides useful links to further investigate the debt.

http://www.publicdebt.treas.gov/opd/opdfaq.htm
This is the U.S. Treasury's debt site. It provides answers to frequently asked questions about the debt and who finances it, and other details of debt and deficit.

State Budgets

http://www.nga.org
The site of the National Governor's Association has material that is of interest to the states and contains the official stand of the National Governor's Association on policy trends coming out of Washington.

http://www.gpo.gov/usbudget
The main budget page for the federal government. Under the category of supporting documents is *Budget Information for the States,* which contains a full summary of state-by-state federal budget obligation by program. This document displays all the major formula grant programs to state and local governments and the amounts of these grants.

Public Opinion Polling

http://www.pollingreport.com/
An interesting site provided by George Washington University with access to a vast number of recent public opinion polls on politics and the economy. The site says it is "An independent, nonpartisan resource on trends in American public opinion." In addition it carries polls on foreign affairs and defense, budget and taxes, crime, education, the environment, civil rights, and race and ethnicity.

DISCUSSION QUESTIONS

1. Explain the difference between mandatory and discretionary expenditures, and give examples of programs that fall under each.
2. Compare Figures 3.2 and 3.3. How do state and federal spending patterns and policy foci differ? (The "All Other" category for state expenditures may be problematic for this question.)
3. List, describe, and give examples of the three categories of regulation placed upon the private sector.
4. Who bears most of the immediate costs of regulation of the private sector? Do you think this is fair? Why?
5. What can you tell about public policy by examining a government's budget?

WEB QUESTIONS

1. Find a policy issue that interests you, and discuss current public opinion about it.

2. What are the major steps in the budget process?

3. What does the National Governor's Association Center for Best Practices do?

4. Go to the U.S. National Debt Clock at http://brillig.com/debt_clock, and look up today's national debt.

5. Go to the U.S. Treasury debt site at http://www.publicdebt.treas.gov/opd/opdfaq.htm, and find out who finances the national debt.

NOTES

1. Executive Office of the President, *Budget of the United States Government: Historical Tables, Fiscal Year 2003* (Washington, DC: U.S. Government Printing Office, 2002). Also available on line at http://www.whitehouse.gov/omb/budget.

2. Executive Office of the President, *A Citizens Guide to the Federal Budget, Fiscal Year 2002*. In *Budget of the United States Government.* http://www.access.gpo.gov/usbudget/fy2002/pdf/guide.pdf (02/22/02).

3. Ibid.

4. The Gallup Poll. Latest: May 18–21, 2000. http://www.pollingreport.com/defense.htm (12/15/00).

5. ABC News.com Poll. April 12–16, 2000. http://www.pollingreport.com/budget.htm (12/15/00).

6. Philip K. Howard, *The Death of Common Sense: How Law Is Suffocating America* (New York: Random House, 1994).

7. Aaron Wildavsky, *The Politics of the Budgetary Process* (Boston: Little, Brown and Company, 1964).

8. Randall B. Ripley, Grace A. Franklin, William M. Holmes, and William B. Moreland, *Structure, Environment, and Policy Actions: Exploring a Model of Policy-Making* (Beverly Hills: Sage Publications, 1973).

9. Wildavsky, *The Politics of the Budgetary Process.*

10. George Thomas Kurian, "Federal Reserve System." In *A Historical Guide to the U.S. Government,* ed. George T. Kurian (New York: Oxford University Press, 1998), 235–241.

11. Ibid.

12. Aaron Wildavsky, *The New Politics of the Budgetary Process,* 2nd ed. (New York: HarperCollins, 1992).

13. Allen Schick, *The Federal Budget: Politics, Policy, Process* (Washington, DC: Brookings, 1995).

14. Ibid.

15. Congressional Budget Office, *CBO's Current Budget Projections.* http://www.cbo.gov/showdoc.cfm?index=1944&sequence=0#table5 (9/11/02).

16. Forbes Magazine, *The 14th Annual List of the World's Billionaires, 2000.* http://www.forbes.com/worldsrichest (12/15/00).

17. Schick, *The Federal Budget,* 116.

18. Martin Neils Baily, Gary Burtless, and Robert E. Litan, *Growth with Equity: Economic Policymaking for the Next Century* (Washington DC: Brookings, 1993).

19. Schick, *The Federal Budget,* 116.

20. Executive Office of the President of the United States, *A Citizen's Guide to the*

Federal Budget: Budget of the United States Government Fiscal Year 2001 (Washington DC: United States Government Printing Office).
http://www.access.gpo.gov/usbudget/fy2001/guide02.html (12/17/00).

21. Ibid.

22. American Council on Intergovernmental Relations, with the Cooperation of the Nelson A. Rockefeller Institute of Government, "Significant Features of Fiscal Federalism: Highlights." In *American Intergovernmental Relations,* ed. Laurence J. O'Toole, Jr. (Washington, DC: CQ Press, 2000), 196–210.

23. Ibid.

24. Christine LaPaille, Jason Feuchtwanger, and Ken Powers, *States' Budget Forecast Cloudy,* National Governor's Association Press Release. http://www.nga.org/Release/PR-18Dec2000Fiscal/asp (12/20/00).

25. National Governor's Association and the National Association of State Budget Officers, *The Fiscal Survey of the States: August 2000* (Washington, DC: National Governor's Association and the National Association of State Budget Officers, 2000).

26. National Association of State Budget Officers, *Policy Resources.* http://www.nasbo.org (1/1/01).

27. David H. Rosenbloom, *Public Administration: Understanding Management, Politics, and Law in the Public Sector,* 3rd ed. (New York: McGraw-Hill, Inc., 1993).

28. Office of Management and Budget, *Report to Congress on the Costs and Benefits of Federal Regulations* (Washington, DC: Office of Management and Budget, June, 2000).

29. Ibid.

30. Cornelius M. Kerwin, *Rulemaking: How Government Agencies Write Law and Make Policy,* 2nd ed. (Washington, DC: CQ Press, 1999).

31. Office of Management and Budget, *Report to Congress on the Costs and Benefits of Federal Regulations.*

32. Walter A. Rosenbaum, *Environmental Politics and Policy,* 4th ed. (Washington, DC: CQ Press, 1998).

33. Robert W. Hahn, "Regulatory Reform: What Do the Government's Numbers Tell Us?" In *Risks, Costs, and Lives Saved: Getting Better Results from Regulation,* ed. Robert W. Hahn (Washington, DC: AEI Press, 1996), 208–253.

34. Office of Management and Budget, *Report to Congress on the Costs and Benefits of Federal Regulations.*

35. Ibid.

36. Ibid.

37. "Over-Regulating America: Tomorrow's Economic Argument," *The Economist,* 340, no. 7976 (July 27, 1996): 19–21.

38. Office of Management and Budget, *Report to Congress on the Costs and Benefits of Federal Regulations* (Washington, DC: Office of Management and Budget, September 1997).

39. Hahn, "Regulatory Reform."

4

Income Security Policy

Income security policy is the largest area of expenditure for the federal government, consuming nearly 38 percent of all federal expenditure. Social Security, the largest income security program, is also the single largest program in the federal government. As Figure 4.1(a) shows, it cost $433.1 billion in 2001. That same year the federal government spent an additional $269.8 billion on other income security programs, for a total expenditure of $702.9 billion.

The federal government carries most of the burden of funding income security programs. As Figure 4.1(b) shows, the states spend a relatively small percentage of their overall funding on income security programs. In 2001 all fifty states spent $23.3 billion, or about 2.3 percent of their total budget expenditures. Much of what they spend is provided by the federal government in the form of grants. In 2001 these grants accounted for $9.9 billion, over 42 percent of the monies the states spent on income security.[1]

How do we explain the enormous expenditure for income security programs? The idea that government should provide some level of income security for people who do not have personal wealth to see them through tough economic times is not new. The long-established English Poor Law tradition, which dates to 1601, held taxpayers in local communities responsible for providing for the needs of the destitute. There was widespread debate regarding who was "deserving" of aid. Nevertheless, the American colonists brought this tradition with them, and the colonies typically required local government units to provide for the deserving needy.[2] This common-law tradition proved sufficient until the aftermath of the Civil War, when there was widespread and

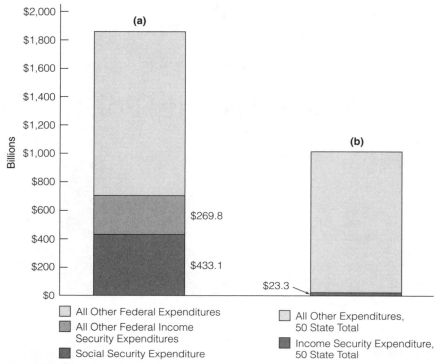

FIGURE 4.1 (a) Federal Expenditure for Income Security, FY 2001.
(b) Estimated 50 State Expenditure for Income Security, FY 2001.

SOURCES: (a) The Budget of the United States FY 2003, summary tables.
[http://www.whitehouse.gov/omb/budget/index.html] (b) National Association of State
Budget Officers, State Expenditure Report 2000, 2001.

urgent need for public support for hundreds of thousands of disabled veterans, war widows, and orphans. In response to this crisis, a pension program very similar to today's Social Security program was developed. However, a program to serve the general population did not emerge until later.[3]

The first comprehensive national program to provide income security can be traced back to Germany in the 1880s, when Chancellor Bismarck led a fight for social insurance programs for victims of industrial accidents. Similar programs were rapidly adopted across Europe and were quickly expanded to include old-age pensions and health benefits.[4] In the United States, social welfare programs took firm root during the Great Depression of the 1930s. These programs came to include retirement pensions, worker accident insurance, unemployment insurance, and public assistance (welfare) for people who were unable to provide for themselves.

U.S. income security programs today share the goal of guaranteeing that people do not fall into poverty, but they differ in eligibility standards and the way benefits are allocated. Benefits can be cash or **in-kind.** Programs that provide in-kind assistance include the Food Stamp and other nutrition programs and housing assistance.

Eligibility can be determined by need, or it may be determined by having paid premiums into an insurance-based program. **Insurance-based programs** are available to people who paid, typically through payroll deductions, into the funds that maintain these programs. The benefit a recipient eventually receives is dependent, to a certain extent, on how much was paid into the fund. Social Security, worker's compensation, and unemployment insurance are insurance-based income security programs.

Eligibility for the second group of income security programs is based not on prior payment into the fund but rather on need. Programs that determine need by current level of income (or means) are called **means-tested.** Temporary Assistance to Needy Families (TANF) is a means-tested income security policy. Supplemental Security Income (SSI) is also determined by need, but neediness is based not only on income but also on age or disability.

For each of the income security programs discussed in this chapter, we begin with a brief description of the program's history and evolution. We next discuss how the program currently operates and issues that are of significance to the program's future evolution.

SOCIAL INSURANCE PROGRAMS

Social Security

The decades of the 1920s and 1930s were difficult economic times for the United States. Beginning in the 1920s a persistent drought had a devastating effect on agriculture on the Great Plains (the Dust Bowl). Unable to grow food, farming families could not sell their crops for cash to feed themselves or repay bank loans. Many thousands lost their land and livelihood when banks foreclosed on farms used as collateral to guarantee loan payments.

Farmers were not the only group to suffer from economic insecurity. The crash of the stock market in 1929 signaled worse times ahead. Wealthy investors lost fortunes in the crash, and many smaller investors saw their funds vanish. The crash was a bellwether of the widespread economic problems that plagued the country (and most of the world) in the 1930s.

The Great Depression, as it came to be called, was a time of extreme economic contraction. Businesses went bankrupt in large numbers, leaving many people without jobs. Unemployment rates were at record highs. Many banks and other financial institutions simply closed their doors, and those who had their money in accounts lost it. Poverty was widespread. Charitable organizations set up "soup kitchens" to feed the millions of hungry. Homeless individuals and families were all too common. As the Depression dragged on year after year, it deepened. More businesses and banks failed; fewer people had jobs or money to spend; and so more businesses and banks failed. The downward spiral seemed unstoppable. A massive public demand for the government to do something arose.[5]

The administration of Herbert Hoover, who was president when the market crashed, unfortunately implemented precisely the wrong policies. Hoover relied on private assistance and voluntary aid to the poor, while at the same time presiding over a tax increase meant to shore up the national budget deficit. These policies exacerbated the financial crisis.

In the 1932 presidential election campaign, Franklin Delano Roosevelt (FDR) promised to take proactive steps to solve the nation's problems. FDR was elected by a nation weary of economic insecurity. His mandate was to provide the same level of income security that Europeans had long known. Shortly after taking residence in the White House, FDR issued Executive Order 6757, which created the Committee on Economic Security. This committee drafted a report to the president with a recommendation for the establishment of what later became the Social Security program.[6]

The **Social Security** Act of 1935 was one of many Roosevelt-era efforts to deal with the financial chaos caused by the Great Depression. Social Security taxes were collected beginning in 1937, and regular pension payments began in 1940. The initial law paid retirement benefits only to contributing workers, but in 1939 the law was changed to add survivors' benefits as well as benefits for the retiree's spouse and children. In 1956 disability benefits were added.[7]

The Social Security Act established a three-member board to administer Social Security, unemployment compensation, and a few other public assistance programs. The board became the Social Security Administration (SSA) in 1946, and in 1953 it was placed under the Department of Health, Education, and Welfare (subsequently renamed the Department of Health and Human Services). In 1994 the Social Security Administration was removed from Health and Human Services; it is now an independent agency.[8]

The Social Security system has played a major role in improving the financial position of retired workers and their families. The system has grown and now covers 96 percent of all jobs in the United States. Between the time benefits were first paid in 1940 and 1972, Congress increased benefit levels ten times. Since 1975, benefits have been indexed for inflation through the use of a cost-of-living adjustment (COLA).[9]

The largest program in the federal government, Social Security accounts for nearly 24 cents of every federal dollar spent. Social Security pays monthly benefits to retirees and people who are disabled as well as a survivor's benefit to families. Social Security is a source of income for more than 44 million Americans.[10]

The money that supports Social Security is raised by a payroll tax of 15.3 percent of gross wages. The employee and the employer each pay 7.65 percent. Social Security taxes also support Medicare, a major health support program for retirees discussed in the next chapter. For people working for an employer, the employer deducts 7.65 percent of the employee's earnings, matches that amount, and sends the money to the Internal Revenue Service (IRS). Self-employed individuals are required to pay the full amount when they file their income tax returns.[11] Social Security payroll taxes are collected under the authority of the Federal Insurance Contribution Act (FICA), which was enacted directly after the creation of the Social Security program in 1935.[12]

The Social Security tax, which is generally referred to as FICA tax, is paid into three trust funds. The Federal Old-Age and Survivors Insurance (OASI) trust fund is used to pay for retirement and survivor's benefits—the part of the program that is commonly called "Social Security." OASI gets the bulk of the funds, receiving 10.7 percent of each employee's gross wages. The Federal Disability Insurance (DI) trust fund, which provides for expenditures associated with payments to the disabled, gets 1.7 percent, and the remaining 2.9 percent goes to support Medicare.[13] Social Security taxes are paid on earnings up to a specified maximum, which was $80,400 in 2001. The portion of the tax going to Medicare, however, continues to be deducted on amounts over the maximum.[14] Since its inception, more than $4.5 trillion has been paid into the trust funds, and more than $4.1 trillion has been paid out in benefits. The remainder is currently on reserve as surplus in the trust funds.[15]

To qualify for Social Security benefits, a worker is required to accumulate a certain number of "credits." Credits are based on earnings associated with a Social Security number. People paying into the program can earn a maximum of four credits per year. Each year the amount of earnings needed for a credit rises as average earning levels rise. In 2001 each $830 paid into the fund earned one credit toward future benefits. The number of credits required varies depending on age and the type of benefits that are claimed. For most taxpayers it takes forty credits, or about ten years of work, to qualify for retirement benefits.[16] Not everyone earns credits. Many federal and state government employees, railroad workers, and children under the age of twenty-one who work in their parents' businesses are not covered by Social Security.[17]

Social Security pays retirement benefits to more than 30 million retirees.[18] Retirement age is currently sixty-five. A reduced benefit is available for people retiring at sixty-two. People who delay receipt of retirement benefits until they reach seventy get a special credit for each month they do not receive benefits until they reach age seventy.

Benefits vary according to how much a person pays into the fund. Most recipients can expect to receive benefits that amount to about 40 percent of their average lifetime earnings.[19] Generally, workers' wages are far lower when they are younger but grow over time, so average lifetime earnings are almost certainly less than the income earned in the last several years at work. In 1999 a low-income worker could expect approximately $13,400 in annual Social Security payments; an average-income worker could expect to receive annual benefits of $29,700; and a high-income worker would receive $72,600. People who are not willing to accept a vastly reduced income in old age need continuing income support in addition to Social Security payments.

As Figure 4.2 shows, the benefits flowing to individuals have increased steadily since 1941. There are several reasons for the increase. Social Security has expanded to include more people since its inception. By 1999 nearly 90 percent of the aged population received Social Security payments; in the early years of the program, far fewer of the elderly had enough credits to qualify. Another reason for the increase is that as women moved into the workforce they became eligible for their own old-age insurance and disability payments, rather than relying on survivor's benefits. Happily, people are living longer and drawing benefits for a longer time. These trends combine to form an increasing pool of individuals receiving benefit payments.

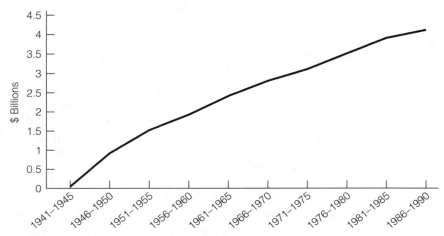

FIGURE 4.2 Average Annual Benefit Payments

SOURCE: United States Social Security Administration

People receiving Social Security benefits are not restricted from earning additional income, provided they have reached full retirement age. There is a cap on how much a person under full retirement age who receives Social Security benefits can earn. In 2001 a person under sixty-five who was collecting Social Security benefits could earn only $10,680 in outside income before his or her Social Security check was reduced $1 for every $2 over the limit. The year the person turns sixty-five, the penalty is $1 in reduced benefits for every $3 earned above $25,000 until the month of full retirement age is reached.[20]

Social Security Amendments of 1954, 1956, and 1960 established a disability insurance program and allowed for cash payments to disabled individuals.[21] Social Security pays benefits to recipients who have accumulated enough credits and have become disabled, regardless of age. The number of credits needed to qualify for disability benefits is based on age. For instance, a person under twenty-four may need only six credits. The number of credits needed increases with age to forty credits at age sixty-two or older.[22]

Disability is defined as a physical or mental ailment that prevents a person from doing what the Social Security Administration refers to as "substantial" work. In 2001 substantial work was the ability to earn $740 or more per month.[23] More than 4 million disabled workers under sixty-five and 1.6 million dependents received Social Security disability benefits in 2001. The average benefit to a disabled worker was $754 a month.[24]

When a person dies, Social Security benefits are payable to certain family members. These payments are called survivor's benefits.[25] Eligibility is restricted to widows or widowers age sixty or over, disabled widows or widowers over fifty, widows or widowers caring for a dependent child, and children under eighteen. A special one-time payment of $255 may be made to a spouse or minor child to help defray burial costs.[26] The amount of the benefit depends on how much the contributor paid into Social Security. Survivors typically get a percentage of the benefits that the contributor would have received had he or she lived to collect them.[27] Average survivor benefits for a household of a widow or widower with two dependent children was $1,611 a month in 2001.[28]

The Social Security trust funds currently have a large surplus because there are more workers than there are beneficiaries. As tax revenues are deposited in the trust funds, Social Security benefits are paid out, and the remainder is invested in U.S. government interest-bearing bonds, thus funding some of the overall debt of the federal government.[29] The interest earned is substantial. In 1998, for instance, the Social Security trust funds earned $49.3 billion in interest from government securities.[30]

This will change when the baby-boom generation (people born between 1946 and 1964) begins to retire. Within the next several decades there will be more retired workers than active workers, and the Social Security trust funds will begin to pay out more in benefits than are deposited in taxes.[31] The surpluses currently in the funds will be drained, and by 2035 the program will have insufficient funds to operate.[32]

Some people think that their Social Security taxes are held in interest-bearing accounts and are earmarked for their own personal use. This is not the case. Social Security is an intergenerational compact. Workers paying in today are providing support for people who are currently receiving benefits. This situation is workable when there is a balance between those paying in and those receiving benefits. In thirty years about twice as many people will receive benefits, and the number of workers per beneficiary will drop from 3.4 to 2.1.[33] Major governmental reforms are necessary to keep the Social Security program solvent beyond 2035, when the trust funds are predicted to be exhausted.

One reform to deal with this future crisis has been to increase the retirement age. The full retirement age for people born before 1938 is sixty-five. It has been increased to sixty-seven for people born in 1967 or later.[34] Some analysts suggest that it should be raised again. Because Americans are living longer, they are spending more years in retirement than ever before. The resulting strain on the system could be eliminated by keeping people in the workforce longer. Some have suggested that Social Security taxes should be paid at all income levels, rather than being capped at a maximum level ($80,400 in 2001). This would permit additional revenues to be paid into the system.

Another suggested reform, and a campaign promise made by President George W. Bush, is to permit people who pay into Social Security to place a portion of their taxes in personal private-sector investment accounts in exchange for a lower level of guaranteed future benefits. Proponents believe that the private sector will return greater benefits to those willing to embrace its risks. This potential reform sounded good to many while the stock market was continuing its unprecedented decade-long climb. Once a recession began shortly after Bush assumed office, fewer people were eager to invest their Social Security funds in the declining stock market. The exact nature of the reforms that will be adopted is not yet certain, but the need to change the system is abundantly clear.

Unemployment Insurance

Unemployment insurance provides temporary income support for workers thrown out of work as a result of economic downturns, downsizing, and other reasons. It was the second large insurance program written into the 1935 Social Security Act.[35] Title IX of the Social Security Act required companies employing more than four people to pay federal payroll taxes unless they participated in a state unemployment insurance program that met federal guidelines. This provision served as an incentive for the states to establish their own unemployment compensation programs, and all fifty states did so.[36]

By 1935, when the United States finally adopted unemployment insurance, unemployment policies had been in place in nineteen European nations as well as Canada and Australia for a number of years. In the United States the onus of unemployment had traditionally fallen on the worker. It was widely assumed that adults who did not have jobs were lazy or incompetent, or had other personal vices. The Great Depression changed those attitudes. With nearly 25 percent of the workforce thrown out of work, it seemed implausible to blame workers. Moreover, the duration of the Great Depression made it clear that there was no relationship between willingness to work and unemployment. Even after unemployment insurance was in place, however, considerable attention was paid to the fear that the program would encourage workers to become unemployed by creating work disincentives.[37]

In 1931 Franklin D. Roosevelt, who was then governor of New York, called a conference of governors of the six northeastern states to discuss the problem of unemployment and potential solutions. Wisconsin became the first state to enact unemployment insurance in 1932. New York, California, Massachusetts, New Hampshire, Utah, and Washington had followed by 1935, but federal intervention was required before the rest of the states adopted unemployment insurance plans. Although the unemployment insurance program has been modified over time (to raise tax rates and to include unemployed veterans, for instance), the essential provisions of the law remain in line with the 1935 act.[38]

Unemployment insurance is provided to workers by the states. Federal guidelines supply some level of state-to-state program consistency, but the amounts paid in benefits and the duration of the benefits differ among the states. In all states, voluntarily leaving a job or being discharged for misconduct are grounds for benefit denial.[39] Unemployed workers are required to appear in person to show that they are able and willing to work. A worker is typically required to accept work if a job is offered, although he or she is not required to become a strikebreaker or work for wages lower than the norm for the position. States are required to make job counseling and placement services available to the unemployed, and federal funds are transferred to the states to help with the operation of these programs. Workers are required to register with the U.S. Employment Service, which is usually located in the same building as the state unemployment benefits office, if they wish to receive benefits.[40]

Unemployment benefits are generally sufficient to provide short-term income support to workers, especially when they are supplemented with union payments or other forms of assistance. Unemployment benefits typically provide workers only with a small percentage of their working salary. Congress has extended and expanded benefits in times of particular economic distress. During the recession of 1991–1992, for instance, Congress added a special supplement to the program.

In and of themselves, however, unemployment benefits are of little long-term help to workers put out of work due to fundamental shifts in the economy. Workers thrown out of manufacturing jobs rarely have the skills to take jobs in the new information-based economy. Unemployment compensation does not address such structural sources of unemployment, and other government programs are necessary in these circumstances.[41]

Who bears the burden of unemployment? There are important demographic, racial, and gender differences in unemployment levels. In recent decades teenagers have had the highest rates of unemployment of any age group, sometimes three times higher than the unemployment rate for society as a whole. Women have higher unemployment rates than men. This weighs heavily on women-headed single-parent families. Minority groups also suffer from persistently higher levels of unemployment.[42]

Worker's Compensation

Worker's compensation provides income security benefits to injured workers and the survivors of workers killed on the job. Prior to the implementation of compensation laws in the early 1900s, injured workers who wanted compensation had to sue their employers for not providing a safe workplace. Winning this sort of lawsuit was difficult, since employers merely needed to show that they were not acting in an intentionally negligent manner.

In the early 1900s most states enacted worker's compensation laws that set money aside to pay workers who had been physically harmed at work, regardless of fault.[43] Since then, worker's compensation has remained a state-based program of income security. Since each state drafted its own law, no two laws are alike, but all provide cash payments to partially replace lost wages, some measure of medical and hospital care for the injured worker, and death benefits to a worker's family.[44]

Typically, the costs of the insurance programs are borne by employers. The programs are funded in several ways. In some states employers pay contributions directly to the state, which maintains a trust fund for all claims. In other states employers are required to show that they have paid premiums to private insurers who agree to provide benefits to injured workers. Still others allow employers to self-insure and directly pay claims to their own workers.[45]

Worker's compensation claims are frequently made for personal injuries due to workplace accidents, such as equipment falling on a worker, and injuries due to workplace demands, such as lifting heavy boxes. More and more worker's compensation claims are coming in the form of class action suits. In a class action suit, a class (a group of people similarly harmed) joins together to seek compensation from an employer for damages they believe they have received. For example, large numbers of employees in an assortment of industries were exposed to asbestos in the workplace before it was determined to be a cancer-causing agent. Now that they are falling ill, they are filing claims against their employers. Another example is the thousands of nuclear industry workers exposed to radioactive substances who are seeking compensation for physical ailments related to that exposure.

More controversial is the extension in some states of worker's compensation benefits to workers traumatized by witnessing or causing a coworker's injury. Some states have allowed claims on the basis of employees' suffering mental harm as a result of these events.[46] Another contentious issue is the requirement by some companies that workers who file claims submit to genetic tests, which can result in denial of claims should the tests show genetic predisposition to the injury. The Equal Employment Opportunity Commission's first lawsuit challenging genetic testing was brought against the Burlington Northern Santa Fe Railroad, which required employee gene tests to ensure that workers filing claims for carpal tunnel syndrome were not genetically predisposed to the condition.[47]

MEANS-TESTED PROGRAMS

Eligibility for a number of income security programs is based on financial means (or income). To qualify for these programs, an applicant must demonstrate economic need. The level of neediness is determined differently by each of the programs, but the calculation typically involves comparing the income of the applicant to the poverty level (or some multiple of it).

The federal poverty level is established annually by the Census Bureau, which uses a set of income thresholds that vary by family size. If a family's total income is below the Census Bureau's threshold, that family and everyone in it are eligible for means-tested program assistance. In 2001 the threshold for a family of four with two children under the age of eighteen was $17,960.[48] Means-tested income support programs may require a family to be at this poverty level to qualify, or they may allow families to earn more. Typical increments are 150 percent or 200 percent above the poverty level. States may also adjust the calculation based upon cost of living in the state.

Welfare

As noted at the start of this chapter, the English Poor Law tradition set the precedent for local care of the needy. Most communities set up or had access to almshouses in which the destitute could find aid in exchange for work. Most also provided some cash assistance so that needy individuals could continue to reside in the community. These so-called mother's pensions were set up in most states in the early 1900s to provide aid to families without a source of support. They were geared to the needs of widows, not deserted wives or unmarried mothers. By 1934 all states except Georgia, Alabama, and South Carolina had mother's pensions in place.[49]

Public assistance for the needy began at the national level in 1935 with the passage of the Social Security Act. Under this act, federal funds were made available for aiding dependent children. To receive funds, each state was required to submit a statewide plan for approval by the Secretary of Health, Education, and Welfare (now Health and Human Services). States could choose how to implement their public assistance programs, but they had to comply with certain federal guidelines regarding program administration and eligibility requirements. For instance, a single agency had to administer the program, and states had to provide people who were denied benefits with the option of a hearing.[50] States determined the level of payments needed by families for basic survival.

The Aid to Families with Dependent Children (AFDC) program was a federal-state partnership with a considerable amount of state-to-state variation in program operation. In the 1960s the emphasis was on providing social services to AFDC recipients, especially children. This casework model emphasized treating each recipient holistically to determine the full range of needs and respond with appropriate services.

A welfare rights movement emerged during the 1960s, and its advocates suggested that the poorer members of society had the right to share in the wealth of the nation. The primary result was to swell the rolls of welfare recipients; the number of people on welfare increased by 36 percent between 1962 and 1967. As eligibility requirements eased in the late 1960s, even more people moved onto the welfare rolls.[51]

By the 1970s there was growing concern about the increasing number of welfare recipients. Movements started in the states to reverse the direction of public assistance. The first attempt involved divesting caseworkers of the role of establishing eligibility for assistance. Since caseworkers were presumably advocates for the poor, removing their authority to enroll clients had the effect of reducing welfare rolls. In the 1980s the reform movement promoted self-sufficiency by demanding work in exchange for benefits.[52]

Welfare reform was the goal of the 1988 Family Support Act (FSA). The FSA modified the structure of Aid to Families with Dependent Children in order to replace AFDC with a support program that emphasized education, training, and work and tried to end long-term welfare dependence. President George H. W. Bush continued the emphasis on welfare reform by encouraging the states to apply for waivers from federal mandates so that they could institute experimental programs with strong incentives to promote self-sufficiency.[53]

Neither the FSA nor the state experiments were successful in stemming the tide of increasing welfare rolls. The average number of children receiving monthly AFDC benefits was a little over 3 million in 1965. By 1970 that number had grown to more than 6 million; by 1980 to over 7 million; and in 1992 to more than 9 million children. These growing numbers caused public concern and became an issue in the 1992 presidential campaign, when one of Bill Clinton's campaign slogans was a promise to "end welfare as we know it."

Little welfare reform was accomplished during the first years of the Clinton administration. With the election of a Republican Congress in 1994, however, welfare reform became a primary goal not only of the president but also of the House of Representatives under the leadership of Republican Speaker Newt Gingrich. In August 1996 the Personal Responsibility and Work Opportunity Reconciliation Act (PRWOR) replaced AFDC with a new program called **Temporary Assistance to Needy Families (TANF).**

PRWOR effectively ended the sixty-year-old system of welfare entitlements. It turned responsibility for assisting the needy over to the states, which were required to implement TANF by July 1997.[54] In exchange for assuming primary responsibility for moving people off of welfare and into work and self-sufficiency, the states were promised five years of funding along with new flexibility to administer welfare programs. They were required to implement programs that promoted work and personal independence. PRWOR affected a number of policy areas in addition to welfare, including child support, immigration, child care, job training activities, food stamps, and Supplemental Security Income (SSI).[55]

Under TANF, each state was to receive a federal block grant earmarked for welfare through the year 2001. Total federal funding was about $16 billion per year to be divided among the states based upon the size of their welfare rolls prior to passage of the welfare reform law. As Table 4.1 shows, TANF recipients fell in all fifty states and most U.S. territories between 1996 and 2000 as a result of the legislation.

By law the states were required to move half of their welfare caseloads into jobs by 2002; if they did not, their block grants would be reduced. Although there are exceptions, federal TANF funds typically may not be spent on any adult who has received a total of five years of welfare support during his or her lifetime or on any adult who fails to find work after two years.

TANF marks a major change in government assistance to the poor. As Figure 4.3 shows, the number of families receiving aid was more than halved been 1995 and 2000. The federal government is no longer responsible for the support of poor families; that responsibility has passed to the states. More important, TANF is not an entitlement program. It does not guarantee income security. The states are free to spend income security funds for other programs, such as pregnancy prevention counseling and job training. TANF also allows states to transfer responsibility for poor families to lower levels of government, including counties and cities.[56]

Welfare reform raises some fundamental fairness issues. Advocates of reform suggest that working and striving for self-sufficiency are positive goods in and of themselves. They imply that the old entitlement system encouraged unmarried women to have children and condemned the children to lives of poverty or near-poverty. Opponents see TANF as punitive. They argue that

Table 4.1 TANF Recipients by State

STATE	1996	2000	Change	STATE	1996	2000	Change
Alabama	100,662	55,168	-45%	Montana	29,130	14,001	-52%
Alaska	35,544	24,389	-31%	Nebraska	38,592	26,841	-30%
Arizona	169,442	82,851	-51%	Nevada	34,261	16,478	-52%
Arkansas	56,343	28,113	-50%	New Hampshire	22,937	13,862	-40%
California	2,581,948	1,272,468	-51%	New Jersey	275,637	125,258	-55%
Colorado	95,788	27,699	-71%	New Mexico	99,661	67,950	-32%
Connecticut	159,246	63,589	-60%	New York	1,143,962	693,012	-39%
Delaware	23,654	17,262	-27%	North Carolina	267,326	97,171	-64%
Dist. Of Col.	69,292	44,487	-36%	North Dakota	13,146	7,734	-41%
Florida	533,801	135,903	-75%	Ohio	549,312	238,351	-57%
Georgia	330,302	135,381	-59%	Oklahoma	96,201	13,606	-86%
Guam	8,314	9,550	15%	Oregon	78,419	42,374	-46%
Hawaii	66,482	42,824	-36%	Pennsylvania	531,059	232,976	-56%
Idaho	21,780	1,382	-94%	Puerto Rico	151,023	90,630	-40%
Illinois	642,644	259,242	-60%	Rhode Island	56,560	44,826	-21%
Indiana	142,604	96,854	-32%	South Carolina	114,273	35,721	-69%
Iowa	86,146	52,293	-39%	South Dakota	15,896	6,702	-58%
Kansas	63,783	36,557	-43%	Tennessee	254,818	143,823	-44%
Kentucky	172,193	85,696	-50%	Texas	649,018	343,464	-47%
Louisiana	228,155	79,745	-65%	Utah	39,073	24,101	-38%
Maine	53,873	14,813	-73%	Vermont	24,331	15,528	-36%
Maryland	194,127	70,910	-63%	Virgin Islands	4,898	2,920	-40%
Massachusetts	226,030	93,890	-58%	Virginia	152,845	67,388	-56%
Michigan	502,354	195,101	-61%	Washington	268,927	146,375	-46%
Minnesota	169,744	116,589	-31%	West Virginia	89,039	31,500	-65%
Mississippi	123,828	33,781	-73%	Wisconsin	148,888	37,381	-75%
Missouri	222,820	122,930	-45%	Wyoming	11,398	1,103	-90%
				U.S. TOTAL	12,241,489	5,780,543	-53%

SOURCE: United States Department of Health and Human Services Administration for Children and Families, December 2000.

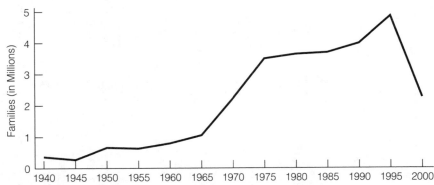

FIGURE 4.3 Families Receiving Public Assistance AFDC 1940–1995; TANF 1996–2000

SOURCE: Department of Health and Human Services Administration for Children and Families

although parents are the target of the punishment, the burden falls on the children. Nearly one in five children in the United States currently lives in poverty, and opponents argue that welfare reform will further exacerbate the problem.[57]

Over the last several decades, the changing wage structure has radically affected the distribution of income in the United States. The shift has been marked by the displacement of middle-income earners and an increase in the numbers of both low-income and high-income earners. There are several potential explanations for this shift. The movement away from a manufacturing-based economy toward a service-sector economy reduced the number of middle-income manufacturing jobs and replaced them with both high-paid (such as information technology workers) and low-paid (such as restaurant help) service-sector jobs. The policies of tax cuts for the wealthy that began in the 1980s are also thought to have increased the number of wealthy households.

Figure 4.4 graphically shows the shift in income distribution over the twenty years between 1974 and 1994. In 1974 there was a more even distribution of wealth among households. By 1994 twice as many households earned over $50,000, while the number of households accounting for the lowest incomes had also increased substantially. The wealthy are able to care for themselves, but the increase in the number of lower-income households poses a challenge for means-tested income security programs. As more households fall into the lower earning categories, a greater demand for government programs to alleviate poverty naturally emerges. Yet over this same time frame, welfare reform has drastically restructured government assistance to the needy. How able the states will be at providing TANF benefits to those who need assistance will depend in large part on future trends in income distribution.[58]

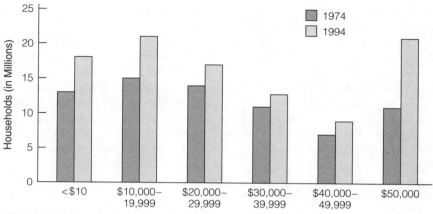

FIGURE 4.4 Annual Income by Household

SOURCE: Joint Center Tabulations of the 1974 American Housing Survey and the 1995 Current Population Survey

Supplemental Security Income

In 1972 the Social Security Administration became responsible for a new program called **Supplemental Security Income (SSI).** SSI replaced several programs that had been in place since the passage of the Social Security Act in 1935. These programs were operated by states or localities and were only partially funded by the federal government. Their main goal was to provide support for the blind, the elderly who had no other sources of income, and the disabled.[59] They had become complicated over time, and when President Richard Nixon undertook their reform, benefits were more than 300 percent higher in some states than in others. Nixon decided to create a single federal program that would replace the plethora of state and local programs, and SSI was created as a federal welfare program for the blind, the elderly, and the disabled.[60]

SSI makes monthly payments to individuals or families who have low incomes and few assets. To qualify, a person must be either disabled or elderly. Children as well as adults qualify for SSI. Income and assets must be below certain threshold levels that place the recipient in the needy category. A recipient's home and personal belongings are not counted in determining need, but cash on hand and bank balances are.[61] Nearly 40 percent of SSI recipients also receive Social Security benefits.

SSI is administered by the Social Security Administration, but it is funded by general tax levies rather than by Social Security taxes. Eligibility is not subject to having paid into the fund. SSI is a means-tested program.[62] It pays benefits to both couples and individuals. For 2001 the monthly payment to individuals was $530 and to couples $796.[63] Some states add money to the federal SSI payment. SSI sets limits on what can be earned outside of SSI. For individuals whose income is from wages only, the maximum that may be earned in a month is $1,145, and for couples it is $1,677.[64] Some states allow SSI recipients to earn more without losing eligibility for SSI benefits.

Welfare reform in 1996 made major changes to SSI. Title II of PRWOR tightened eligibility for disabled children and added accountability requirements. Children could not qualify as disabled unless they had a "medically determinable physical or mental impairment, which results in marked and severe functional limitations, and which can be expected to result in death or which has lasted or can be expected to last for a continuous period of not less than 12 months."[65] As a result of this definition, more than 120,000 children lost SSI benefits in the first four months of the law's implementation.[66]

The welfare reform law also initially denied SSI benefits to legal immigrants until they either had worked in the United States for ten years or became citizens. This section of the law was changed in 1997 to permit all legal immigrants to qualify for SSI benefits, regardless of when they became disabled.

Food Stamps

The idea of having the government distribute food to the hungry dates back to the Great Depression. The government wanted to dispose of excess agricultural supply so that the prices of farm goods would increase. An outcry arose when milk was dumped on the ground, so excess food began to be distributed to the poor. People who qualified for the program had to purchase orange stamps at full price, and they received one-dollar's worth of free blue stamps for each two-dollars' worth of orange stamps they purchased. Orange stamps could be used to buy any food item, but blue stamps could be used only to redeem surplus agricultural goods. In this way, the needy were able to get free food, and the Agriculture Department was able to dispose of excess production.[67] This program had two clear features. First, it sought to increase consumption. Second, by requiring the needy to purchase some stamps to get additional free stamps, the program reduced access to the program by the very poor. The orange and blue plan was cancelled in 1943 when World War II reduced agricultural surpluses.

In the 1950s Congress became interested in reintroducing food stamps to dispose of the large stores of food surplus building up under government farm-price supports. Instead the Eisenhower administration implemented a commodities distribution program called the Needy Family Program, in which local distribution centers gave away excess agricultural production. At its peak, the program served more than 4 million families.

In the 1960s the Kennedy administration reintroduced a simplified **Food Stamp program,** which was put in place by the Food Stamp Act of 1964 and ran alongside the Needy Family Program.[68] The program provided an income subsidy to low-income individuals and families by reducing the cost of food. Stamps of only one color were issued, and needy families were able to purchase them for a fraction of face value. Stamps could be spent on any food commodity, rather than being restricted to the purchase of agricultural surpluses.

An income requirement was built into the program, whereby the purchase price of the stamps rose along with family income. The Food Stamp program gradually replaced the Needy Family Program in more and more localities.[69]

The program was put in place just as public concern began to focus on hunger in America. Under the Nixon administration in the 1970s uniform national income eligibility standards were set, and the federal government agreed to pay half the program's administrative costs. With these changes, even more localities decided to participate. The program was serving 16.3 million people in 1975, up from 4.3 million in 1970. By the end of the 1970s all states were required to serve all eligible people applying for food stamps, thus making it an entitlement program. Reforms in the late 1970s removed the requirement that poor households purchase stamps, and this reform added another 3.6 million people to the program.[70] By 1992 about 25 million households were receiving food stamps.

The Food Stamp program is an in-kind federal assistance program run by states or localities. Every county in every state has at least one food stamp office. The Department of Agriculture pays for 100 percent of the cost of food stamps and supplements the states and localities by paying for about two-thirds of their administrative costs.

Households that meet eligibility requirements receive some number of food stamps, which are redeemable at grocery stores for food items. They can be used to buy foods accepted by the government as nutritious, including breads and cereals, fruits and vegetables, meat, and dairy products. Food stamps cannot be used to pay for beer, wine, liquor, tobacco, pet food, soap, paper products, any item to be eaten in the store, or hot foods.[71]

Each person in the household must be a U.S. citizen or, if a legal immigrant, must have accumulated forty qualifying work credits under Social Security Administration guidelines. Noncitizens who are legal permanent residents of the United States and are active-duty members or honorably discharged veterans of the U.S. armed forces are also eligible. American Indians who are members of federally recognized tribes are entitled to food stamps. Noncitizens may be eligible after living in the United States for seven years if they came to the country as refugees. To receive food stamps, individuals must register for work or participate in an employment and training program. Typically, households may not have more than $2,000 in resources, including cash, bank accounts, and other property, but not including a home and the land it is on. Households must also be below an income limit. Income limits vary by family size and by the amount of mortgage or rent paid, utility costs, and child-care costs to allow adults to work.[72]

Because eligibility requirements are less stringent, many people who are not eligible for cash assistance under TANF qualify for food stamps. In 1995 approximately 25 million American households received food stamps.[73]

By the beginning of the 1980s, emphasis shifted from expanding the Food Stamp program to reducing administrative costs and fraud. Some changes made it more difficult to qualify for food stamps. One of the greatest barriers is the federal requirement for frequent in-person eligibility recertification interviews. These reviews are especially problematic for people who are newly employed, in particular those making the transition from welfare to work under welfare reform. Food Stamp program caseloads have fallen along with welfare caseloads, regardless of the fact that those moving off of welfare probably still qualify for the program.[74]

Housing

Housing availability and affordability have been issues of social concern for many years. Housing assistance first began on a national level during the Great Depression, when one-third of the nation was considered ill-housed even by Depression standards.[75] In response, Congress passed the U.S. Housing Act of 1937, also known as the Wagner-Steagall Act. The act had two main goals. One was to build public housing units or repair existing stock so that it might become public housing, and the other was to provide rental assistance to low-income families.

There are major differences in these two goals. The construction and provision of public housing put the government in the potential position of competing with the private sector, while the provision of monetary assistance so that poor people could find housing in the private sector did not. The Housing Act, as part of wider Depression-era legislation, focused on reducing unemployment and was careful not to compete with private-sector development efforts. For each new unit of public housing constructed, it required local housing authorities to eliminate one unit of substandard or unsafe housing. This provision was put in place so that public efforts to improve housing would not increase the overall supply of housing units and thus drive down their prices.[76]

These early attempts to build public housing ended when World War II needs replaced all other government concerns. The building of public housing units resumed after the war with the passage of the 1949 Housing Act, which restricted access to these units to very low-income families.[77] During the 1960s and 1970s, in response to urban disorder, there was increased interest in building more housing units, and the Housing Act of 1968 established a production goal of 26 million units in ten years. By the mid-1970s public housing programs were being widely attacked as contributing to the economic and racial segregation of American cities.[78]

Public housing assistance was not restricted to providing dwellings. Section 8 of the 1937 Housing Act authorized programs to provide eligible families with vouchers or certificates that could be used to defer some of the cost of renting dwellings from private landlords. Landlords could redeem Section 8 vouchers for the difference between what a family could afford to pay for housing and the rent for the home.[79] These rent supplement programs were continued in later legislation and remain a major part of housing assistance today.

To live in public housing today, families and individuals must meet federal requirements, which include income limitations. Public housing is available to low-income families, the elderly, and the disabled. Rent varies, but it cannot represent more than 30 percent of a family's total annual income. Family income is certified annually to reevaluate rent scale. Public housing residents sign leases, which are subject to termination after two weeks should the tenant fail to pay the rent.

Slightly more that 1 million public housing units are currently available nationwide.[80] This is a decidedly small number of units, given the demand. Moreover, the physical condition of this very limited supply of public housing is poor, and buildings are in need of repair. The Department of Housing and Urban Development's (HUD) Urban Revitalization Demonstration program (HOPE VI) has provided funds to redevelop a few of the nation's public housing units. Much needs to be done to redevelop the remaining units. Not only are buildings deteriorating, but the families living in them also experience serious socioeconomic problems. Eighty percent of the people living in public housing units have incomes below the poverty line. Crime and drugs flourish in public housing neighborhoods. Because of these problems and the isolation associated with grouping the poor together in centralized public housing units, many cities are trying to restructure their public housing initiatives. In several cities, large public housing units are being torn down. Attempts are being made to integrate poor families into new developments where they will live side-by-side with middle- or upper-income families.

A larger population is served by Section 8 housing assistance. The Quality Housing and Work Responsibility Act of 1998 merged the Section 8 voucher and certificate programs of the 1937 Housing Act into the Housing Choice Voucher Program. Eligible families can apply for Section 8 assistance as long as no more that 40 percent of their income has to be used to pay the rent in the first year.[81] The Section 8 housing voucher program is administered by local public housing authorities or other local government agencies. The administering housing authority or government agency is required to inspect the rental unit to ensure that it complies with Department of Housing and Urban Development quality guidelines. The housing authority also must verify that the rent charged is in accord with free market rates and that it meets HUD's guidelines.[82] The Section 8 Housing Choice Voucher Program is the largest U.S. housing subsidy program, with more than 3 million households participating.

The number of low-income Americans continues to grow, and the pressure increases for affordable housing. It is estimated that more than 5 million very low-income families use more than half of their income on housing. The quantity of affordable housing continues to shrink, making the situation worse. The housing needs of minority households increased dramatically in the last decade. The elderly, people with disabilities, and children are disproportionately affected.[83]

Welfare reform offers substantial challenges to HUD. Difficulties arise in moving welfare recipients to work when their housing is distant from potential employers and transportation to the workplace is not available. HUD has tried to meet this challenge with its Welfare-to-Work Voucher system. HUD provides vouchers so that families can move into apartments close to available jobs, child-care facilities, and public transportation. The vouchers are made available to communities on a competitive basis. Communities receiving the

HUD special program vouchers are required to work with welfare and work-force development agencies.[84]

SUMMARY

Income security programs are a major expenditure of the federal government. Their goal is to prevent people from falling into poverty. The numerous programs differ in eligibility standards and the way benefits are allocated. Eligibility can be determined by need, or it may be determined by having paid premiums into an insurance-based program. Social Security, worker's compensation, and unemployment insurance are insurance-based income security policies. Programs that determine need by current level of income are called means-tested. Temporary Assistance to Needy Families (TANF) is a means-tested income security policy. For the Supplemental Security Income (SSI) program, neediness is determined not only by income but also by age or disability. Some programs do not offer cash payments as benefits, but rather provide in-kind assistance. These programs include food stamps and other nutrition programs and housing assistance.

Social Security expenditures account for nearly 24 cents of every federal dollar spent, making Social Security the single largest federal program. It pays monthly benefits to retirees and the disabled as well as a survivor's benefit to families. Social Security is a source of income for more than 44 million Americans. The money that supports Social Security is raised by a payroll tax of 15.3 percent of gross wages—7.65 percent each from the employer and the employee. The Social Security trust funds currently have a large surplus. However, within the next several decades there will be more retired workers than active workers. When this happens, the trust funds will begin to pay out more in benefits than it receives in taxes, and the program will have insufficient funds to operate.

Unemployment insurance provides temporary income support for workers who have lost their jobs. Unemployment insurance was the second large insurance program written into the 1935 Social Security Act, and it provided incentives to the states to establish unemployment compensation programs through the enactment of a payroll tax on all employers. Unemployment benefits, in and of themselves, are of little long-term help to workers put out of work due to fundamental shifts in the economy. There are important demographic, racial, and gender differences in unemployment levels. The young, women, and minorities are affected by higher unemployment rates.

Worker's compensation provides income support benefits to injured workers and to the survivors of workers killed on the job. Worker's compensation is a state-based income security program. Each state provides income support to partially replace lost wages, some measure of medical and hospital care for the injured worker, and death benefits to a worker's family.

Public assistance for the needy began at the national level with the passage of the Social Security Act of 1935. Under this act, federal funds were made available for dependent children. For sixty years, the Aid to Families with Dependent Children program was the main component of welfare. In August 1996 the Personal Responsibility and Work Opportunity Reconciliation Act (PRWOR) replaced AFDC with a new program called Temporary Assistance to Needy Families (TANF), effectively ending the system of welfare entitlements. This reform turned responsibility for assistance to the needy over to the states, which assumed responsibility for moving people on welfare to work and self-sufficiency. PRWOR has affected a number of policy areas in addition to welfare, including child support, immigration, child care, job training activities, food stamps, and SSI.

The major sources of in-kind income support are food stamps and housing assistance. Households that meet eligibility requirements receive some amount of food stamps, which are redeemable at grocery stores for food items. Because eligibility requirements are less stringent, many people who are not eligible for cash assistance qualify for food stamps. Housing assistance is provided to eligible individuals or families in the form of public housing units or Section 8 vouchers to defer the cost of private-sector rental units.

KEY TERMS

Food Stamp program	Social Security	unemployment insurance
in-kind benefits	Supplemental Security Income (SSI)	
insurance-based programs		worker's compensation
means-tested programs	Temporary Assistance to Needy Families (TANF)	

WEB SITES

Social Security

http://www.ssa.gov/pubs
The Social Security Administration maintains a very useful Web site that provides detailed information about disability benefits, retirement benefits, survivors' benefits, and Supplemental Security Income (SSI). Also included is an assortment of information on how the program is financed and administered, how Social Security numbers are issued, how to apply for benefits, and how to compute credits.

Welfare

http://www.welfareinfo.org
A versatile Web site maintained by the Welfare Information Network and dedicated to charting the process of welfare reform. This site has information on the reauthorization of TANF, state welfare reform programs, laws and regulations, and links to just about every issue of interest associated with welfare

reform. It also provides access to data files that are useful in exploring the effect of welfare reform efforts.

http://www.nasbo.org/resource/welfare/welfare.htm
The National Association of State Budget Officers maintains this site, which provides information on how the states are dealing with welfare reform. It has many useful links to items of interest, including child support, legal immigrants, child care, job training activities, food stamps, and Supplemental Security Income.

Supplemental Security Income

http://www.ssa.gov/notices/supplemental-security-income
A site maintained by the Social Security Administration that contains both general and detailed information about SSI. There are discussions of regulations, SSI law, the SSI payment schedule, and historical information on payment amounts from 1975 to 2001.

Food Stamps

http://www.ssa.gov/pubs/10101.html
The Social Security Administration maintains this site that provides general facts on who is eligible for food stamps and how to apply.

http://www.frac.org/html/federal_food_programs/federal_index.html
A site maintained by the Food Research Action Center that provides information on government food programs, including the Food Stamp program, the National School Lunch program, the School Breakfast program, the Summer Food Service Program for Children, the Supplemental Nutrition Program for Women, Infants and Children (WIC), the Child and Adult Care Food Program (CACFP), and the Emergency Food Assistance Program (TEFAP)

Housing Assistance

http://www.nahro.org
The National Association of Housing and Redevelopment Officials site has useful entries on housing issues. Included are links to studies detailing the state of current U.S. housing stock. The site also contains links to sites on community development block grants, legislative initiatives, public housing, and Section 8 assistance.

DISCUSSION QUESTIONS

1. Explain the difference between insurance-based and means-tested programs. Give examples of each.
2. What are the major issues facing Social Security, and what are the proposed solutions?

3. List the social programs created by President Franklin Delano Roosevelt in response to the Great Depression.

4. How did PRWORA change the welfare system? How does this policy reflect the changing ideology regarding public assistance?

5. Name one income security program developed by the federal government and administered by the state.

6. What were the two reasons that the Food Stamp program was initiated? What agency is responsible for the administration of the program today?

WEB QUESTIONS

1. Discuss the purpose of the Promising Practices section of the Welfare Information Network's Web site at www.welfareinfo.org/promising.htm, and describe one of the programs listed.

2. Several government food programs are listed on the Food Research Action Center's Web site at http://www.frac.org/html/federal_food_programs/federal_index.html. Discuss the history, purpose, benefits, participation, eligibility, and funding of a federal program other than the Food Stamp program.

3. What issues or programs are on the current legislative agenda of the National Association of Housing and Redevelopment Officials (NAHRO), whose site is at http://www.nahro.org/legislative/index.html? List the Senate and House committees and subcommittees that NAHRO considers to be "Key Players" in accomplishing these goals.

NOTES

1. National Association of State Budget Officers, *State Expenditure Report 2000* (Washington, DC: National Association of State Budget Officers, 2001).

2. Elizabeth Wisner, *Social Welfare in the South: From Colonial Times to World War I* (Baton Rouge, LA: Louisiana State University Press, 1970).

3. Margaret C. Jasper, *Social Security Law* (Dobbs Ferry, NY: Oceana Publications, 1999).

4. Alexander Hicks, *Social Democracy and Welfare Capitalism: A Century of Income Security Politics* (Ithaca, NY: Cornell University Press, 1999).

5. Jasper, *Social Security Law.*

6. Edwin E. Witte, *The Development of the Social Security Act* (Madison, WI: University of Wisconsin Press, 1963).

7. Merton C. Bernstein and Joan Brodshaug Bernstein, *Social Security: The System That Works* (New York: Basic Books, 1988).

8. Jasper, *Social Security Law.*

9. National Research Council, *Assessing Policies for Retirement Income: Needs for Data, Research, and Models* (Washington, DC: National Academy Press, 1997).

10. Social Security Administration, *Social Security Basic Facts.* Social Security Administration Publication No. 05-10080, March 2000. http://www.ssa.gov/pubs/10080.html (1/30/01).

11. Social Security Administration, *A "Snapshot."* Social Security Administration Publication No. 05-10006, July 2000. http://www.ssa.gov/pubs/10006.html (1/30/01).

12. Jasper, *Social Security Law.*

13. Social Security Administration, *How It's Financed.* Social Security Administration Publication No. 05-10094, August 1999. http://www.ssa.gov/pubs/10094.html (1/30/01).

14. Social Security Administration, *Update 2001.* Social Security Administration Publication No. 05-10003, January 2001. http://www.ssa.gov/pubs/10003.html (1/30/01).

15. Jasper, *Social Security Law.*

16. Social Security Administration, *Update 2001.*

17. Social Security Administration, *How You Earn Credits.* Social Security Administration Publication No. 05-10072, January 2001. http://www.ssa.gov/pubs/10072.html (1/30/01).

18. Social Security Administration, *Social Security Basic Facts.*

19. Social Security Administration, *A "Snapshot."*

20. Social Security Administration, *Update 2001.*

21. Jasper, *Social Security Law.*

22. Social Security Administration, *Update 2001.*

23. Social Security Administration, *How You Earn Credits.*

24. Social Security Administration, *Social Security Basic Facts.*

25. Jasper, *Social Security Law.*

26. Social Security Administration, *A "Snapshot."*

27. Joseph F. Stenken, ed., *Social Security Manual* (Cincinnati, OH: National Underwriter Company, 2000).

28. Social Security Administration, *Social Security Basic Facts.*

29. Social Security Administration, *How It's Financed.*

30. Ibid.

31. National Research Council, *Assessing Policies for Retirement Income.*

32. Social Security Administration, *How It's Financed.*

33. Social Security Administration, *The Future of Social Security.* Social Security Administration Publication No. 05-10055, August 2000. http://www.ssa.gov/pubs/10055.html (1/29/01).

34. Social Security Administration, *A "Snapshot."*

35. Mark E. Rushefsky, *Public Policy in The United States: Toward the Twenty-First Century* (Pacific Grove, CA: Brooks/Cole, 1990).

36. Thomas R. Dye, *Understanding Public Policy,* 8th ed. (Englewood Cliffs, NJ: Prentice-Hall, 1995).

37. Tax Foundation, *Unemployment Insurance: Trends and Issues* (Washington, DC: Tax Foundation, Inc., 1982).

38. Robert Black, *Estimating Outlays for Unemployment Compensation Programs* (Washington, DC: Congressional Budget Office, 1976).

39. Saul J. Blausteing, *Unemployment Insurance in the United States: The First Half Century* (Kalamazoo, MI: W.E. Upjohn Institute for Employment Research, 1993).

40. Dye, *Understanding Public Policy.*

41. Clarke E. Cochran, Lawrence C. Mayer, T. R. Carr, and N. Joseph Cayer, *American Public Policy: An Introduction,* 6th ed. (Boston: Bedford/St. Martin's Press, 1999).

42. Richard K. Vedder and Lowell E. Gallaway, *Out of Work: Unemployment and Government in Twentieth-Century America* (New York: New York University Press, 1997).

43. William D. Haders, *The Paralegal's Guide to Administrative Law* (Cincinnati, OH: Anderson Publishing, 1994).

44. Frank Lang, *Workmen's Compensation Insurance* (Chicago: Richard D. Irwin, Inc., 1947).

45. Haders, *The Paralegal's Guide to Administrative Law.*

46. T. C. Brown, "High Court Says Workers' Comp Covers Mental Hurt," *Cleveland Plain Dealer,* February 4, 2001.

47. Greg Toppo, "Gene Map May Create Discrimination," *New York Times,* February 12, 2001.

48. U.S. Bureau of the Census, *Current Population Survey.* http://www.census.gov/hhes/poverty/threshld/thresh01.html (9.20/02).

49. Robert Stevens and Rosemary Stevens, *Welfare Medicine in America* (New York: The Free Press, 1974).

50. Vicky N. Albert, *Welfare Dependence and Welfare Policy: A Statistical Study* (New York: Greenwood Press, 1988).

51. Mary Jo Bane and David T. Ellwood, *Welfare Realities: From Rhetoric to Reform* (Cambridge, MA: Harvard University Press, 1994).

52. Ibid.

53. Ibid.

54. Cochran et al., *American Public Policy.*

55. National Association of State Budget Officers, *Welfare.* http://www.nasbo.org/resource/welfare/welfare.htm (1/4/01).

56. Cochran et al., *American Public Policy.*

57. The CQ Researcher, *Issues in Social Policy* (Washington, DC: CQ Press, 2000).

58. Joint Center for Housing Studies, *The State of the Nation's Housing* (Cambridge, MA: Joint Center for Housing Studies of Harvard University, 1996).

59. Jasper, *Social Security Law.*

60. Ibid.

61. Social Security Administration, *A "Snapshot."*

62. Ibid.

63. Social Security Administration, *Update 2001.*

64. Ibid.

65. Personal Responsibility and Work Opportunity Reconciliation Act (PRWOR), Public Law 104–193, Section 211.

66. Cochran et al., *American Public Policy.*

67. James C. Ohls and Harold Beebout,

The Food Stamp Program: Design Tradeoffs, Policy, and Impacts (Washington, DC: The Urban Institute, 1993).

68. Committee on Agriculture, House of Representatives, *Food Stamps Program* (Washington, DC: U.S. Government Printing Office, 1976).

69. Ohls and Beebout, *The Food Stamp Program.*

70. Ibid.

71. U.S. Department of Agriculture, *Food Stamps Online.* http://www.fns.usda.gov/fsp/MENU/FAQS/faqs.htm (9/20/02).

72. Social Security Administration, *Food Stamp Facts.* Social Security Administration Publication No. 05-10101, March 1998. http://www.ssa.gov/pubs/10101.html (1/30/01).

73. Social Security Administration, *Social Security Bulletin, Annual Statistical Supplement, 1996* (Washington, DC: U.S. Government Printing Office, 1996).

74. National Governor's Association, *Food Stamps.* National Governor's Association Online, December, 19, 2000. http://www.nga.org/106Congress/Foodstamps.asp (1/4/01).

75. Committee for Economic Development, *Financing the Nation's Housing Needs* (New York: Committee for Economic Development, 1973).

76. J. Paul Mitchell, "The Historical Context for Housing Policy," in *Federal Housing Policy and Program: Past and Present* ed. J. Paul Mitchell (New Brunswick, NJ: Center for Urban Policy Research, 1985).

77. Rachel G. Bratt, *Rebuilding a Low-Income Housing Policy* (Philadelphia: Temple University Press, 1989).

78. J. Mitchell, "The Historical Context for Housing Policy."

79. National Association of Housing and Redevelopment Officials, *Rental Assistance Programs.* http://www.nahro.org/programs/rent_s8/voucher/ (2/13/01).

80. National Association of Housing and Redevelopment Officials, *Public Housing.* http://www.nahro.org/programs/phousing/index.html (2/13/01).

81. National Association of Housing and Redevelopment Officials, *Rental Assistance Programs.*

82. Ibid.

83. U.S. Department of Housing and Urban Development, *Rental Housing Assistance—The Worsening Crisis*

(Washington, DC: U.S. Department of Housing and Urban Development, 2000).

84. National Association of Housing and Redevelopment Officials, *Welfare to Work Vouchers.* http://www.nahro.org/programs/rent_s8/welfare_work.html (2/13/01).

5

Health Care Policy

Unlike many nations that rely on their governments to provide basic health care to citizens, in the United States health care is provided almost entirely by the private sector. While there are an assortment of public hospitals and clinics, the overwhelming number of health care facilities are privately owned and operated. Despite the fact that government is not a large provider of health services, government is heavily involved in funding them. This chapter discusses a number of health care programs that are made possible by government funding in the context of private-sector provision of services.

The health care industry is a large part of overall U.S. economic activity; in fact it is the largest single industry in the United States.[1] Total health care expenditures amounted to more than $1.2 trillion in 1999, which comes to more than $4,300 for every person in the United States. Health care constitutes 13 percent of all national spending; in other words, 13 cents of every dollar spent in America goes to the health care industry.

Government programs for health consume considerable federal and state resources. As Figure 5.1(a) shows, at the federal level the major health care program is Medicare. It is the fourth-largest federal program overall. In 2001 Medicare expenditures came to $270 billion, or over 14 percent of all federal expenditure. The federal government spent an additional $172.6 billion on other health programs in 2001. Together, these programs cost a total of $442.6 billion and accounted for nearly 24 percent of all federal expenditure.

The states carry a significant load when it comes to health care for the needy. As Figure 5.1(b) shows, the states spent $198.7 billion—nearly 20 percent of their overall funding—on Medicaid in 2001. States raise that money in

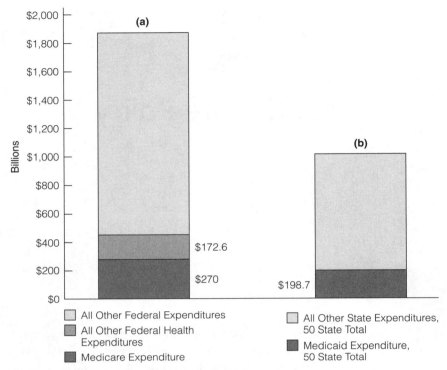

FIGURE 5.1 (a) Federal Expenditure for Health, FY 2001.
(b) Estimated 50 State Expenditure for Health, FY 2001.

SOURCES: (a) The Budget of the United States FY 2003, summary tables.
[http://www.whitehouse.gov/omb/budget/index.html] (b) National Association of State
Budget Officers, State Expenditure Report 2000, 2001.

a variety of ways. Federal government grants provided 56 percent of state funding of Medicaid, and the states independently raised the other 44 percent.[2]

How do we explain the enormous expenditure on health care programs? This chapter begins with a discussion of the evolution of health care in the United States, paying particular attention to the role of government. The organization of the U.S. health care system and how it is financed is discussed. The chapter then turns to the major government programs and concludes with a discussion of some of the dilemmas confronting the American health care system.

THE EVOLUTION OF HEALTH
CARE IN AMERICA

Prior to the discovery of disease transmission through germs, the practice of medicine relied heavily on tradition rather than science. Health care was largely dispensed in the home by a practitioner who traveled to the patient. For the most part, general hospitals were nonexistent. Poorhouses and almshouses took in sick people who had no families to care for them, but aside from these wretched places, health care was almost always provided in the home.

In early America, local government played a prominent role in the provision of health care to the poor. Just as the English Poor Law tradition that was transplanted to America had institutionalized local cash assistance to the poor, so was medical aid relegated to counties and towns. By the early 1900s counties and cities had built hospitals for the care of the indigent.[3] With the discovery of the science of disease transmission and anesthesia, however, surgery became painless and much safer, and hospitals became the place where surgery was performed.[4] Many additional hospitals were established by local governments, nonprofit community groups, and churches in the years following these discoveries, often with funding from millionaire philanthropists. The number of hospitals grew from a few dozen in 1875 to four thousand by 1900. These hospitals prospered by serving the rapidly expanding American middle class on a fee-for-service basis.[5]

There were a few limited federal efforts in the arena of health care prior to the Great Depression of the 1930s. One such effort was the establishment of Public Health Service Hospitals to serve seamen as called for by the 1798 Act for the Relief of Sick and Disabled Seamen. Seamen were seen as essential to the future of the nation, and the act tried to ensure their recovery from injury and illness. The federal government also assumed responsibility for providing places for the isolation of people sick with contagious diseases in times of epidemics.[6]

The Great Depression and the passage of the 1935 Social Security Act gave rise to an opportunity to provide health care benefits to the general population. In European nations government-provided health care services were part of the social welfare system. President Franklin Delano Roosevelt (FDR) believed, however, that the American public was not ready for major federal involvement with health care, so he did not insist on adding it to the 1935 act. Instead, the act provided federal grants to the states for maternal and child health care services and services for disabled children. From 1935 through the 1960s, while the federal government continued to support maternal and child health care services, the major federal thrust was building infrastructure (hospital construction) and conducting medical research (the National Institutes of Health).[7]

The structure for private-sector medical insurance emerged in the late 1920s when Blue Cross hospitalization insurance began in Dallas, Texas. Blue Cross spread across the country during the 1930s, and Blue Shield, which pays for physician services, was started. Over time a growing number of commercial insurers entered the health care market. The overall prosperity of the 1950s, combined with the strength of labor unions determined to negotiate generous benefits for their members, gave rise to the widespread adoption of employer-provided health insurance. Such insurance remains the foundation of the current heath care system.[8]

A new major role for the federal government came with the passage of the Social Security Amendments Act of 1965, which established the Medicare and Medicaid programs. **Medicare** helps pay for health care for the elderly, and

Medicaid was initially seen as a program to maintain the incomes of deserving elderly faced with large medical bills.[9] Medicaid was later expanded to include many low-income families unable to pay for health care in the dominant for-profit system.

THE U.S. HEALTH CARE SYSTEM

Today's health care system is dominated by private-sector for-profit organizations mixed with some not-for-profit health care providers. Government plays a relatively modest role in the direct provision of service through local health clinics that offer free or low-cost inoculations and general health care. Government also provides for health inspections, veterans' hospitals, and contagious disease control. Private-sector not-for-profit organizations play a critical role in raising money for research (for example, the March of Dimes) and providing targeted services (such as Planned Parenthood).

The bulk of the U.S. health care system is composed of private for-profit hospitals, physicians, and health care organizations. Health care professionals work either on a **fee-for-service** basis, whereby they receive payment for services provided, or in a **managed care** environment, whereby large groups of health care professionals negotiate a fixed rate of payment to care for a known population of patients. As shown in Figure 5.2, a complex system of private insurers and government regulators pay for these services. For most Americans, health care is funded by private health insurance or by one of several large government programs (Medicare, Medicaid, and the State Children's Health Insurance Program). Employers provide private health insurance for most working Americans and their families.

One of the major issues confronting the health care system over the last several decades is rapidly increasing costs. Costs have risen dramatically since the 1980s, when they consumed 8.8 percent of the gross domestic product (GDP). They hit 13.4 percent in 1993. Costs stabilized in the late 1990s and even fell to 13.2 percent of the GDP by 2000. In raw dollars, however, costs have skyrocketed, going from $245.8 billion in 1980 to nearly $1.3 trillion in 2000.[10] Particularly sharp cost increases between 1980 and 1990 led many citizens and government leaders to rethink the way health care is provided in the United States. Table 5.1 shows the growth in the national expenditure for health care, the per capita expenditure, the percent of gross domestic product spent on health care, and the average annual percentage growth of the costs from 1980 to 2000.

In an attempt to hold down costs in the 1980s and 1990s, many employers shifted from the traditional fee-for-service method of reimbursing health care providers to **health maintenance organizations (HMOs)** and **preferred provider organizations (PPOs).** HMOs and PPOs try to minimize costs by requiring patients to see only those physicians who have agreed to provide

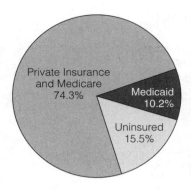

FIGURE 5.2 Health Insurance Coverage, 1999

SOURCE: U.S. Census Bureau, *Statistical Abstract of the United States, 2001* (Washington, DC.: U.S. Government Printing Office, 2001), p. 102.

services for fixed or reduced prices. HMO health care professionals receive fixed salaries and get bonuses if they keep costs low. PPO health care professionals agree to serve at a specified reduced rate based on the average market rate charged by all physicians. Other cost containment methods are employed. Primary care physicians control access to more expensive specialists; patients can see specialists only if referred by the primary care physician. There is widespread use of nurses and physician assistants, who earn less than physicians. Perhaps most controversial, physician recommendations are reviewed by the payers, who decide whether costly services are necessary. As a result, by the mid-1990s, cost increases began to slow, and annual percentage increases in health care costs went down to below 5 percent.

The result of putting so much pressure on cost escalation was serious concern about the quality of care. Physicians complained, and in an unprecedented move fifteen thousand voted to join the AFL-CIO-affiliated Service Employees International Union, arguing that they were employees of health care organizations that deprived them of decision-making authority. Denial of care became all too common, and patients pushed politicians to do something about access. President Bill Clinton proposed a "patient's bill of rights," and several members of Congress picked up the issue. The fact that many health care organizations are exempt from state law and cannot be sued became a central political issue for reformers.[11] Cost stabilization in the health care industry was short-lived, and in 2000 inflation rates were at 6.9 percent.[12] Employers once again expect double-digit inflation in health insurance costs in the coming years.

One explanation of the sharp increases in health care costs that began in the 1980s is that the phasing in of so-called **third-party payers** stimulated an uncritical demand for services. These third-party payers included the insurance companies that paid the bills of most health care users and the government, which paid for Medicare and Medicaid coverage. According to this explanation, consumers of medical care do not treat the health care system as a market. Patients do not shop for the best price for care. As a result, competition

Table 5.1 National Health Expenditures, 1980–2000

Year	Amount (in billions)	Per Capita Amount	Percent of Gross Domestic Product	Average Annual Percent Growth
1980	$245.8	$1,067	8.8%	11.7%
1990	$696.0	$2,738	12.0%	11.7%
1995	$990.3	$3,698	13.4%	5.7%
2000	$1,299.5	$4,637	13.2%	6.9%

SOURCE: Centers for Medicare and Medicaid Services, Department of Health and Human Services, *National Health Expenditures Aggregate and per Capita Amounts, 1980–2000.* http://cms.hhs.gov/statistics/nhe/historical/t1.asp (9/24/02).

does not bring down costs in the health care arena. Consumers receive services without any concern about the price. Furthermore, the phasing in of Medicare and Medicaid led to an increased use of services. A basic law of economics is that when demand goes up, so does price. The health care system was not an exception to this rule.[13]

Another reason for cost escalation is the use of the expensive technology responsible for many of the advances we have come to expect in modern medicine. To provide quality health care, physicians and hospitals must have access to the newest and best technology. Sometimes, however, the cost of new equipment cannot be justified by the amount of use it receives. Competing hospitals must have equivalent equipment if they wish to stay competitive, even if they cannot fully utilize it. The result is that equipment costs are passed through to other services that the hospital provides, thus raising overall prices.[14]

Medicine is a labor-intensive industry. Even though most workers do not command high salaries, their numbers have continued to increase, and the salaries add up. As the aging of society increases the burden on the health care system, the numbers will grow even more, as will the costs.[15]

Pre-tax medical accounts, a benefit often provided by employers to reduce employees' out-of-pocket health care costs, are another reason for increases in medical costs. These accounts allow a person to put aside a specified amount of money for medical expenses during the course of a year. Since any money that has not been spent is lost, these accounts encourage the use of all the money set aside. This in turn increases the demand on the health care system.[16]

Court cases may have an effect on costs in the future. Under the provisions of the Employee Retirement Income Security Act (ERISA) of 1974, 48 million Americans are currently prohibited from suing their health care plans, but some do have the right to sue. In a precedent-setting decision, a California superior court ordered Aetna US Healthcare to pay $120.5 million to the widow of a cancer patient whose doctor's request to use an experimental treatment was rejected by the insurance company. Whether a reform of ERISA will allow other policyholders to sue remains to be seen, but there is little doubt that health care plans must weigh denial of care decisions carefully.[17]

GOVERNMENT HEALTH CARE PROGRAMS

Millions of people rely on the government to provide them with medical insurance. Under the auspices of the Medicare, Medicaid, and S-CHIP programs, federal and state governments pay for the health care of targeted groups of people. Medicare provides coverage to those over sixty-five; Medicaid serves low-income individuals; and S-CHIP provides health care access to children whose lower-income families are not covered by private health insurance plans.

Medicare

Medicare is a federal health insurance program for the elderly and the disabled administered by the Social Security Administration and private insurance companies that contract with the government to process medical claims.[18] Eligibility is not determined by income; rather, Medicare is an entitlement program available to everyone aged sixty-five and older and those with disabilities who paid into the system (see Chapter 4).[19]

On July 30, 1965, President Lyndon Johnson signed the Medicare Bill in Independence, Missouri, the home of President Harry S. Truman. Years before, President Truman had tried to push some form of national health insurance coverage through Congress—as had President Roosevelt before him and Presidents Dwight Eisenhower and John Kennedy after him. Fearing that the opposition of the powerful American Medical Association (AMA), which opposed government health insurance, would damage his Social Security bill, President Roosevelt had moved away from the controversial issue. President after president was unable to place health care onto the national agenda. By adopting an incremental approach that phased in government involvement with health care by applying it only to the aged, Johnson was able to see his policy through to success.[20]

Medicare was originally designed in two parts. **Medicare Part A** covered all recipients for hospital stays, while the optional **Medicare Part B** provided medical insurance for health care not requiring a hospital stay. In 1997 Congress passed a law expanding newly covered preventive care services. This change acknowledged the weaknesses in Medicare coverage as it was originally defined and gave recipients a choice regarding future health care options.[21] Commonly called the **Medicare+Choice** program, it gave participants the right to select additional health care options that would be covered under Medicare.

Even with these options, Medicare does not pay all of a recipient's medical expenses, and recipients often purchase additional **Medigap** insurance to supplement their Medicare benefits. These policies generally pay for expenses not reimbursed by Medicare, such as hospital deductibles and copayments.[22]

Medicare is funded with both tax dollars and private contributions, and the monies are divided into two Medicare trust funds: the Federal Hospital Insurance (HI) trust fund, which pays for the services covered under Part A (the hospital insurance provisions) of Medicare, and the Federal Supplementary Medical Insurance (SMI) trust fund, which pays for services under Part B (the medical insurance provisions). Of the 15.3 percent Social Security tax on wages (discussed in Chapter 4), 2.9 percent goes into the HI trust fund. Social Security taxes are not put into the SMI trust fund. Its revenues come from general taxes collected by the Treasury Department and from private contributions in the form of enrollee premiums.[23]

Medicare Part A pays benefits only after substantial deductibles are met. For the first sixty days of hospitalization in 2001, Medicare required the patient to pay $792. For the sixty-first through ninetieth day, the patient is required to pay $198 a day before Medicare pays its share. At these rates, someone hospitalized for roughly three months would pay $6,732 before Medicare covered its share of hospital expenses. Should a person be unfortunate enough to have to stay in the hospital beyond three months and up to five months, Medicare requires $396 per day in deductible costs—nearly $12,000 over the full five months. Deductible amounts for a stay in a skilled nursing facility are lower. For the first twenty days, there are no patient payments. After twenty-one days, the patient is required to pay $99 a day for care.[24]

The insured person pays a premium of $50 per month to be covered by Medicare Part B. After patients have paid a $100 annual deductible, Medicare pays 80 percent of the cost of covered services.[25] These include certain physician services, therapy services, outpatient care, laboratory and diagnostic tests, and medical equipment such as wheelchairs.

Additional health care options available under Medicare+Choice include the Medicare Managed Health Care Plan, the Private Fee-for-Service Plan, and the Medicare Medical Savings Account Plan. The Medicare Managed Health Care Plan is an approved network of doctors, hospitals, and other health care providers that agree to provide care in return for monthly payments from Medicare. Providers may be HMOs, provider-sponsored organizations (PSOs), PPOs, or HMOs with a point of service (POS) option. HMOs usually require participants to use doctors and hospitals in the network, and relatively few direct costs are charged to patients. A PPO or PSO usually allows patients to use service providers outside of the network, but a patient who does so must pay out-of-pocket expenses.

A Private Fee-for-Service Plan (PFFS) is a Medicare-approved private health insurance plan. Medicare pays the plan a premium for Medicare-covered expenses, and the PFFS provides all Medicare-covered benefits to participants. The PFFS decides how much to pay for the covered services a participant receives, and the participant pays the difference.

A **Medicare Medical Savings Account Plan** (MSA) is a health insurance plan with a high annual deductible. The participant establishes a Medicare MSA, and Medicare deposits money into it. The participant uses this money to pay for medical care throughout the year. If money is left over, the participant can keep the balance to pay extra medical costs.[26]

As discussed in Chapter 4, the Social Security trust funds currently have large surpluses because there are more workers than beneficiaries. With expected increases in the number of retirees and fewer active workers paying into the funds, they will begin to pay out more in benefits than they will receive. The HI trust fund will be depleted earlier than the income security trust funds because of anticipated increases in the cost of medical care, and by 2016 the program will have insufficient funds.[27]

Despite efforts to control rising health care costs, they are likely to grow faster than income. This creates problems for everyone, particularly for the elderly. Their out-of-pocket expenses for medical care are higher than those of the general population; they typically spend a greater percentage of their incomes on medical care because they require more than younger people; and they must absorb the gaps in Medicare coverage, which include copayment requirements, prescription drug costs, insurance premiums, and deductibles. If medical costs continue to increase, retirement income that otherwise would have been sufficient will fall below the threshold of adequacy.[28]

Fees paid to providers who accept Medicare payments are tightly controlled by **diagnosis-related groups (DRGs).** DRG payment scales reduce costs, but if treatment costs more than the DRG rate, the hospital must take a loss. This results in the **"quicker and sicker" syndrome:** the patient is released from the hospital faster or the patient is diagnosed in a DRG that provides a higher level of coverage, even if it is not the appropriate DRG. Most often, however, the DRG system results in underpayment to hospitals and physicians, and they raise the prices they charge other patients and payers for service (called cost shifting).[29]

Medicare does not cover all health-related expenses. For instance, it does not pay for dental care, eye exams or glasses, hearing aids, prescription drugs, routine physical checkups, orthopedic devices, or non-skilled nursing home care. Medicare will not cover expenses associated with experimental procedures. These items amount to a large portion of medical needs of the elderly.[30]

Medicaid

Medicaid was passed along with Medicare in 1965. It was originally intended to help elderly Americans faced with health bills that Medicare would not cover.[31] Later Medicaid expanded to include many low-income families unable to pay for health care through the dominant for-profit health care system.

Those who qualify for Medicaid include the elderly who qualify for Medicare but cannot afford the Part A hospital deductible or the Part B premium. About 25 percent of Medicare recipients qualify for Medicaid. Disabled people, pregnant women, and children from low-income households are also eligible. One of Medicaid's main constituencies is women and children in households receiving public financial assistance.[32] Other very poor people may not be able to qualify.[33]

The law that established Medicaid directed each state to formulate and administer its own program, following federal guidelines. The federal government provides matching dollars, but the states are free to create programs that fit their needs. Because of this, there is reasonably wide variation from state to state. States set their own eligibility criteria, and these levels can be below federal poverty thresholds. States, however, are required to provide Medicaid benefits to SSI (Supplemental Security Income) beneficiaries and those who qualified for welfare under pre-TANF (Temporary Assistance for Needy Families) rules.

Medicaid coverage is more comprehensive than Medicare coverage, but it often pays health care providers so little that they do not want to participate in the program. To change this, provider payment rates are often increased. This has had an adverse effect, however, causing Medicaid costs to increase rapidly. Costs grew at rates of 20 to 30 percent each year in the early 1990s, then settled at about 8 percent per year through the rest of the decade.[34] Cost increases reemerged as a major problem by 2000, when the states found themselves devoting more and more of their resources to support Medicaid programs. With costs rising 9 percent in 2000, the states began to pressure Washington for a radical restructuring that would permit them to combine Medicaid with private health insurance so that more people would be covered.[35]

State Children's Health Insurance Program

The **State Children's Health Insurance Program (S-CHIP)** was established by the Balanced Budget Act of 1997, which required all states to provide health insurance coverage by 2000 for children in families with incomes lower than 200 percent of the federal poverty level. The goal was to cover children in families whose incomes were too high to qualify for Medicaid yet too low to afford private health insurance. S-CHIP was another incremental move toward providing universal health care in a system that has failed to do so.[36]

S-CHIP allows the states and territories to develop insurance plans for the children and provides federal matching grants. States were permitted to extend their Medicaid programs or to set up separate S-CHIP insurance programs. Since inception, they have enrolled more than 2.5 million children in these health insurance programs.[37] Of the fifty states, Washington, D.C., and two territories, nineteen have expanded their Medicaid programs to cover uninsured children; fifteen have set up independent S-CHIP programs; and another nineteen have done both.[38] The S-CHIP program has grown, and state expenditures totaled $3.7 billion by fiscal 2001.[39]

DILEMMAS CONFRONTING THE SYSTEM

While many people believe that health care in the United States is good, perhaps an equal number of observers point to problems in the system. The central problem, discussed earlier in this chapter, is finance. Health care is expensive. Managing the expense creates a second tier of issues that warrant discussion.

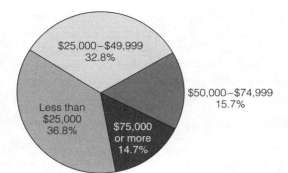

FIGURE 5.3 Uninsured Population by Household Income, 1999

SOURCE: U.S. Census Bureau, *Statistical Abstract of the United States, 2001* (Washington, DC: U.S. Government Printing Office, 2001), p. 102.

Access to Health Care

A key issue is access. More than 15 percent of Americans are not covered by insurance (see Figure 5.2) and must either bear the full cost of health care should they become ill or have someone else pay for their care. Americans under age sixty-five who can afford the system have entrée to health care, while those who cannot afford the price are denied access. About 70 percent of the uninsured are from lower income levels. Nearly 37 percent come from households with annual incomes under $25,000, as shown in Figure 5.3. Another 33 percent come from households below, at, or just slightly above the median household income ($42,228 in 2000). The very poor who qualify for a government-funded program have health care benefits. Those who are above the income level that would qualify them for government assistance, yet below the financial threshold that would permit them to purchase health insurance, do not have access to available health care. The system rations health care to those who can afford it.

This inequity is a moral and ethical issue of considerable importance. For example, the fact that the death rate from breast cancer is 50 percent higher for American women who lack insurance than for those who have medical insurance[40] clearly shows the consequences of a system structured to provide medical care only to paying customers. To those who consider health care a basic human right, this outcome is distressing.

Uninsured individuals typically do not seek medical care until they are ill. The lack of preventive care means that when they do get medical assistance, they are sicker than they would be if they had access to routine care. Sicker patients cost more to treat. They also have few options of where to go for care, so they often go to emergency rooms, even if the illness does not warrant an emergency room visit. Emergency room care is very expensive, thus exacerbating the financial problems of the health care system.

Lack of access to treatment is not only a problem for the uninsured. One of the major complaints about managed care organizations and insurance companies is their refusal to pay for medical care they deem too expensive. Public backlash over **denial of benefits** resulted in attempts to remedy the situation legally. In 1997 alone, forty-two states instituted managed care regulations or legally mandated benefits.[41] Attempts to legally address denial of benefits reached the national stage when President Clinton called for the passage of a **patient's bill of rights** in 1998. Partisan differences stalled the measure, even though both parties introduced bills in Congress with the intent of protecting managed care consumers.

The Price of Prescription Drugs

The escalating cost of prescription drugs became a political issue in the 2000 election campaign between Al Gore and George W. Bush. Both candidates agreed that elderly people should have some protection against the rising price of medicine. Both favored a modest and incremental expansion of Medicare to include coverage for prescription drugs. Neither was willing to advocate for universal health care coverage.

Perhaps that is not surprising, considering the resounding failure of the Clinton administration on universal health care coverage. The defeat of Clinton's universal health care plan signaled the return to incremental strategies for those who favored the expansion of health care benefits. It is also not surprising that a conservative, Bush, and his liberal opponent both favored the expansion of health care benefits for the elderly. Older people vote. Soon after the election, however, the relative importance of the passage of a drug benefit supplement to Medicare faded as other matters rose to national prominence.

The major issue surrounding the extension of benefits to include prescription drugs has to do with the increasing importance of drugs in health care. When Medicare was passed, prescription drugs were a minor part of health care, so a drug benefit was not included in the original legislation. New drugs have been remarkably effective in improving the quality of life and reducing hospital stays and surgery. As a consequence, demand has been increasing. The pharmaceutical industry, one of the most profitable industries in the United States, opposes a Medicare prescription drug benefit, believing that it would put the drug industry under the same cost constraints and controls that currently affect physicians who accept Medicare insurance payments for services.[42]

Americans spent in excess of $100 billion on prescription drugs in 1999. This is nearly double what was spent just ten years earlier.[43] With the aging of the population and the increasing power of drugs, it is reasonable to expect large increases in drug sales over the next decade. Unless legislation is passed to provide a prescription drug benefit, the increasing cost will fall on the elderly.

The Right to Die

A controversial issue in health care has to do with laws that prohibit individuals from taking their own lives and physicians from helping them. Euthanasia has been condemned by the medical profession, some religious leaders, and the government, but for many years there has been a groundswell of support for people's right to die. Supporters of the right to die argue that people should be allowed to control their own bodies, even if that means terminating their own lives. Opponents argue for the more liberal use of painkilling drugs and hospice care that allows for natural death with dignity. Some religious groups prohibit suicide. Others fear that a system that allows medically assisted suicide could be easily abused.

As medicine is able to keep people alive in advanced stages of illness, allowing a person to opt for death over what some consider to be unwarranted intervention to prolong life has attracted a considerable following. Suicide is legal in many parts of the world, and assisted suicide is practiced in both the Netherlands and Belgium.[44] Oregon legalized the practice in 1998. Hawaii later voted against legalizing euthanasia.

Debate over the Oregon law continues, especially at the national level. In the Bush administration, Attorney General John Ashcroft is attempting to have Oregon's Death with Dignity Act struck down. In April 2002 a federal judge in Portland blocked the Justice Department from taking punitive actions again Oregon doctors who act in accord with the Oregon law. Ashcroft, acting for the Bush administration, filed suit in the U.S. Court of Appeals for the Ninth Circuit in September 2002, asking the court to reverse the lower court's decision and hold doctors criminally liable if they prescribe lethal does of medication as permitted by the law. If the Court of Appeals decision is not satisfactory to the state of Oregon or to the Bush White House, an appeal could be made to the U.S. Supreme Court.

SUMMARY

Unlike most advanced industrialized nations, the United States does not provide health care benefits to all citizens as part of standard governmental services. Most Americans either have private health insurance or are covered by one of several large government programs (Medicare, Medicaid, and the State Children's Health Insurance Program). Many are not covered at all, and if they become ill, they must either bear the full cost of their health care or rely on charity.

One of the major issues confronting the health care system in recent years is rising costs. Particularly sharp increases after 1980 caused many to rethink how health care is paid for in the United States. In an attempt to hold down costs, many employers shifted from traditional fee-for-service insurance plans to HMOs and PPOs, which try to control costs by requiring patients to see network physicians who agree to provide services for fixed or reduced prices.

Medicare, Medicaid, and S-CHIP are the three major government health insurance programs. Medicare is an entitlement program available to all those sixty-five years and older and those with disabilities. Medicare Part A covers hospital insurance, and Medicare Part B is medical insurance. Enrollment in Medicare Part B requires payment of a premium. Medicaid was passed along with Medicare in 1965. Originally intended to help elderly Americans with health bills that Medicare would not cover, Medicaid later expanded to include many low-income families unable to afford private health insurance, including the elderly who qualify for Medicare but cannot afford the Part A hospital deductible or the Part B premium, people who are disabled, pregnant women, and children from low-income households. The State Children's Health Insurance Program provides health insurance coverage for children in families with incomes too high to qualify for Medicaid and too low to afford private health insurance.

Many controversies regarding health care consume national attention. Among these are euthanasia, how to find coverage for the uninsured, ever-increasing health care costs, and the necessity to assist elders with a prescription drug benefit.

KEY TERMS

denial of benefits

diagnosis-related groups (DRGs)

fee-for-service

health maintenance organization (HMO)

managed care

Medicaid

Medicare

Medicare Medical Savings Account Plan

Medicare Part A

Medicare Part B

Medicare+Choice

Medigap

patient's bill of rights

preferred provider organization (PPO)

"quicker and sicker" syndrome

State Children's Health Insurance Program (S-CHIP)

third-party payers

WEB SITES

http://www.medicare.gov/
The official government site for information on Medicare, this site has search and compare tools that allow you to look for information on health plans, nursing homes, Medigap policies, Medicare participating physicians, and prescription drug assistance programs. It also contains many articles on Medicare updates and changes in the program as well as enrollment procedures and current cost and benefits amounts.

www.kff.org
The Henry J. Kaiser Family Foundation site provides valuable information on Medicaid and the uninsured, Medicare, minority health issues, public opinion, women's health policy, and marketplace issues for health policy. The site also provides information on a host of other related subjects, including access to care, the elderly, HIV/AIDS, the health care industry, and S-CHIPS.

www.urban.org
The site of the Urban Institute provides enormous amounts of material on

Medicare, Medicaid, and S–CHIP as well as valuable information on the condition of the urban poor and their access to government programs. It contains multiple papers about the implication of budgetary, demographic, and policy reform changes on the major government health programs.

http://www.apha.org/ppp/schip/
The American Public Health Association's (APHA) Web site, with a great deal of information on S–CHIP, also links to the American Academy of Pediatrics site, which also contains a great deal of information on children's medical care.

http://www.medicarewatch.org/
A project of the Century Foundation, this site concentrates on Medicare reform. It is particularly good at pointing out issues associated with social and economic inequalities among Americans, and reforms that might reduce or eliminate the disadvantages faced by vulnerable populations covered by Medicare. The site has links to recent reports on Medicare provided by health care foundations, think tanks, and consulting firms.

DISCUSSION QUESTIONS

1. List and explain the reasons for high rates of price increase in the health care industry.
2. List and explain the three primary government-funded health care programs.
3. Do you think that the government's role in the provision of health care services is sufficient? Why?
4. Define and discuss the patient's bill of rights.
5. In what ways is Medicare in the same type of financial trouble as Social Security?

WEB QUESTIONS

1. The Henry J. Kaiser Family Foundation (http://www.statehealthfacts.kff.org/) provides valuable information on a variety of health issues. Look up and explain your state's HIV/AIDS policies.
2. Discuss some of the issues surrounding long-term care for the elderly as reported by the Urban Institute at http://www.urban.org/health/long-term-care.html.
3. What are some of the opportunities and threats to public health programs created by the S–CHIP program (http://www.apha.org/ppp/SCHIP/SCHIP.pdf)?

NOTES

1. Kant Patel and Mark E. Rushefsky, *Health Care Politics and Policy in America,* 2d ed. (Armonk, NY: M. E. Sharpe, 1999).

2. National Association of State Budget Officers, *State Expenditure Report 2000* (Washington, DC: National Association of State Budget Officers, 2001).

3. Robert Stevens and Rosemary Stevens, *Welfare Medicine in America* (New York: The Free Press, 1974).

4. Odin W. Anderson, "Health Services in the United States: A Growth Enterprise for a Hundred Years," in *Health Politics and Policy,* ed. Theodor J. Litman and Leonard S. Robins (New York: John Wiley & Sons, 1984), 67–80.

5. Ibid.

6. Stevens and Stevens, *Welfare Medicine in America.*

7. Ibid.

8. Craig Ramsay, *U.S. Health Policy Groups: Institutional Profiles* (Westport, CT: Greenwood Press, 1995).

9. B. Guy Peters, *American Public Policy: Promise and Performance,* 5th ed. (New York: Chatham House Publishers, 1999).

10. Centers for Medicare and Medicaid Services, Department of Health and Human Services, *National Health Expenditures Aggregate and Per Capita Amounts, 1980–2000.* http://cms.hhs.gov/statistics/nhe/historical/t1.asp (09/24/02).

11. The CQ Researcher, *Issues in Social Policy* (Washington, DC: CQ Press, 2000).

12. Ibid.

13. Clark E. Cochran, Lawrence C. Mayer, T. R. Carr, and N. Joseph Cayer, *American Public Policy: An Introduction,* 6th ed. (Boston: Bedford/St. Martin's Press, 1997).

14. Ibid.

15. Ibid.

16. Ibid.

17. The CQ Researcher, *Issues in Social Policy.*

18. National Association of State Budget Officers, *Medicaid.* http://www.nasbo.org/resource/medicaid/medicaid.htm (1/4/01).

19. Margaret C. Jasper, *Social Security Law* (Dobbs Ferry, NY: Oceana Publications, 1999).

20. Theodore R. Marmor, *The Politics of Medicare,* 2nd ed. (New York: Aldine De Gruyter, 2000).

21. Connacht Cash, *The Medicare Answer Book* (Provincetown, MA: RacePoint Press, 1999).

22. Jasper, *Social Security Law.*

23. Social Security Administration, *How It's Financed,* Social Security Administration Publication No. 05-10094, August 1999. http://www.ssa.gov/pubs/10094.html (1/30/01).

24. Social Security Administration, *Update 2001,* Social Security Administration Publication No. 05-10003, January 2001. http://www.ssa.gov/pubs/10003.html (1/30/01).

25. Ibid.

26. Jasper, *Social Security Law.*

27. Social Security Administration, *How It's Financed.*

28. National Research Council, *Assessing Policies for Retirement Income: Needs for Data, Research, and Models* (Washington, DC: National Academy Press, 1997).

29. Jasper, *Social Security Law.*

30. Ibid.

31. Stevens and Stevens, *Welfare Medicine in America.*

32. Patel and Rushefsky, *Health Care Politics and Policy in America.*

33. National Association of State Budget Officers, *Medicaid.* (http://www.nasbo.org/resource/medicaid/medicaid.htm (1/4/01).

34. Ibid.

35. Robert Pear, "Governors Offer Radical Revision of Medicaid Plan," *New York Times,* February, 25 2001. http://www.nytimes.com/2001/02/25/politics/26GOVS.html.

36. Patel and Rushefsky, *Health Care Politics and Policy in America*.

37. National Governors' Association, *The State Children's Health Insurance Program*. http://www.nga.org/106Congress/ SCHIP.asp.

38. American Academy of Pediatrics, *State Children's Health Insurance Program*. http://www.aap.org/ (2/23/2001).

39. National Association of State Budget Officers, *State Expenditure Report, 2000*.

40. Stephen M. Ayres, *Health Care in the United States: The Facts and the Choices*

(Chicago: American Library Association, 1996).

41. Patel and Rushefsky, *Health Care Politics and Policy in America*.

42. The Center for Responsive Politics, *Prescription Drugs: What's the Issue?* www.opensecrets.org (5/24/2002).

43. Ibid.

44. Agence France-Presse, "Belgium Euthanasia Law Approved," *New York Times* On-Line, May 17, 2002, International Section.

6

Protection Policy

Protection is a major duty of government. We look to the government to protect us from foreign attacks, terrorist acts, and criminal activities. We count on the government to keep international waters and airspace free from pirates and others who would interfere with trade. We expect government to ensure that we are safe in our homes, workplaces, and communities as well as when we travel. A considerable percentage of our tax dollars goes to providing these services.

The federal government is primarily responsible for national and homeland defense. The military services (the Army, Air Force, Navy, Marines, and Coast Guard) play a critical role in defending the nation's security. The newly created Department of Homeland Security has the mission of coordinating federal, state, and local response to terrorist threats. Each state provides a National Guard unit that is at the disposal of the standing federal military, should more assistance be needed. The states and localities are the first to respond in the event of a terrorist threat or activity.

Federal, state, and local governments also play roles in crime control and law enforcement. The federal government restricts its police functions to the pursuit of terrorists, international criminals, kidnappers, drug dealers, and domestic criminals who cross state lines. The Federal Bureau of Investigation (FBI) and the Federal Marshall Service have specific crime prevention obligations in these matters. However, most of the job of protecting citizens from crime falls on states and localities, and most law enforcement activities are the

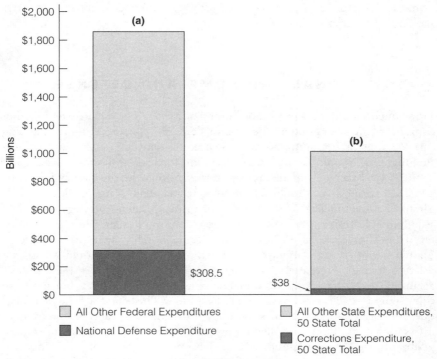

FIGURE 6.1 (a) Federal Expenditure for National Defense, FY 2001.
(b) Estimated 50 State Expenditure for Corrections, FY 2001.

SOURCES: (a) The Budget of the United States FY 2003, summary tables.
[http://www.whitehouse.gov/omb/budget/index.html] (b) National Association of State
Budget Officers, State Expenditure Report 2000, 2001.

responsibility of state and local police forces. The federal government provides some prisons, but most incarcerated people serve their time in state prisons and local jails.

Government protection programs consume considerable federal and state resources. As Figure 6.1(a) shows, expenditures for the major program at the federal level, national defense, came to $308.5 billion, or more than 16 percent of all federal spending in 2001. National defense represents the second-largest single expenditure of the federal government.

The states carry a share of the load when it comes to protection policy. As Figure 6.1(b) shows, $38 billion—or nearly 4 percent of overall state funding—went to police and corrections in 2001. In 2001, the fifty states received only about 3 percent of the funds they spent on protection from federal grants. They independently raised the vast majority of the money spent on protection.[1] As more emphasis is placed on homeland security, the federal government will likely find itself providing more grants to states and localities.

This chapter provides an overview of federal, state, and local protection policies. The discussion focuses on national and homeland defense, domestic crime, and the role of federal, state, and local governments in ensuring that our nation and communities are safe.

NATIONAL AND HOMELAND DEFENSE

How much should we spend on defending ourselves? The debate over whether to pay for "guns" or "butter" (defense or domestic policies) is a long-standing one. What is the optimum ratio of expenditures between defense and domestic programs? Should we maintain a standing force of professional soldiers, or should we rely on well-trained reserve forces? Should we put money into conventional weapons, or should we continue to maintain a large nuclear arsenal? Should massive nuclear retaliation be our primary defense strategy, or should we build a defensive system that can stop incoming missiles? How many military bases should we have? How do we decide which military bases to close? Should we worry only about our own national defense, or should we assume a larger role in international military affairs? How do we protect ourselves against terrorist attack? Should we launch pre-emptive attacks against those we think might attack us some time in the future? These and a host of related questions are the basis of discussion of national and homeland defense policy.

National and homeland defense policy is made up of a collection of programs run by different groups. Often these programs do not work together without some degree of conflict. Although each branch of the military service is part of the Department of Defense, there is considerable interservice rivalry, especially in the competition for resources. Even when military leaders can agree on a direction for the country to follow, Congress often fails to follow their advice. The Department of Defense may take one position, while the State Department takes another. The new Department of Homeland Defense must deal with integrating and coordinating the activities of a host of federal, state, and local organizations, each dealing with one aspect of homeland defense. International events or the election of a new president can quickly alter national defense priorities. Furthermore, the environment for today's national and homeland defense policymaking is rooted in prior decisions and actions, some of which go back decades. The best way to understand current issues in national and homeland defense policy, therefore, is to frame the issues in the geopolitics of the last several decades.

The Cold War

The United States has a tradition of **isolationism** that began with the formation of the nation and persisted to the twentieth century. Part of the tradition of separation from the rest of the world is a result of America's advantageous geography. Bordered on the east and west by oceans and on the north and south by traditionally friendly nations, the country developed without the need to focus on the affairs of other countries. While it is true that the United States fought a war with Mexico and had some disagreements with Canada, generally speaking, the nation has never had to worry much about its immediate neighbors. With rare exceptions, the wars fought by the United States have not taken place on American soil. Until the Second World War, the United States followed the custom of disbanding its standing army at the end of hostilities, maintaining only a small permanent military force.

Traditional American isolationism was abandoned in the middle of the twentieth century. The United States, which entered World War II hesitantly and only after a direct attack on Pearl Harbor, emerged from it in 1945 as a superpower with ongoing alliances and responsibilities. World War II was followed immediately by the **Cold War** between the Free World and the communist nations. Instead of disbanding the armed forces, the United States increased its military might to confront the Union of Soviet Socialist Republics (USSR). Cold War military readiness dominated the American defense posture for nearly fifty years following the end of World War II.

The Cold War began when Allied forces battling the German Axis met in Germany in 1945. The Soviet Red Army entered Germany from the east, while Allied forces under the command of American General Dwight D. Eisenhower pushed into Germany from the west. They met in Berlin. With military actions over, the conquering armies proceeded with restoring civilian rule to the war-torn nations of Europe. In the West, democratic governments supporting free market capitalist economies were returned to power. In the East, the Red Army installed dictators loyal to Stalin's regime who shared the Soviet craving for socialist economic systems.

Europe was thus split into two blocs divided by what British Prime Minister Winston Churchill called an "**iron curtain.**" The nations of the Eastern bloc became socialist dictatorships allied with the Soviet Union for common defense through a treaty called the **Warsaw Pact.** East Germany became part of the Eastern bloc, as did all of the countries that lay between Russia and Germany. West Germany became a capitalist democracy allied with the Western powers and a member of the **North Atlantic Treaty Organization (NATO).**

Two critical features made the conflict between the Soviet Union and the Western powers extremely volatile. First, the USSR was an avowed expansionist power that considered the socialist economic system superior to capitalism and the communist "dictatorship of the proletariat" an enemy of Western democracies. The Soviet Union's threat to expand throughout the world and eventually overtake the great powers of the West provoked an American policy response that came to be called **containment.**[2] Under this policy, the United States and its NATO allies were quick to counter any perceived Soviet expansion anywhere in the world. As the Cold War wore on, the entire globe came to be divided along the lines that divided Europe in 1945. Many developing nations accepted socialist ideology and allied with the Soviet Union. Periodic small wars, which came to be termed brushfire wars, were fought to prevent the further spread of communist ideology. The Korean conflict and the war in Vietnam were both justified under the containment rationale.

The second factor that made the Cold War clash between the Soviet Union and the United States frighteningly unstable was the **arms race.** Both nations vied for military superiority by building vast stockpiles of nuclear weapons and an assortment of land-based and sea-based delivery systems. The development of long-range **intercontinental ballistic missiles** ended forever the belief that geographic distance meant safety. Both sides sought another way to defend themselves, and their answer was a strategy aptly named **MAD (mutually assured destruction).** MAD meant that each side had to have so many weapons that a first strike by one nation would not wipe out the other nation's capacity to retaliate. The country that launched the first strike would be destroyed by a retaliatory strike. Mutually assured destruction strategies on both sides led to the arms race. Each country needed to be absolutely sure that it had sufficient nuclear capacity to withstand a surprise attack and still respond with a retaliatory strike able to destroy the enemy. If one side built a new weapons system, the other side had to match it. As the Cold War progressed, each side amassed more than enough nuclear bombs to blow up the world many times over.[3]

MAD was exceptionally costly. Building and maintaining enormous weapons complexes consumed considerable national resources for both the United States and the USSR. MAD was also a flawed strategy. It might deter a planned strike, but it did nothing to prevent an accidental one.[4] Indeed, the sheer number of warheads and weapons systems encouraged by MAD increased the odds that a system would malfunction and precipitate an accidental attack.

The cost and the insecurity eventually created willingness on both sides to reduce the sizes of their arsenals, and a series of treaties and talks resulted. The **Strategic Arms Limitation Talks (SALT)** and the **Strategic Arms Reduction Talks (START)** were both efforts to end the arms race and to retire some of the weapons. In 1972 SALT I froze new offensive nuclear weapons deployment, and the **Antiballistic Missile (ABM) Treaty** limited the deployment of systems designed to defend against ballistic missile attack. The ABM Treaty codified the strategy of deterrence through the threat of retaliation. A 1974 amendment to the ABM Treaty permitted each side one land-based antiballistic missile system. SALT II, signed in 1979, limited the production of offensive missiles.

In 1991 the Soviet Union collapsed, and the Cold War ended. Russia assumed control of the former Soviet Union's weapons, and its new democratic government was interested in negotiating deep cuts in the arsenals. START I was negotiated in 1991, soon after the collapse of the Soviet Union, and START II in 1993.[5] In START II each side agreed to radical reductions in the number of nuclear weapons in their stockpiles.

Post–Cold War Defense Policy

The gradual weakening of the Soviet state and of its influence on Eastern bloc nations had begun in the late 1980s. First in Poland and then in nation after nation, the Soviets lost their grip. In 1989 the Berlin Wall came down, leading the way to the reunification of Germany. In 1991 a coup in Russia led to the

Table 6.1 Defense Spending as a Percentage of GDP, NATO Allies

	1990	1991	1992	1993	1994	1995	1996	1997	% Change 1996–1997	% Change 1990–1997
Belgium	2.40	2.33	1.86	1.77	1.72	1.65	1.60	1.59	−0.98%	−34%
Canada	2.01	1.90	1.90	1.86	1.74	1.60	1.44	1.28	−11.08%	−36%
Denmark	2.05	2.06	2.00	1.99	1.87	1.81	1.77	1.75	−1.36%	−15%
France	3.56	3.56	3.41	3.41	3.34	3.11	3.02	2.98	−1.30%	−16%
Germany	2.82	2.30	2.13	1.95	1.78	1.71	1.66	1.58	−4.52%	−44%
Greece	4.66	2.30	2.13	1.95	1.78	1.71	1.66	1.58	−4.52%	−44%
Italy	2.14	2.11	2.05	2.09	2.00	1.78	1.94	1.93	−0.63%	−10%
Luxembourg	0.94	0.99	0.98	0.84	0.86	0.82	0.81	0.80	−0.95%	−15%
Netherlands	2.62	2.50	2.46	2.26	2.12	2.03	2.00	1.94	−3.24%	−26%
Norway	2.94	2.79	3.01	2.74	2.76	2.32	2.36	2.20	−6.78%	−25%
Portugal	2.78	2.77	2.75	2.66	2.56	2.67	2.50	2.61	4.78%	−6%
Spain	1.84	1.72	1.57	1.73	1.54	1.55	1.48	1.42	−3.98%	−23%
Turkey	3.53	3.76	3.88	3.93	4.05	4.14	4.12	4.04	−2.18%	14%
United States	5.33	4.74	4.89	4.54	4.15	3.84	3.58	3.41	−4.83%	−36%
United Kingdom	4.04	4.24	3.82	3.60	3.37	3.06	3.00	2.81	−6.26%	−31%

SOURCE: U.S. Department of Defense.

fall of Soviet leader Mikhail Gorbachev. Democracy and capitalism soon emerged. With the end of the Cold War, a half century of U.S. defense strategy was no longer applicable. America became the world's sole superpower, and no other nation was powerful enough to counter it. As one would expect (see Table 6.1), U.S. military expenditure fell in the years after the Cold War ended, but the United States still spent a considerable sum to maintain superpower status.

The demise of the USSR had enormous consequences. The rivalry between the United States and the USSR had been a stabilizing force across the globe. Without the domination of the world's two superpowers, various national and ethnic conflicts arose. Nations that had been kept united by Soviet-supported dictators suddenly fell to pieces.[6] The division was peaceful in Czechoslovakia but so brutal in Yugoslavia that the United Nations intervened with troops to end the ethnic conflict there.

Because of the changes in the type and mix of threats that confronted the United States in the post–Cold War era, the nation began to reconsider its military policy.[7] This reorientation occurred in both nuclear and conventional forces.[8] One of the largest shifts was the adoption of the role of **peacekeeper.** In the post–Cold War era, conventional military forces increasingly participated in nontraditional peacekeeping operations.[9] For example, American forces were sent to Bosnia to prevent further "ethnic cleansing" in the aftermath of Yugoslavia's breakup.

Regardless of the scope of peacekeeping activities, downsizing the military was proposed and debated. Some suggested reducing the active component of the military and transferring resources to the National Guard and reserve forces.[10] With no pressing need for large forces to patrol the world, some suggested that professional forces were no longer required and that a citizen's army was adequate. Others argued that the size of military forces should be kept stable, but that the military should be reorganized to be more flexible and should be reequipped with new technology to be more lethal. These debates were not fully resolved before the September 11, 2001, terrorist attacks pushed discussions of military downsizing off the national agenda. The ensuing wars in Afghanistan and Iraq even resulted in some discussion of increasing the level of forces.

The end of the Cold War made the United States keen to reduce its stockpile of nuclear weapons. START I required the United States and Russia to trim their stock of strategic offensive nuclear weapons by more than a third, down to 6,000 warheads each. The START II treaty required both nations to cut their arsenals further, to between 3,000 and 3,500 warheads. At the Helsinki summit in March 1997 President Bill Clinton and Russian President Boris Yeltsin agreed to commit their governments to negotiate another reduction, to 2,000 to 2,500 weapons each. In addition, the testing of nuclear weapons was voluntarily halted.[11]

The reduction in the number of weapons meant that the MAD strategy was giving way to defensive strategies that included some form of antiballistic missile system. The Clinton administration continued a research, development, and testing program for antiballistic missile defense, and the George W. Bush administration announced the intention of withdrawing from the ABM Treaty and deploying such a system.[12] The Bush administration believes that terrorists, crime syndicates, drug cartels, and dictators cannot be deterred by MAD. More important, they fear that North Korea or Iran might soon acquire the ability to use long-range missiles to attack the United States.[13] The general spread of weapons is of concern, although the United States is in a dubious position to criticize it. As Figure 6.2 shows, the United States is the leading exporter of weapons.

The possibility of the use of biological and chemical weapons caused increasing alarm in the 1990s. Iraq and the former USSR had large biological weapons development programs and arsenals, and domestic terrorists were known to be trying to acquire biological agents. The Clinton administration and Congress began a civilian biological defense program. Beginning in 1999 Congress allocated $121 million in emergency funding to the Centers for Disease Control and Prevention (CDC) to begin to enhance the nation's biological defense. A national pharmaceutical stockpile was also established to help the National Disaster Medical System manage mass casualties that would result from a biological attack. In the name of national defense, health agencies began working to develop new drugs, diagnostic tests, and vaccines to prepare a response in the event of biological warfare.[14]

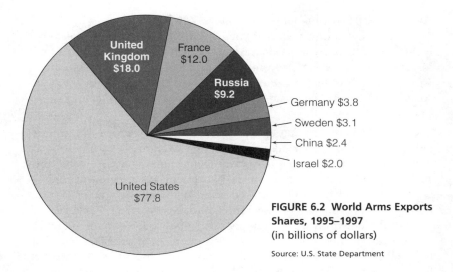

FIGURE 6.2 World Arms Exports Shares, 1995–1997
(in billions of dollars)

Source: U.S. State Department

The War on Terrorism

After the end of the Cold War, the United States found itself increasingly deal-ing with threats from nations that previously had not been at the center of U.S. policy. These nations included Iran, Iraq, North Korea, Afghanistan, Algeria, and other so-called rogue nations.[15] The fear that these unstable countries would be able to secure weapons of mass destruction and launch attacks dominated pol-icy discussions.[16] Nuclear, chemical, and biological warfare all seemed plausi-ble.[17] Terrorist groups given shelter in these countries were also a cause for concern, and the September 11, 2001, terrorist attacks on the World Trade Center and the Pentagon confirmed the fears of security analysts.

The September 11 attacks resulted in a **war on terrorism** in Afghanistan against the **al Qaeda** terrorist network considered to be responsible for plan-ning and carrying them out. The United States, with allies from many nations, defeated the **Taliban** rulers of Afghanistan who supported al Qaeda, driving them from power. Since then, the first steps have been taken toward the instal-lation of a democratic government for Afghanistan.

The determination of the United States to block future acts of terrorism led to the decision to engage in a wider antiterrorist campaign. The Bush administration declared that terrorists and the nations harboring them would be targeted. In his 2002 State of the Union address, George W. Bush outlined the wider goals of the war on terrorism:

> Our military has put the terror training camps of Afghanistan out of busi-ness, yet camps still exist in at least a dozen countries. A terrorist under-world, including groups like Hamas, Hizballah, Islamic Jihad, Jaish-e-Mohammed, operates in remote jungles and deserts and hides in the centers of large cities. While the most visible military action is in

Afghanistan, America is acting elsewhere. We now have troops in the Philippines, helping to train that country's armed forces to go after terrorist cells that have executed an American and still hold hostages. Our soldiers, working with the Bosnian Government, seized terrorists who were plotting to bomb our Embassy. Our Navy is patrolling the coast of Africa to block the shipment of weapons and the establishment of terrorist camps in Somalia. . . .

Our second goal is to prevent regimes that sponsor terror from threatening America or our friends and allies with weapons of mass destruction. Some of these regimes have been pretty quiet since September the 11th, but we know their true nature. North Korea is a regime arming with missiles and weapons of mass destruction, while starving its citizens. Iran aggressively pursues these weapons and exports terror, while an unelected few repress the Iranian people's hope for freedom. Iraq continues to flaunt its hostility toward America and to support terror. The Iraqi regime has plotted to develop anthrax and nerve gas and nuclear weapons for over a decade. This is a regime that has already used poison gas to murder thousands of its own citizens, leaving the bodies of mothers huddled over their dead children. This is a regime that agreed to international inspections, then kicked out the inspectors. This is a regime that has something to hide from the civilized world. States like these and their terrorist allies constitute an axis of evil, arming to threaten the peace of the world. By seeking weapons of mass destruction, these regimes pose a grave and growing danger. They could provide these arms to terrorists, giving them the means to match their hatred. They could attack our allies or attempt to blackmail the United States. In any of these cases, the price of indifference would be catastrophic.

We will work closely with our coalition to deny terrorists and their state sponsors the materials, technology, and expertise to make and deliver weapons of mass destruction. We will develop and deploy effective missile defenses to protect America and our allies from sudden attack. And all nations should know: America will do what is necessary to ensure our Nation's security.[18]

The extent and duration of the war on terrorism is undetermined. What is clear is that expenditures that were targeted for decreases are now on the increase. As mentioned earlier, national defense expenditures amounted to $308.5 billion, or over 16 percent of all federal spending, in 2001. The Bush administration has asked Congress for substantial increases in national defense spending for 2002 and beyond: an increase of $40 billion for 2002, another $31 billion for 2003, $14.8 billion for 2004, and $19.7 billion for 2005. If Congress approves these increases, federal defense spending will increase by 34 percent over four years.[19] The war with Iraq will further increase defense spending. The states are also expected to put more resources into protection programs and policies as they seek to deal with security concerns in the post–September 11 world.

The Bush administration sent a new national security strategy to Congress in September 2002. The **Bush Doctrine** abandons containment and deterrence as the primary national defense strategies and advocates preemptive strikes against countries that appear to have the capacity and intent to attack the United States with weapons of mass destruction.[20] The war in Iraq was its first use.

National and Homeland Defense Spending

Levels of defense spending are highly sensitive to shifts in the world's balance of power. They are also responsive to leaders' preferences. Presidents who are inclined to maintain a higher degree of defense readiness call for more spending than do presidents who prefer to concentrate resources on domestic policies and programs. It is important to point out that willingness to engage the country in war or to maintain a strong international presence is not the result of party differences. Since the Second World War, both Republican and Democratic presidents have engaged American forces in military actions. Members of Congress consider both the international situation and the president's recommendations when they vote to allocate funds for national defense.

In addition, members of Congress are particularly cognizant of the impact of military spending in their own districts. They are concerned about the negative effect of defense cutbacks on the economies of the communities in which their constituents live. Even when the Department of Defense recommends base closures, it is difficult to get enough congressional votes to close the bases. Similarly, representatives from states and localities in which defense-related industries are located favor weapons systems that will bring jobs and money to their districts and states.

Defense spending targeted to homeland defense is expected to play an increasingly important role in coming years. One of the consequences of the September 11 attacks and the war on terrorism is the realization by state and local governments that traditional law enforcement activities increasingly overlap with national concerns. Localities and states are the first line of defense in incidents of domestic terrorist attack. Just as New York City's mayor and New York State's governor were central players in the first days after the attack on the World Trade Center, so will all local and state officials play central roles in the event of other acts of terrorism.

DOMESTIC LAW ENFORCEMENT

Threats to safety do not come only from foreign countrie[s]
Criminal activities committed within the nation's borders co[ ]
to public safety. How do we decide how much to spen[d]
Should we put a police officer on every corner? H[ ]
should we build to hold the people we arrest and c[ ]
should we keep in prison? Questions about expen[ ]

corrections form the foundation of the debate about domestic law enforcement. States currently spend nearly 4 percent of their overall funds for crime control and corrections. In 2001 that amounted to about $38 billion.[21] While this does not approach the level of spending for health care or education, crime control is a substantial activity of states and localities.

There are many types of crime. **Violent crime**—murder, manslaughter, extortion, criminal endangerment, assault, robbery, rape, and sexual assault—is perhaps the most vexing. **Property crimes**—burglary, larceny, embezzlement, fraud, possession and sale of stolen property, destruction of property, trespassing, arson, vandalism, theft, forgery and counterfeiting, and motor vehicle theft—all impose heavy costs on society. **Violations of public order** include possession of illegal weapons, drunk driving, flight to avoid prosecution, court offenses, and obstruction of justice. More controversial are violations of morals and decency regulations and the crimes of illegal drug possession and use, some of which are termed **victimless crimes.**

How society decides to deal with all these crimes determines public protection policy. There are basically two approaches to dealing with criminals: rehabilitating offenders or punishing them. Supporters of **punitive approaches** often offer victims' rights arguments for their stand. They also insist on the usefulness of keeping dangerous individuals away from society and on the threat of punishment as a deterrent of other criminal behavior. Those who favor the **rehabilitative approach** suggest that it is in the best interest of society to have criminals discover the error of their ways and resume roles as productive citizens. The United States has attempted both punitive and rehabilitative approaches.

The first prisons were opened shortly after the American colonies won independence from England. In 1779 the **penitentiary,** the first type of prison to be developed, used solitude and work to reform criminals. The theory behind the development of the penitentiary was that criminal behavior was caused by the poor environment in which the lawbreaker lived. Called the Pennsylvania or solitary system, the penitentiary provided a structured environment in which criminals were expected to reform and become useful citizens. These early prisons were harsh. Prisoners were subject to solitary confinement for the duration of their incarceration and were beaten if they [broke] the rules.[22] Prisoners had no rights and were treated as "slaves of the [state]." [They] worked alone in their cells and were supposed to meditate on their [wrongs. Some went] likely insane from the lack of social interaction.

[In the early 19]00s solitary confinement was replaced by the so-called [Auburn] system. [In this] system, prisoners were permitted to interact in [the daytime while making goods in] prison [fact]ories. These goods were sold to generate [revenue. Nineteenth cen]tury prisons also widely engaged in [leasing prisoners to private ente]rprises, which treated the prisoners [harshly.]

[The reformatory movement began] in the 1870s and 1880s, in large part [as a reaction to these abuses.] It emphasized humane treatment of [prisoners and education and m]editation to encourage rehabilitation.

Education, vocational training, and religious instruction were provided. Prisoners were given rewards for good behavior, including the privilege of receiving visitors and parole. Prisons continued to evolve in this more humane direction into the twentieth century.[24] During the 1960s and 1970s there was a widespread prisoners' rights movement, and treatment replaced harsh sanctions, even those implemented with the goal of rehabilitating the prisoner.

As crime rates increased in the 1960s and 1970s, opinions shifted. A series of studies in the 1970s found that compassionate alternative rehabilitative strategies were not effective. These studies seemed to suggest that the individual traits of offenders as well as the environments to which they returned had far more influence on subsequent criminal behavior than prison reform programs. By the 1980s there was a loud outcry for "law and order." Interest shifted from trying to find ways to rehabilitate lawbreakers to keeping them away from society for as long as possible. The goal was no longer to reform criminals but rather to punish and remove them from interaction with society.[25] The deterrent role of punishment was emphasized.

Perhaps no single issue highlights shifting social attitudes about the proper treatment of lawbreakers more than execution. **Capital punishment** has been a long-standing dilemma in the United States. In 1972 the Supreme Court ruled in *Furman* v. *Georgia* that the death sentence constituted "cruel and unusual" punishment and was thus unconstitutional. The death sentences of more than six hundred prisoners were commuted to life terms. In response, many states revised their statutes to conform with Supreme Court guidelines issued in the *Furman* and other cases that followed in the 1970s and 1980s, and by 1977 some states reinstituted the death penalty.[26] As Figure 6.3 shows, the number of executions increased after the reimposition of the death penalty. By 1999, the number of executions returned to 1950 levels. The number of prisoners on death row swelled, as Figure 6.4 shows, and by the end of 1999 the prison systems of thirty-seven states and the federal government held more than 3,500 prisoners on death row.[27]

Concern about the death penalty, particularly about errors in convicting people, began to surface in the late 1990s. Criticism came not only from opponents of capital punishment but also from judges, attorneys, and supporters of the death penalty. By 2002 more than a hundred death-row inmates had been freed because of questions about their guilt. A study by Columbia University argued that errors occur in 68 percent of capital cases. DNA testing has indicated that some inmates did not commit the crimes they were convicted of, and other inmates have been released because of the incompetence of their court-appointed attorneys. For example, one Texas lawyer slept in court during his client's trial.

When Illinois Governor George Ryan, a death penalty supporter, found out that more people on his state's death row had been found innocent and freed than had been put to death, he halted executions in 2000. In 2002 Maryland Governor Parris Glendening, also a death penalty supporter, halted executions over allegations of racial bias, and in April of that year a U.S. district judge from New York declared the death penalty unconstitutional because of

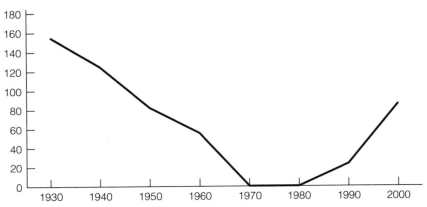

FIGURE 6.3 U.S. Executions—All States, 1930–2000

SOURCE: United States Department of Justice

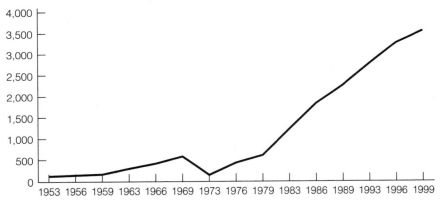

FIGURE 6.4 Prisoners on Death Row, 1953–1999

SOURCE: United States Department of Justice

racial discrimination associated with its imposition.[28] In September 2002 a federal judge in Vermont also ruled that the death penalty was unconstitutional.[29] In a surprise decision in June 2002, the U.S. Supreme Court ruled that execution of the mentally retarded was cruel and unusual punishment and in violation of the Eighth Amendment of the Constitution.[30]

Criminal Activity

Crime rates in the United States increased from the end of World War II through the 1970s. That trend has been reversed, and as Figure 6.5 shows, the rates of both violent crimes and property crimes have declined during the past years. Between 1973 and 1999 violent crime rates decreased from 47.7 per 1,000 in the population to 32.1 per 1,000. Overall, violent crime rates have declined about 31 percent since 1994.[31] Property crime has fallen off from

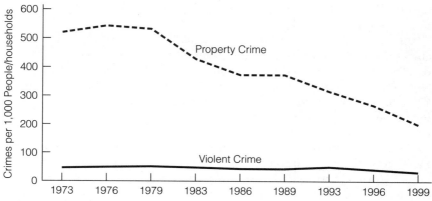

FIGURE 6.5 Overall Crime

SOURCE: United States Bureau of Justice Statistics

519.9 per 1,000 households in 1973 to 198 in 1999.[32] Property crime rates have shown a remarkable decline of 58 percent since 1975.[33]

Despite these reductions, crime is still a concern. In 2001 approximately 24 million crimes were committed. For every one thousand people, there was one rape or sexual assault, two assaults resulting in serious injury, and three robberies. Murder was the least common crime. There were six murder victims for every one hundred thousand persons in 2001.[34] Violent crime has clear characteristics. About one-quarter of violent crime incidents occurred at or near the victim's home; almost half occurred within a mile of the victim's home; and about three-quarters took place within five miles. Only 4 percent of victims of violent crime reported that the incidents took place more than fifty miles from home.

While at work, more than 2 million people become victims of violent crime each year. Some jobs are more dangerous than others. Law enforcement officers are the most vulnerable, while security guards, taxi drivers, prison guards, jail guards, and bartenders also experience high rates of workplace violence.

School violence is a concern, especially in the wake of several well-publicized school shootings. In 1997 between 7 and 8 percent of students in grades nine to twelve reported being threatened or injured with weapons such as guns, knives, or clubs on school property in the prior twelve months. That same year, about 9 percent of students reported bringing such weapons to school in the prior thirty days. Thirty-five school-age children were victims of school-associated homicides between July 1, 1997, and June 30, 1998.

Urban residents had the highest violent victimization rates, followed by suburban residents. Rural resident had the lowest rates. In 1999 nine urban residents, seven suburban residents, and five rural residents per one thousand were victims of aggravated assault. Urban residents were robbed at almost four times the rate of rural residents. Urban and suburban residents were victims of simple assault at equal rates. Surveys of twelve cities in 1998 found that, in a majority of the cities, black residents in urban areas experienced a higher rate of violent crime than urban whites.[35]

In one-quarter of the incidents of violent crime, offenders used or threatened to use weapons. Offenders had or used weapons in slightly less than half of all robberies, compared with 5 percent of all rapes and sexual assaults in 1999. Homicides are most often committed with guns, especially handguns. In 1998, 52 percent of homicides were committed with handguns, 13 percent with other guns, 13 percent with knives, 5 percent with blunt objects, and 17 percent with other weapons.[36]

Property crime occurs most often to people living in rented property. In 1999 property crime rates were 48 percent higher for households in rented property than for households in owner-occupied property. Burglary rates were 85 percent higher for renters; motor vehicle theft rates were 55 percent higher; and theft rates were 40 percent higher.

Urban households have historically been the most vulnerable to property crime, burglary, motor vehicle theft, and theft in the United States. In 1999 suburban households were more likely to experience overall property crime, motor vehicle theft, and theft than were rural households. Rural households, however, were burglarized at rates significantly greater than suburban households.[37]

Age is a key indicator of propensity toward crime. Crime is primarily a phenomenon of the young. Crime rates peak between the ages of sixteen and eighteen, then fall off rapidly as people enter their early twenties. Since youth is so closely connected to crime, the larger the percentage of the population in their younger years, the higher the overall crime rate the community can expect.[38]

Gender is also a factor. Crime is mainly a male phenomenon. The number of women incarcerated in state and federal prisons was 93,000 by 2001, compared to nearly 1.3 million men.[39]

For many years researchers on sentencing practices in federal, state, and local courts have reported differences based on race and ethnicity. Not only are there differences from judge to judge, but there also seem to be differences in the way certain groups are charged and sentenced. Some racial and ethnic groups are more likely to be charged with crimes that typically incur the most severe sentences. Studies have shown, for instance, that African Americans and Hispanics are more likely than whites to be sentenced to imprisonment and that African Americans are more likely to receive longer sentences.[40] On any given day in 1996, for example, approximately 30 percent of African American men between the ages of twenty and thirty were in jail, in prison, or on parole.[41] In 2001 there were 3,535 African American male inmates per 100,000 African American males in the United States, compared to 1,177 Hispanic male inmates per 100,000 Hispanic males and 462 white male inmates per 100,000 white males.[42] Of persons under sentence of death in 2000, 1,990 were white and 1,535 were African American—a number that vastly outweighs the percentage of African Americans in society.[43]

Federal, State, and Local Law Enforcement Efforts

When the United States was formed, the individual states did not adopt a federal criminal code. Rather, each remained responsible for crime committed within its jurisdiction. The practice of state sovereignty in criminal matters continued as new states joined the Union. Although a few crimes were considered federal matters, in large part the role of criminal justice was reserved to the states. Each state set up its own law enforcement system, hired its own law enforcement officers, and built its own jails and prisons.[44] Today law enforcement remains mostly under the jurisdiction of state and local authorities. They run the jails and the state prisons that house the vast majority of those incarcerated.

The federal role in law enforcement was originally limited to crimes committed on federal property, against federal officials, by federal officials, or in other narrowly defined areas of jurisdiction. The federal government had practically no role in housing prisoners prior to the 1890s. State, county, and municipal governments operated nearly all the country's jails, prisons, and workhouses, and the federal government contracted with states and localities to house federal prisoners.

A growing number of federal prisoners and opposition to the federal government leasing state prison space led to the need for federal prisons. The first federal prisons were established by the **Three Prisons Act of 1891,** and by 1930 there were seven of them. As of 2000 ninety-eight federal institutions housed federal prisoners. These include penitentiaries, federal correctional institutions, federal prison camps, and federal medical centers operated by the Bureau of Prisons.[45]

The answer to the question of who winds up in a federal prison has changed over time. Federal law has shifted with political winds. For some time, federal criminal law was deeply concerned with the transportation of young women for immoral purposes, but today such crimes are not generally treated as a federal offense. During prohibition, alcohol production and consumption dominated federal prosecution. Today drug prosecutions have replaced the emphasis on alcohol.[46] The **war on drugs,** culminating with the Anti-Drug Abuse Act of 1988 and the Crime Bill of 1994, gave the federal government a far more active role in funding and participating in drug-related law enforcement.[47] In 2001 about 58 percent of federal prisoners were serving time for drug offenses.

The United States sends more people to prison and for longer periods than most other industrialized nations.[48] Nearly 2 million people are currently in U.S. jails, state prisons, and federal prisons. Jails are local (mostly county) institutions used to confine persons awaiting trial or adults serving short sentences.[49] Local jails were responsible for nearly 702,000 persons awaiting trial or serving sentences at midyear 2001. Of these, about 70,800 were serving their sentences in the community; the rest were being held in the jails.[50] In that same year, state and federal prisons held 1.4 million inmates (federal prisons accounted for a mere 157,000 of that total).[51] Figure 6.6 shows the rate of

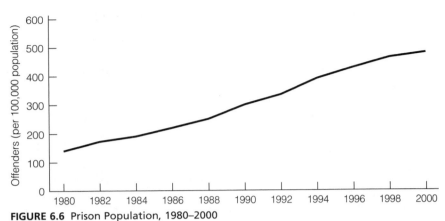

FIGURE 6.6 Prison Population, 1980–2000

SOURCE: United States Bureau of Justice Statistics.

increase in prison populations since 1980. In 2001, 3.1 percent of U.S. adult residents—6.6 million people—were on probation, in jail or prison, or on parole.[52]

One of the major problems affecting the prison population is overcrowding. Incarceration rates over the fifty-year period from the 1920s to the 1970s were fairly stable, averaging 110 persons per 100,000 of population. In the 1970s this stability broke down, and by the 1980s the populations of both state and federal prisons had increased more than 150 percent. By 1993 the incarceration rate was 351 per 100,000, three times the earlier rate. State and federal prisons held over 948,000 prisoners by the middle 1990s.[53] By 2001 the number had skyrocketed again, and nearly 1.4 million people were in federal or state prisons, and almost 2 million people were either in prisons or local jails.

Part of the reason for this growth was the passage of federal mandatory sentencing laws. The Comprehensive Crime Control Act of 1984 and the Anti-Drug Abuse Act of 1986 imposed minimum sentences on many crimes.[54] The 1994 crime bill imposed additional mandatory sentences, especially for drug crimes. These laws have had a disproportionate effect on racial and ethnic minorities.[55] Some drug laws imposed stricter sentences for possession of types of drugs more commonly found in inner-city African American communities than for drugs more commonly used by affluent whites. It takes, for instance, five hundred grams of powder cocaine (used by more affluent people) to trigger a five-year minimum sentence, while five grams of crack cocaine (used by less affluent people) earns the same penalty. The Congressional Black Caucus and other groups seek equalization in drug laws.[56]

As a result of the increase in the number of prisoners, two or three people shared a cell meant for only one, and others slept in shower rooms, corridors, dayrooms, infirmaries, and rooms designed for other purposes. Some states placed tents in prison courtyards to house the growing population. Increased population resulted in inmate aggression toward other inmates, riots, and other major disturbances.[57] Overcrowding also resulted in the lack of adequate medical care for prisoners.

By 1990 the majority of states were under federal court order to relieve prison overcrowding, but the number of inmates continued to grow. One response was prison building, which became a major industry in the 1990s. This has not ended the overcrowding problem. By the end of 1999 state prisons were between 1 percent and 17 percent above capacity, while federal prisons were 32 percent above capacity.[58]

Another response to prison overcrowding involved finding inventive ways to house and manage the increasing number of prisoners. **Prison privatization,** which emphasizes management for profit rather than nonprofit service delivery, has become a popular solution.[59] In many cases, privatization involves contracting for privately delivered services, such as medical care, facility construction, educational services, drug treatment, staff training, vocational programs, and counseling. Full privatization, which involves delegating almost all correctional functions to a private firm, is more controversial, particularly when it involves private-sector management of secure punishment facilities for adults.[60] Such private facilities as community treatment centers, halfway houses, and special placement treatment programs are generally well tolerated.

SUMMARY

The United States entered World War II hesitantly and only after a direct attack on Pearl Harbor, but emerged from the war as a superpower with ongoing worldwide alliances and responsibilities. When World War II ended, divisions between the Free World and the communist nations gave rise to Cold War conflicts between the Soviet Union and the Western powers. These conflicts were extremely volatile because the Soviet Union was an expansionist power and because the Soviet Union and the United States challenged each other in an arms race. The development of intercontinental ballistic missiles that could be fired well within the borders of either Russia or America and hit a target in the other country ended the era of safety through geographic distance. Both sides used the strategy of mutually assured destruction, and its cost and the insecurity it created eventually produced willingness on both sides to reduce armaments. The Strategic Arms Limitation Talks (SALT) and the Strategic Arms Reduction Talks (START), combined with the end of the Cold War, changed the nature of national security concerns for the United States.

Since the end of the Cold War the United States has had to deal with threats from nations to which it previously had paid little attention. Iran, Iraq, North Korea, Afghanistan, Algeria, and other so-called rogue nations became the focus of foreign policy. The September 11, 2001, terrorist attack launched a new era. The United States, with the support of allies, began the war on terrorism with an attack on the Taliban rulers of Afghanistan who supported and protected the al Qaeda terrorist network. The war with Iraq was the first test of the Bush Doctrine of pre-emption.

National and homeland defense policies are primarily the responsibility of the federal government, although the threat of terrorist activity is forcing states and localities to become more concerned with these activities as well. The war on terrorism has created a new partnership between federal, state, and local governments for protection of the country. The states and localities now see themselves as the first responders in the event of a terrorist attack on American soil.

Violent crime, property crime, and violations of the public order need to be controlled by federal, state, and local authorities. The United States has tried both punitive and rehabilitative approaches to dealing with criminals. Early corrections activities, while harsh, were focused on rehabilitation. Later prison reform movements were more concerned with ensuring that prisoners' rights were not violated. A shift to more punitive methods came as a result of an increase in crime rates in the mid-1900s. The shifts in approaches can be clearly seen in attitudes about capital punishment, which was first permitted, then outlawed, then reinstated.

Violent crime rates have fallen about 31 percent since 1994, and property crime rates have dropped 58 percent. Despite these reductions, crime is still a concern for the public and for government officials. Age, race, and gender are key indicators of who will be arrested for criminal behavior. Crime is primarily a phenomenon of the young, and the larger the percentage of the population in their younger years, the higher the overall crime rate. Crime is dominantly a male phenomenon, although the number of women engaged in criminal activities is rising. Race and ethnicity are also factors. The number of African Americans in jail, in prison, or on parole far exceeds what one would expect if all races were equally accountable for criminal activities. Research on sentencing practices in federal, state, and local courts has raised concerns about the lack of fairness of the law enforcement and judicial systems.

More than 2 million people are currently in jails, state prisons, and federal prisons in the United States. Overcrowding in prisons has resulted in institutional violence and riots. By 1990 the majority of states were under federal court order to relieve prison overcrowding. One response has been to build more prisons. Prison privatization has also been attempted.

KEY TERMS

al Qaeda	congregate system	destruction (MAD)
Antiballistic Missile (ABM) Treaty	containment	North Atlantic Treaty Organization (NATO)
arms race	intercontinental ballistic missile	peacekeeper
Bush Doctrine	iron curtain	penitentiary
capital punishment	isolationism	prison privatization
Cold War	mutually assured	property crime

punitive approach

rehabilitative approach

Strategic Arms
Limitations Talks (SALT)

Strategic Arms
Reduction Talks

(START)

Taliban

Three Prisons Act of
1891

victimless crime

violations of public

order

violent crime

war on drugs

war on terrorism

Warsaw Pact

WEB SITES

http://www.defenselink.mil/
The site of the Department of Defense's Defense Link will take you to any
of the military services. The site also contains current news material as well as
information about the Defense Department and the Pentagon.

http://www.state.gov/
The State Department's home page, with information about the organization
of the State Department, its bureaus and offices, and the U.S. embassies and
consulates. There is material about the secretary of state and discussions of
the secretary's travel. The site has information on travel and living abroad as
well, and information on employment in international organizations.

http://www.state.gov/www/global/arms/bureauac.html
The site of the Bureau of Arms Control within the State Department,
responsible for international agreements on conventional, chemical/biologi-
cal, and strategic forces. There is a great deal of information on treaties,
weapons of mass destruction, missile defense, and monitoring compliance,
plus links to other bureaus, including the Bureau of Nonproliferation, the
Bureau of Political-Military Affairs, and the Bureau of Verification and
Compliance.

http://www.ojp.usdoj.gov/
The U.S. Department of Justice Office of Justice Programs official site. From
this site you can follow links to find out about funding, training, programs,
and statistics about a host of topics, including the justice system (law enforcement, the courts, prosecution, indigent defense, juvenile justice, corrections,
and managing offenders), crime victims (victims of crime, violence against
women, and family violence), fighting crime (technology to fight crime, terrorism and domestic preparedness, substance abuse, community-based programs, American Indian and Alaska native affairs).

http://www.ojp.usdoj.gov/bjs/
The Bureau of Justice Statistics site provides information and statistics about
crimes and victims, characteristics of crimes, characteristics of victims, drugs,
homicide trends, and firearms. The site contains links to the *World Factbook of*

Criminal Justice Systems, the FBI's *Uniform Crime Reports,* juvenile justice statistics, and international statistics. It also includes information on courts and
sentencing, corrections, jails, prisons, and parole.

http://www.fbi.gov/
The home page of the Federal Bureau of Investigation (FBI). This lively site
contains information on the FBI and its programs as well as the most-wanted
federal criminals and major investigations. The site also contains new articles
on issues of current interest.

DISCUSSION QUESTIONS

1. What two factors made the conflict between the Soviet Union and the
    Western powers so volatile?
2. Discuss the U.S. policy of containment, and identify the conflicts that
    resulted from it.
3. Discuss the U.S. role as global peacekeeper. What is your opinion about
    this initiative?
4. To what extent should Americans be willing to curtail their freedoms to
    gain security against terrorists?
5. Look at Figure 6.2. Where do you think these weapons go? Why does the
    United States export so many weapons?
6. Should we punish criminals or attempt to rehabilitate them?
7. What role do race and ethnicity play in judicial practices?
8. Discuss the roles of federal, state, and local government in law
    enforcement.
9. What government policies have contributed to prison overcrowding, and
    what solutions have been attempted?

WEB QUESTIONS

1. Visit http://www.defenselink.mil/pubs/dod101/budget.html. What is the
    total annual budget of the Department of Defense, and how are expendi-
    tures broken down?
2. What are the CINCs, and how do they execute public policy
    (http://www.defenselink.mil/pubs/dod101/commands.html)?
3. What is the role of the State Department
    (http://www.state.gov/r/pa/rls/dos/index.cfm?docid=4078), and how
    does it carry out that task?
4. Visit http://www.state.gov/www/global/arms/bureau_ac/wmd_ac.html.
    Discuss the significance of one of the following treaties: the Biological

Weapons Convention, the Chemical Weapons Convention, the Comprehensive Nuclear Test-Ban Treaty.

5. What is the COPS program (http://www.usdoj.gov/cops/home.htm), and how does it differ from traditional approaches to law enforcement?

6. Explain two of the current issues of public interest listed on the FBI's Web site at http://www.fbi.gov/home.

7. Look at this year's *Uniform Crime Report* at www.fbi.gov/ucr, and discuss some crime indexes.

NOTES

1. National Association of State Budget Officers, *State Expenditure Report 2000* (Washington, DC: National Association of State Budget Officers, 2001).

2. William F. Burns, "The United States in a Changing World," in *U.S. Defense Policy in an Era of Constrained Resources,* ed. Robert L. Pflatzgraff, Jr., and Richard H. Shultz, Jr. (Lexington, MA: D.C. Heath and Company, 1990), 1–12.

3. Peter J. Roman, *Eisenhower and the Missile Gap* (Ithaca, NY: Cornell University Press, 1995).

4. James M. Lindsay, "The Nuclear Agenda," *Brookings Review* 18 (4): 8.

5. James M. McCormick and Daniel B. Bullen, "Disposing of the World's Excess Plutonium," *Policy Studies Journal* 26 (4): 682–702.

6. Isaiah Wilson III, "Dueling Regimes: The Means-Ends Dilemma of Multilateral Intervention Policy," *World Affairs* 163 (3): 99.

7. Daniel Smith, "Why We Need a Real Defense Review in 2001," *CDI Quadrennial Defense Review Project.* http://www.cdi.org/issues/qdr/whyneed2001.htm (2/8/01).

8. Daniel Smith, "Making the World Safe for the United States," *Weekly Defense Monitor* 5 (5). http://www.cdi.org/weekly/2001/issue05.htm (2/6/01).

9. Brian J. Reed and David R. Segal, "The Impact of Multiple Deployments on Soldiers' Peacekeeping Attitudes, Morale,

and Retention," *Armed Forces and Society: An Interdisciplinary Journal* 27 (1): 57.

10. Earl H. Tilford, Jr., "Reviewing the Future," *Parameters* 30 (3): 148.

11. Lindsay, "The Nuclear Agenda."

12. Kerry Gildea, "Bush Team Plans Overhaul for Ground Based NMD, Senators Say," *Defense Daily* 209 (2).

13. Lindsay, "The Nuclear Agenda."

14. Ali S. Khan, Stephen Morse, and Scott Lillibridge, "Public-Health Preparedness for Biological Terrorism in the USA," *The Lancet* 356 (9236): 1179.

15. Carl Conetta and Charles Knight, "Defense Sufficiency and Cooperation: A US Military Posture for the Post-Cold War Era," *Defense Policy Review: Future Visions for US Defense Policy*, March 12, 1998. http://www.comw.org/pda/opdfin.htm (2/8/01).

16. Kenneth G. Weiss "The Limits of Diplomacy: Missile Proliferation, Diplomacy, and Defense," *World Affairs* 163 (3): 110.

17. Khan, Morse, and Lillibridge, "Public-Health Preparedness for Biological Terrorism in the USA."

18. George W. Bush, Address Before a Joint Session of the Congress on the State of the Union, January 29, 2002. Weekly Compilation of Presidential Documents, the 2002 Presidential Documents Online via GPO Access at frwais.access.gpo.gov (3/1/02).

19. The Budget of the United States FY 2003, summary tables. http://www.whitehouse.gov/omb/budget/index.html (2/20/02).

20. George W. Bush, *The National Security Strategy of the United States.* http://www.whitehouse.gov/nsc/mss.html (10/07/02).

21. National Association of State Budget Officers, *State Expenditure Report 2000.*

22. Clemens Bartollas, "The Prison: Disorder Personified," in *Are Prisons Any Better? Twenty Years of Correctional Reform,* ed. John W. Murphy and Jack E. Dison (Newbury Park, CA: Sage Publications, 1990), 11–21.

23. John W. Roberts, "Introduction," in *Escaping Prison Myths,* ed. John W. Roberts (Washington, DC: American University Press, 1994), 1–23.

24. Ibid.

25. Alfred Blumstein, "Prisons," in *Crime,* ed. James Q. Wilson and Joan Petersilia (San Francisco: Institute for Contemporary Studies, 1995), 387–419.

26. Dennis L. Peck and John O. Smykla, "Legal Mandates and Changes in Prisons," in *Are Prisons Any Better? Twenty Years of Correctional Reform,* ed. John W. Murphy and Jack E. Dison (Newbury Park, CA: Sage Publications, 1990), 23–41.

27. U.S. Department of Justice, Bureau of Justice Statistics, *Capital Punishment Statistics.* http://www.ojp.usdoj.gov/bjs/cp.htm (3/8/01).

28. David Pasztor, "Execution Errors Erode Convictions in Death Penalty," Cox News Service, Austin, Texas, June 1, 2002.

29. Pam Belluck, "National Death Penalty Ruling," *New York Times,* September 29, 2002, section 4, p. 2.

30. Neal Conan, "Evolution of the Death Penalty in America." Talk of the Nation, National Public Radio, June 26, 2002.

31. Jan M. Chaiken, "Crunching Numbers: Crime and Incarceration at the End of the Millennium," *National Institute of Justice Journal,* January 2000: 10–17.

32. U.S. Department of Justice, Bureau of Justice Statistics, *Characteristics of Crime.*

http://www.ojp.usdoj.gov/bjs/cvict_c.htm (3/15/01).

33. Chaiken, "Crunching Numbers."

34. U.S. Department of Justice, Bureau of Justice Statistics, *Criminal Victimization, Summary Findings.* http://www.ojp.usdoj.gov/bjs/cvictgen.htm (10/09/02).

35. Ibid.

36. Ibid.

37. Ibid.

38. Blumstein, "Prisons."

39. U.S. Department of Justice, Bureau of Justice Statistics, *Prison Statistics.* http://www.ojp.usdoj.gov/bjs/prisons.htm (10/09/02).

40. Douglas C. McDonald and Kenneth E. Carlson, *Sentencing in the Federal Courts: Does Race Matter?* A Discussion Paper from the Bureau of Justice Statistics, Federal Justice Statistics Program, U.S. Department of Justice, December 1993.

41. Chaiken, "Crunching Numbers."

42. U.S. Department of Justice, *Prison Statistics.*

43. U.S. Department of Justice, *Capital Punishment Statistics.*

44. Law Enforcement Assistance Administration, *Two Hundred Years of American Criminal Justice: An LEAA Bicentennial Study* (Washington, DC: U.S. Department of Justice, 1976).

45. Federal Bureau of Prisons, *Federal Bureau of Prisons Quick Facts.* http://www.bop.gov/fact0598.html (2/9/01).

46. Norval Morris, "Foreword," in *Escaping Prison Myths,* ed. John W. Roberts (Washington, DC: American University Press, 1994), vii–ix.

47. John J. DiIulio, Jr., Steven K. Smith, and Aaron J. Saiger, "The Federal Role in Crime Control," in *Crime,* ed. James Q. Wilson and Joan Petersilia (San Francisco: Institute for Contemporary Studies, 1995), 445–464.

48. Clemens Bartollas, "The Prison."

49. Advisory Commission on Intergovernmental Relations, *Jails: Intergovernmental Dimensions of a Local*

Problem (Washington, DC: Advisory Commission on Intergovernmental Relations, 1984).

50. U.S. Department of Justice, Bureau of Justice Statistics, *Corrections Statistics*. http://www.ojp.usdoj.gov/bjs/correct.htm (10/09/02).

51. Federal Bureau of Prisons, *Federal Bureau of Prisons Quick Facts*.

52. U.S. Department of Justice, *Corrections Statistics*.

53. Blumstein, "Prisons."

54. Peck and Smykla, "Legal Mandates and Changes in Prisons."

55. Chaiken, "Crunching Numbers."

56. Lance Gay, "Clinton Stole Crime Issue, Report Says," *Plain Dealer,* February 19, 2001: 2A.

57. Bartollas, "The Prison."

58. U.S. Department of Justice, *Prison Statistics*.

59. Suzanne Smalley, "For-Profit Prisons Offer Privatization Lessons," *Government Executive Magazine*. http://www.goveexec.com/daily/fed/0599/050399b2.htm (2/9/01).

60. T. Don Hutto, "The Privatization of Prisons," in *Are Prisons Any Better? Twenty Years of Correctional Reform*, ed. John W. Murphy and Jack E. Dison (Newbury Park, CA: Sage Publications, 1990), 111–127.

7

Education Policy

Education policy is not a large expense for the federal government. As Figure 7.1(a) shows, when all federal expenditure for education, training, employment, and social services are added together (which is the way the federal government computes the expenditure), the total for 2001 was $57.3 billion, which made up 3 percent of the federal budget. Of this amount, $35.1 billion was direct education funding: $22.8 billion for elementary, secondary, and vocational education; $9.5 billion for higher education; and another $2.8 billion for research and general education aids. The rest of the money went to employment training and other labor social services.[1]

Education is the single largest area of expenditure for the states. Slightly more than one-third of all state expenditure goes to support elementary and higher education. As Figure 7.1(b) shows, the states spent $339 billion for education in 2001. Of this, $229.4 billion went to support elementary and secondary education, and $109.6 billion was spent on state colleges and universities. About 88 percent of the monies spent on elementary, secondary, and higher education came from independently raised state funds, while the federal government provided about 12 percent to assist the states.[2]

Many nations do not regard education as a public function, but instead expect families to pay to educate their own children. Why did the United States develop a public system of education and fund it with tax dollars? Why do we invest so much public money in education? What are some of the major issues confronting our system of publicly supported schools? This chapter looks at these issues.

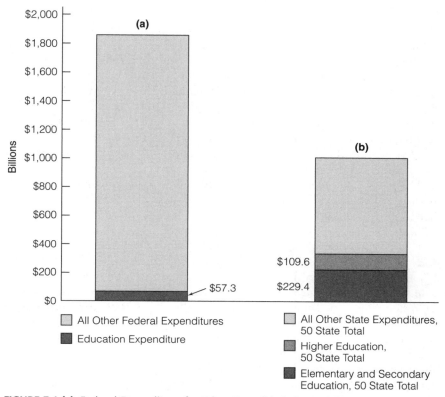

FIGURE 7.1 (a) Federal Expenditure for Education. **(b)** Estimated 50 State Expenditure for Education, FY 2001.

SOURCES: (a) The Budget of the United States FY 2003, summary tables. [http://www.whitehouse.gov/omb/budget/index.html] (b) National Association of State Budget Officers, State Expenditure Report 2000, 2001.

EVOLUTION OF ELEMENTARY AND SECONDARY SCHOOL POLICY

One of the deeply held religious beliefs of the Protestants who first settled the American colonies was that each person should be able to read the Bible. Linked thus to religion, education was an important social value and was treated as a high priority by communities. This tradition generally transferred to civil society after the disappearance of the early religious communities. Most people were expected to obtain some amount of education—at least to be literate—and schools were typically provided for the education of youth. A major exception was the slave population: education for slaves was considered dangerous and was outlawed in many of the slaveholding states.

During the seventeenth and early eighteenth centuries, schools were primarily established to teach religion. Church-state partnerships were common in New England, and schools entirely run by churches were the norm in the rest of the colonies. Vocational (apprenticeship) training was also provided in some schools.

In the late eighteenth century many early state constitutions included provisions for the establishment of schools. Thomas Jefferson, for instance, proposed that Virginia set up a three-year elementary school system funded by tax dollars for all the nonslave children in Virginia. Other states followed similar paths.[3] Few in number and randomly placed across the country, these early schools were different in character from the schools that emerged later.[4]

The schools that emerged in the later nineteenth century were part of a much larger institutional system. The system was characterized by age-graded and hierarchically ordered schools administered by professionals who had been trained to teach in and administer academic institutions. Previous schools had been informal and under local control, while these newer schools were formal institutions designed to socialize children into the society of the state.[5]

Public education served an essential function in this nation of immigrants.[6] One of the major outcomes of universal free public education was the assimilation of the children of newly arrived immigrants into the majority population. Schools acted as leveling fields that created a unified American citizenry who spoke the same language, read the same literature, knew the same history, and honored the same heroes.[7]

Education is one of the exceptions to the demand for limited government prevalent in the United States. Part of the reason Americans support government provision of education is the belief in equality of opportunity, and education is seen as a key enabler of equality of opportunity. With education, a person can rise in society and attain success. Support for education in the United States has been intimately linked to the general belief in providing each citizen with the tools necessary for personal achievement.[8]

From time to time the federal government has played an active, albeit restricted, role in elementary and secondary education. One of the earliest federal roles was the use of land—a resource it had vast amounts of—to provide funding for education. In the **Northwest Ordinance of 1787,** the federal government required that one section of land in each township be set aside for the support of education.[9]

Several major federal education programs for kindergarten through twelfth grade (K–12) education were put in place beginning in the 1950s. The first of these was the **National Defense Education Act of 1958,** which provided federal support to strengthen science, math, and foreign language instruction. This federal action was taken in response to the Soviet Union's launch of *Sputnik,* the first satellite to orbit Earth, which drew federal attention to the national defense importance of a well-educated citizenry. The National Defense Education Act provided funding to train a new generation of college faculty and scientists.[10]

In 1965 the role of the federal government in K-12 education expanded with the passage of the **Elementary and Secondary Education Act.**[11] This act provided financial assistance to local schools for textbooks, libraries, and other instructional materials. **Title 1** provided funds to schools with high concentrations of children from low-income families. In 1968 the act was amended to provide financial aid for handicapped children.[12] As with other Great Society programs initiated by President Lyndon Johnson's administration, the Elementary and Secondary Education Act and its amendment imposed regulations on schools in exchange for federal largess. Title 1 funds remain a key source of funding for schools in economically depressed areas.

Although many of these programs were useful to localities and the states, by the end of the 1970s there was increasing opposition to federal involvement in K–12 education. Federal regulations came to be seen as substantial burdens, and the election of Ronald Reagan in 1980 brought a champion of deregulation to the White House. Reagan vowed to eliminate the Department of Education and to return control of schools to the localities. He was unable to eliminate the Education Department, but his rhetoric focused national attention on improving education.[13]

The decline of America's public schools became a critical issue in the 1980s. The schools were perceived to be failing to equip students for success in increasingly technical jobs. Global economic competition revealed that American students were lagging behind German and Japanese students. There was fear that the United States would be unable to compete in the international marketplace unless the schools started turning out better prepared graduates.

Despite widespread acceptance that American schools were in need of reform, no single solution to the problems of K–12 education emerged. States and localities instituted a series of reforms and pilot projects. Some created magnet and charter schools that provided training in the arts, math and science, or other areas. Charter schools also addressed concerns that traditional school administration was the root of the problem in educational performance. Central in the debates on educational reform was the question of how to improve failed urban schools that struggled with reduced tax bases so as to provide for the needs of inner-city children. These issues are discussed later in the chapter.

The election of George W. Bush in 2000 refocused attention on the role of the federal government in elementary and secondary education. During his campaign, Bush strongly favored education reform, particularly increased accountability for school performance. Bush argued for mandatory annual testing of students to ascertain their learning and determine the effectiveness of the teachers and schools. Shortly after coming to office, he was successful in getting Congress to pass school reform legislation.

EVOLUTION OF POLICY FOR
HIGHER EDUCATION

The states—and before them the colonies—have played a role in higher education since the founding of Harvard in 1636. During the seventeenth and eighteenth centuries, individual colonies granted charters for colleges. Most of the colleges were private sectarian institutions.[14] A few nonsectarian state colleges, including the Universities of Georgia, North Carolina, and Virginia, were established before the Civil War.[15]

A major shift came in the nineteenth century with the establishment of public (state-supported) universities across the entire nation.[16] The federal government played a key role in initiating the state university systems, but thereafter the states had the major responsibility for funding them.

Federal support first came in the form of the **land-grant college system,** in which federal lands were given to each state for the establishment of a college under the terms of the **Morrill Acts of 1862 and 1890.**[17] The first Morrill Act provided thirty thousand acres for each of the state's members of Congress. Direct monetary appropriations were provided to these schools through the second Morrill Act, which was responsible for the establishment of the traditionally black land-grant colleges set up in the South at this time, and through the Bankhead-Jones Act. The original mission of the land-grant colleges was to teach agriculture and the "mechanic arts." They sought to provide a practical education to the children of people of ordinary means and emphasized pragmatic studies over the classics that were being taught at private institutions.[18]

Over time the land-grant colleges and universities evolved into a larger system designed to support both education and targeted research. An important early component of the land-grant system, agricultural experiment stations were created by the **Hatch Act of 1887.** The amount of the federal appropriation for experiment stations varied each year and was determined by the number of small farmers in the state. States were required to provide matching funds. Another component of the land-grant system was the Cooperative Extension Service, which was created by the **Smith-Lever Act of 1914.** Its purpose was to disseminate the findings of the research at the agricultural experiment stations. This act authorized ongoing federal support (with state matching money) on a formula similar to that used by the Hatch Act.[19]

Today there are 105 land-grant universities—at least one in each state and territory and including 29 Native American tribal colleges set up in 1994. The Department of Agriculture (USDA) plays a large role in administering the land-grant system. USDA's Cooperative State Research Service (CSRS) administers funds from both the Hatch Act and the Morrill Acts. The Extension Service of USDA administers Smith-Lever funding and cooperates with states to set priorities and to facilitate the sharing of information within the Cooperative Extension System.[20]

What is interesting about land-grant colleges and universities is the land-grant model itself. The mission as Morrill conceived it was threefold: research, teaching, and extension (or service). Practical focus and outreach or extension were key elements. Extension was designed to link the land-grant school's academic and research programs to societal needs. Fiduciary responsibility and a public service ethos were part of the mission. At the time almost 50 percent of the U.S. population lived on farms, so agriculture was a prime focus of the land-grant institutions. What is truly significant is that the land-grant system created a partnership between the government, the university, and the private sector for the advancement of research and transfer of technology. Since the 1860s, the percentage of the population living on farms and deriving their income from farming has declined, and the private sector has shifted from farming to industry. The successful land-grant model remains, with its prime features of practicality, research associated with national needs, and government–university–private sector partnerships.[21]

Land-grant colleges are not the only ones to emphasize practical and applied research and partner with the private sector and the federal and state governments. World War II drove universities in the direction of forging wider linkages with the government and the private sector, as did the crisis of economic competitiveness that emerged in the 1970s. Private universities tended to adopt the land-grant model to adapt to a changing world.

As the nation emerged from World War II, American colleges and universities grew rapidly. **The Servicemen's Readjustment Act of 1944,** commonly known as the **GI Bill,** [22] triggered enrollment increases that ushered in a boom period for colleges and universities.[23] The creation of the national laboratory system strengthened the link between the universities and the federal government and fueled research. Universities grew increasingly dependent on federal funding from such departments and agencies as the Department of Defense (especially the Defense Advance Research Projects Agency), the Department of Energy, the National Institutes of Health, NASA, and the National Science Foundation.[24] One of the key changes in the postwar era was bipartisan acceptance of the appropriate role of the federal government in funding university research. The consensus was that the country would reap a great social benefit from university research, and therefore it should be funded. While the rationalization for the appropriateness of the government's funding of university research was generally restricted to basic research, the reality of the situation was that vast amounts of money were directed toward applied research and development (R&D) as well. Universities became heavily dependent on federal funding to support all their R&D efforts.

Widespread student protests over involvement in the Vietnam War wracked college campuses in the late 1960s and early 1970s. The protests brought visibility to the role that universities were playing in that war by providing the Department of Defense with research. This concern led to a reevaluation of the link between higher education and the federal government, and many universities legally separated themselves from their contract research units.[25] With the end of American involvement in Vietnam, however, the scrutiny of university research eased.

By the late 1970s fear of the diminution of U.S. economic competitiveness reopened the debate over the appropriate role of university research. Comparisons with Japan and Germany raised the question of whether the United States ought to be putting so much R&D funding into military (rather than civilian) programs. Questions arose about the nature of the link between basic research and commercialization of new and improved products and processes. Many policy analysts and politicians began to advocate federal funding for targeted research associated with national needs and an emphasis on civilian R&D. A series of national acts were passed, including the Stevenson-Wydler Technology Innovation Act of 1980, the Bayh-Dole Act of 1980, the Small Business Innovation Development Act of 1982, the National Cooperative Research Act of 1984, the Trademark Clarification Act of 1984, the Federal Technology Transfer Act of 1986, the Omnibus Trade and Competitiveness Act of 1988, and the National Competitiveness Technology Transfer Act of 1989. While each has unique features, the general intent was to involve the universities in applied research directly applicable to business needs and to move university-developed technologies to the private sector for commercialization. The hoped-for outcome was improvement in the nation's economic competitiveness as the fruits of science and technology rapidly diffused into the society.[26]

While the nation's policymakers drew on the success of the land-grant model to design this new legislation, they fundamentally altered the traditional implementation mechanism. The original land-grant model rested on the idea of direct government funding for universities based on the notion of not-for-profit public service and the transfer of research results to improve society. The fundamental incentive was the fiduciary responsibility of the university. The "competitiveness legislation" that emerged in the 1980s, by contrast, created financial incentives for universities to transfer the results of R&D to society. It sets a new direction by allowing universities to make a profit from patenting and licensing technologies developed by professors on their campuses.

FUNDING AND ORGANIZATION
OF PUBLIC SCHOOLS

Elementary and secondary education in the United States has predominantly been the obligation of states and localities. As Figure 7.2 shows, the percentage of revenue coming from federal sources is small compared to that coming from states and localities. Federal support has declined over the last thirty years, as has local support, while state support has increased slightly. In the 1996–1997 school year, as shown in Figure 7.3, federal aid comprised approximately 6 percent of the funding that supported public elementary and secondary education. States, on average, provide 48 percent of funds, and localities 45 percent.

The local funds are often raised through local property taxes, which creates inequity because school districts in affluent areas are more able to provide resources for education than are districts in poor areas. Poor districts may have tax rates four or five times higher than rates in wealthy districts and still not be able to match the per-pupil funding of affluent districts.

Mexican American parents in San Antonio, Texas, objected to the reliance on property taxes to fund education, and in 1973 the Supreme Court ruled against them (*San Antonio Independent School District* v. *Rodriguez*), stating that education "is not among the rights afforded explicit protection under our federal constitution."[27] However, basing their decisions on state constitutions that

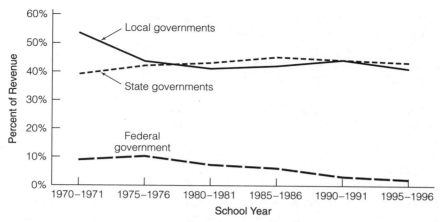

FIGURE 7.2 Sources of Revenue for Public Elementary and Secondary Schools, 1970–1971 to 1995–1996.

SOURCE: U.S. Department of Education, National Center for Education Statistics, Statistics of State School Systems; Revenues and Expenditures for Public Elementary and Secondary Education; and Common Core of Data Surveys.

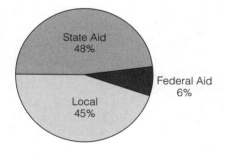

FIGURE 7.3 Distribution of School Revenues for Public Elementary and Secondary Education by Source, 1996–1997.

SOURCE: U.S. Department of Education, National Center for Education Statistics, Common Core Data, "National Public Education Financial Survey," School Year 1996–1997.

guarantee equal education to all children, courts in many states have determined that education is a right. *Serrano* v. *Priest,* a 1971 California case, held that education is a fundamental right that cannot be made a condition of the wealth of a child's parents. The *Serrano* decision prompted a flood of lawsuits attempting to overturn other states' reliance on property taxes to fund education. The New Jersey supreme court focused on language in the state constitution calling for "a thorough and efficient system of free public schools" and found New Jersey's property tax funding of schools to be unconstitutional. In the mid-1980s Kentucky's courts ruled its school financing system unconstitutional as well. In the late 1980s, with per-pupil disparities between rich and poor districts having grown from the $238 difference that had sparked the *Rodriguez* case to $1,300 per pupil, the Texas supreme court found the Texas school funding scheme unconstitutional.[28] By 1997 seventeen states had initiated some type of change in funding to assist less wealthy districts. Other states continue to struggle over the constitutionality of their state funding systems.

Ohio, for instance, has had three waves of cases make their way to the state supreme court. The most recent, heard in 2001, was remanded for arbitration and is now back on the court's docket. Michigan, New Hampshire, Pennsylvania, and Alaska are also actively engaged in a debate regarding the constitutionality of their school funding.

The federal government has attempted to provide some funding for schools in poor districts. The largest source is Title 1 of the Elementary and Secondary Education Act of 1965. In 2001 federal funding through Title 1 amounted to $9.5 billion. This money goes to K–12 schools with high concentrations of low-income families. The law was rewritten in 1994 to state explicitly that educationally disadvantaged students served by Title 1 should be held to the same academic standards as other children. The states were required to develop content standards to define what all children are expected to learn and performance standards to measure how well each child is meeting the content standards.[29]

Elementary and secondary schools are typically controlled by **school districts,** separate government units set up to direct public school systems. The United States has over fourteen thousand school districts.[30] Most states use school districts to organize and deliver elementary and secondary education. However, there are exceptions. In Hawaii, for instance, the state government provides for all education. In Maine, education is provided by the state government in some areas, and by townships, municipalities, or school districts in other areas.[31]

Institutions of higher education draw their funding from a mix of sources, including student tuition, private gifts, endowment income, revenue from royalties on patents and licenses, and government funding.[32] Government higher education funding comes primarily from the state, with federal assistance in the form of grants and loans. The federal government assists students with tuition through Pell grants (Department of Education grants of up to $3,125 per year to undergraduate students with financial need), Stafford loans (loans to undergraduate and graduate students on which the government pays the interest until the student graduates), and the GI Bill. The federal government also provides research grants to university professors, and a percentage of these grants goes to support the university infrastructure and operating costs. Each state provides some level of support to its state universities, but the level varies.

CURRENT ISSUES

Schools today are at the center of considerable debate. At the core of the debate are two questions: how can we best educate students, and how can we provide equitable access to educational institutions. In trying to decide how best to educate students, policy analysts have focused on the declining quality of education and have sought educational reforms. Some of these reforms have been controversial, especially when the reformers have proposed changes that critics see as violating the separation of church and state. Efforts to seek equity in access to quality educational institutions have also proved controversial. Earlier efforts under affirmative action guidelines written to assure minority access to institutions of higher education have been challenged. Attempts to desegregate K–12 educational institutions has proved to be a perennial problem. The following sections discuss these issues.

The Quality of Schools

Several factors combined to put the issue of educational quality on the national agenda. One was publicity about high school graduates who were unable to balance their checkbooks or read directions.[33] In 1975 the disclosure by the College Board that scores on the Scholastic Aptitude Test (SAT) had fallen sharply since 1963 resulted in a tidal wave of questions concerning the decline in American educational achievement.[34] Some experts blamed lax curricula, large class sizes, and poor teaching. Others pointed to the lack of safety in schools, the negative influence of television, and reduced parental supervision. Still others suggested that declining test scores were the result of widening the pool of test takers to include weaker students who once would never have considered going on to higher education.

While the debate raged, America set out to reform education. Several changes were suggested, including the creation of charter schools, national testing of student performance, mechanisms to allow parents to move their children out of failing schools, merit pay increases for teachers, and national qualification and testing of teachers.[35]

The idea behind national testing of student performance was that information on student progress would make it possible to correct poor learning while the child could still be helped. Some testing plans included mandatory retention in the current grade should a child fail to score at grade level. Critics suggested that mandatory retention punished children instead of fixing the system that failed them.

Perhaps most controversial was the call for school choice by providing vouchers that parents could use to send children to private school or to transfer them to another, presumably better, public school. The idea behind vouchers was that the school system was in essence a monopoly. Children attended school by virtue of where they lived. Short of their parents moving them out of the district, children are virtual captives of the school district. The notion behind school choice is that parents would have the power to move their children out of failing schools. In this way, the monopoly would be ended and schools would have to compete for students. The theory suggested that this would improve school performance. Arguments in favor of educational choice rest on the inequity of choices under the monopolistic system, in which economically advantaged parents have greater choices in both the public and private sector to seek schools of excellence for their children. Critics point out that the voucher system could result in the collapse of the free, universal public school system, especially if vouchers are used to pay for tuition at private or religious schools.[36]

National qualification and testing of teachers along with reward schemes such as teacher merit pay were aimed at improving teaching performance. They have been vigorously opposed by teachers' unions, although they have been implemented in several states. Many states have also opened **charter schools,** nonsectarian public schools that do not have to abide by many of the regulations that apply to traditional public schools. The charter is a performance contract establishing the school and describing its mission, program, goals, methods of assessment, and ways to measure success. Charters are typically granted for from three to five years, after which the school must report its academic results to the sponsoring agency (usually the state or local school board). If results are not positive, the charter may be revoked. The idea is to allow schools increased autonomy in exchange for increased accountability.

One of the most radical changes came with the passage of President Bush's **No Child Left Behind Act** in 2002. This act promised a stronger federal government role in K–12 education, primarily through increased funding. It mandates yearly testing in grades three through eight and provides a mechanism for students to transfer out of failing schools.[37] The act allows for recruitment of more math, science, and special education teachers by forgiving part of their college loans in exchange for a five-year commitment to teaching in poor schools. Whether the act will have an effect on schools is yet unclear.

Religion and the Schools

The appropriate relationship between religion and the schools has been an issue for a long time. In 1947, for instance, the Supreme Court ruled that New Jersey could use tax money to pay the bus fares of students attending Catholic parochial school, despite the fact that the school taught religious as well as academic subjects (*Everson* v. *Board of Education*). The Court shocked many Americans in 1962 when it ruled that the nondenominational prayer used by the New York Board of Regents violated the First Amendment's establishment clause, which requires the separation of church and state (*Engle* v. *Vitale*). The next year the Court extended this ruling to prohibit required reading of the Bible and recitation of the Lord's Prayer (*School District of Abington Township* v. *Schempp*). Other Court actions have repeatedly stuck down religious observances in schools, including before-school and after-school use of buildings for religious meetings, the performance of religious pageants, and religious displays.[38]

Restrictions against prayer in school are repeatedly challenged. Student-led prayer has been substituted for teacher-led prayer, for example. Opponents of the ban on prayer contend that the upsurge of school violence can be traced to the lack of prayer in schools. After several students and a teacher were murdered in a Columbine, Colorado, high school in 1999, there were efforts to have a copy of the Ten Commandments posted in schools. The Court has not thus far approved of any such efforts.

In 2002 the U.S. Supreme Court ruled that the provision of school vouchers to students who attend parochial schools was constitutional. The test case was a pilot program in the Cleveland school system. In a close decision, the conservative members of the Court upheld the constitutionality of the program, saying that such vouchers did not violate the separation of church and state (*Zelman, Superintendent of Public Instruction of Ohio, et al.* v. *Simmons-Harris, et al.*).

Racial Equality

School segregation was sanctioned by *Plessy* v. *Ferguson,* an 1896 case in which the Supreme Court upheld a Louisiana law that mandated "separate but equal" railroad accommodations for whites and blacks. Schools remained segregated until the Court ruled in *Brown* v. *Board of Education* (1954) that "separate education facilities are inherently unequal." A year later, the Court ruled that lower courts should provide remedies to bring about school desegregation "with all deliberate speed." Over the next decade, virtually no progress was made toward desegregating the schools, and in 1971 the Court ordered **busing** as the remedy in *Swann* v. *Charlotte-Mecklenburg Board of Education.* This ruling allowed suburban white students to be bused to inner-city, predominately black schools.[39]

Busing was particularly unpopular among white parents who did not want their children bused to schools outside their neighborhoods. In 1974 the Supreme Court, which now had a number of more conservative justices, ruled against cross-district busing, resulting in a return to high levels of segregation. African American students were trapped in underfunded inner-city school districts, while white students typically attended more affluent suburban schools. By the late 1980s, schools across the United States were more segregated than they had been in the 1960s.[40]

The policy of **affirmative action** has been extensively used to correct for racial injustice. The term was first used by President John Kennedy in 1961 in an executive order requiring federal contractors to take "affirmative action" to ensure that they did not discriminate. Presidents Lyndon Johnson and Richard Nixon went beyond mere nondiscrimination and required active recruitment of minorities and imposition of minority-hiring goals. Colleges and universities began using affirmative action strategies in the 1970s to increase minority enrollment.[41]

In 1978 the Supreme Court heard the precedent-setting case *University of California Regents* v. *Bakke.* Allan Bakke, a white applicant, sued the University of California after he was denied admission to law school and less-qualified minority applicants were admitted under affirmative action guidelines. The Court ruled in his favor, outlawing the use of racial quotas in university admissions, but did agree that race could be used as a factor in admission decisions. Attacks on affirmative action increased in the 1980s and 1990s, and in 1996 California voters passed Proposition 209, which eliminated the use of race-based and gender-based preferences in hiring, contracting, and education. Texas and Florida quickly followed, eliminating race-based admissions policies for colleges and universities.[42] Race-based admission practices of other colleges and universities across the country are currently being questioned in court cases.

In 2001 the University of California Board of Regents reversed the earlier ban on affirmative action. This move, which may not stand the test of state law, was a response to the drastic decrease in the number of minority applicants as a result of the affirmative action ban. Whether affirmative action will be put back in practice remains to be seen.

SUMMARY

Education policy has deep roots in American tradition. The early Protestant settlers' belief that each person should be able to read the Bible, along with the belief in equality of opportunity, are the foundation on which education policy rests. Education also played a key socializing role in a nation of immigrants.

The first American schools were established to teach religion. Church-state partnerships were widespread in New England, and church-run schools were common elsewhere. Many early state constitutions included provisions for the establishment of state-funded schools. Nineteenth-century school systems were characterized by age-ranked schools run by trained experts.

The federal government has played an active but restricted role in K–12 education over time. The major influence has been through the Elementary and Secondary Education Act, which provided funds to schools with high concentrations of children from low-income families. By the end of the 1970s, the strong arm of the federal government was increasingly being opposed, and federal regulations came to be seen as substantial burdens.

Most pre–Civil War colleges were private sectarian institutions. In the nineteenth century public land-grant universities sought to educate the children of people of ordinary means and emphasized pragmatic studies over the classics. Land-grant colleges and universities evolved into a larger system designed to support both education and targeted research, and the land-grant model of research, teaching, and extension became the organizing principle of all modern universities. World War II moved universities in the direction of forging wider linkages with both the government and the private sector.

After World War II, the GI Bill prompted enrollment increases, and the creation of the national laboratory system strengthened the ties of universities to the federal government and fueled research. Student protests over involvement in the Vietnam War in the late 1960s and early 1970s led to a reevaluation of the link between higher education and the federal government. The desire to link universities to industry and thus improve national economic well-being became public policy in the 1980s.

Elementary and secondary education has predominately been the obligation of states and localities. Federal aid comprises approximately 6 percent of elementary and secondary education funding, while states on average provide 48 percent of funds and localities 45 percent. The local funds often come from local property taxes, which creates inequity across schools districts. State courts have played key roles in the area of school finance. The courts in many states are guided by state constitutions, which they interpret to guarantee equal education to all children. The federal government has attempted to provide funding for poor districts through Title 1 monies associated with the Elementary and Secondary Education Act of 1965.

Institutions of higher education draw their funding from a mix of sources. These include student tuition, private gifts, endowment income, revenue from royalties on patents and licenses, and government funding. Government higher education funding comes primarily from states with federal assistance in the form of grants and loans.

Education policy provokes many issues of national concern. A major issue is school performance and quality. School reform efforts have included the creation of charter schools, national testing of student performance, mechanisms to allow parents to move their children out of failing schools, merit pay increases for teachers, and national qualification and testing of teachers.

The judiciary has played a critical role in education policy. Religion in schools has been an issue since the Supreme Court banned prayer in schools. The Court played a major role by instituting school desegregation and later by striking down affirmative action policies designed to correct for racial injustice.

KEY TERMS

affirmative action

busing

charter schools

Elementary and Secondary Education Act

Hatch Act of 1887

land-grant college system

Morrill Acts of 1862 and 1890

National Defense Education Act of 1958

No Child Left Behind Act

Northwest Ordinance of 1787

school districts

Servicemen's Readjustment Act of 1944 (GI Bill)

Smith-Lever Act of 1914

Title 1

WEB SITES

http://www.ed.gov/
The home page of the U.S. Department of Education has links to educational statistics, disabilities education, ERIC digests for research on education, and numerous resources on financial aid.

http://www.accesseric.org/
The Educational Resources Information Center (ERIC) is an information network that acquires, catalogs, summarizes, and provides access to education

information from all sources. The database and ERIC document collections are housed in about three thousand locations worldwide, including most major public and university library systems. ERIC produces a variety of publications and provides extensive user assistance, including AskERIC, an Internet-based electronic question-answering service for teachers.

http://www.ed.gov/free/
The site of Federal Resources for Educational Excellence affords access to all other federal government agencies that provide educational material for the arts, educational technology, foreign languages, health and safety, language arts, mathematics, physical education, science, social studies, and vocational education. The site also allows a search of all federal educational resources by key word.

http://www.eriche.org/main.html
The site of the ERIC clearinghouse on higher education. Along with providing answers to frequently asked questions about higher education, it provides resources for administrators, faculty, students, and parents.

http://caspar.nsf.gov/
The National Science Foundation database that provides statistical data on U.S. universities and colleges and their science and engineering resources. This site allows easy downloads.

http://coe.ilstu.edu/grapevine/
The University of Illinois Grapevine site that reports on state efforts for higher education. The available data include tax appropriations for universities, colleges, community colleges, and state higher education agencies. You can look at the higher education spending of individual states or access a fifty-state summary.

DISCUSSION QUESTIONS

1. How did land-grant colleges and universities get established? How did they change the way Americans thought about higher education?

2. How does the current system of public school funding create inequity across school districts? What policies address this issue?

3. List and explain the policy actions taken to improve the quality of public schools.

4. One of the suggested explanations of decreasing SAT scores is the "widening pool of test takers who would never have gone on to higher education in the past." What government policies have contributed to widening the pool?

5. What are the arguments for and against providing parents with school choice?

6. Affirmative action policies have involved several levels of government. List and explain the policy actions taken, and identify the level of government responsible for them.

WEB QUESTIONS

1. What are some of the current initiatives of the federal government regarding education policy (http://www.ed.gov/about/priorities.jsp)?

2. What is the mission of the Department of Education (http://www.ed.gov/offices/OUS/fedrole.html), and what percent of total education spending is the department responsible for?

3. How much did the Department of Education spend on postsecondary education in the last budget year (http://www.ed.gov/offices/OUS/Budget02/History.pdf)? How much of this spending was mandatory, and how much was discretionary? What was the largest program that the department financed?

NOTES

1. Executive Office of the President, *The Budget for Fiscal Year 2003, Historical Tables* (Washington, DC: U.S. Government Printing Office, 2002).

2. National Association of State Budget Officers, *State Expenditure Report 2000* (Washington, DC: National Association of State Budget Officers, 2001).

3. Francesco Cordasco, *A Brief History of Education* (Totowa, NJ: Littlefield, Adams & Co., 1976).

4. Ibid.

5. Michael B. Katz, *Reconstructing American Education* (Cambridge, MA: Harvard University Press, 1987).

6. Phillip C. Schlechty, *Schools for the 21st Century: Leadership Imperatives for Educational Reform* (San Francisco: Jossey-Bass Publishers, 1990).

7. Diane Ravitch, "Desegregation: Varieties of Meaning," in *Shades of Brown: New Perspectives on School Desegregation,* ed. Derrick Bell (New York: Teachers College Columbia University, 1995), 31–47.

8. John Kingdon, *America the Unusual* (New York: St. Martin's Press, 1998).

9. Paul T. Hill, "Getting It Right the Eighth Time: Reinventing the Federal Role," in *New Directions: Federal Education Policy in the Twenty-First Century,* ed. March Kanstoroom and Chester E. Finn, Jr. (New York: The Thomas B. Fordham Foundation, 1999), 147–169.

10. Ibid.

11. Ibid.

12. Clarke E. Cochran, Lawrence C. Mayer. T. R. Carr, and N. Joseph Cayer, *American Public Policy: An Introduction,* 6th ed. (Boston: Bedford/St. Martin's Press, 1999).

13. David K. Cohen, "Standards-Based School Reform: Policy, Practice, and Performance," in *Holding Schools Accountable: Performance-Based Reform in Education,* ed. Helen F. Ladd (Washington, DC: Brookings, 1996), 99–127.

14. Louis W. Bender, *Federal Regulation and Higher Education* (Washington, DC: The American Association for Higher Education, 1977).

15. Cordasco, *A Brief History of Education.*

16. The Carnegie Foundation for the Advancement of Teaching, *The States and Higher Education: Proud Past and Vital Future* (San Francisco: Jossey-Bass, 1976).

17. National Association of State Universities and Land-Grant Colleges, *The Land Grant Tradition* (Washington, DC: NASULGC, 1995).

18. National Research Council, the Committee on the Future of the Colleges of Agriculture in the Land Grant University System, *Colleges of Agriculture at the Land Grant Universities: Public Service and Public Policy* (Washington, DC: National Academy Press, 1996).

19. National Association of State Universities and Land-Grant Colleges, *The Land Grant Tradition.*

20. National Research Council, *Colleges of Agriculture at the Land Grant Universities.*

21. National Association of State Universities and Land-Grant Colleges, *The Land Grant Tradition.*

22. Ibid.

23. Bender, *Federal Regulation and Higher Education.*

24. Dianne Rahm, John Kirkland, and Barry Bozeman, *University-Industry R&D Collaboration in the United States, the United Kingdom, and Japan* (Dordrecht: Kluwer Academic Publishers, 2000).

25. Robert M. O'Neil, *The Courts, Government, and Higher Education* (New York: Committee for Economic Development, 1972).

26. Rahm, Kirkland, and Bozeman, *University-Industry R&D Collaboration in the United States, the United Kingdom, and Japan.*

27. John C. Hogan, *The Schools, the Courts, and the Public Interest* (Toronto: Lexington Books, 1974).

28. Christopher E. Smith, *Courts and Public Policy* (Chicago: Nelson-Hall Publishers, 1993).

29. Independent Review Panel, *Improving the Odds* (Washington, DC: Independent Review Panel for the Assessment of Title 1, 2001).

30. Richard Stillman II, *The American Bureaucracy: The Core of Modern Government,* 2d ed. (Chicago: Nelson-Hall, 1996).

31. Robert D. Reishauer, "Government Diversity: Bane of the Grants Strategy in the United States," in *American Intergovernmental Relations,* ed. Laurence J.

O'Toole, Jr. (Washington, DC: CQ Press, 2000), 108–120.

32. Rahm, Kirkland, and Bozeman, *University-Industry R&D Collaboration in the United States, the United Kingdom, and Japan.*

33. Mitchell Lazarus, *Goodbye to Excellence: A Critical Look at Minimum Competency Testing* (Boulder, CO: Westview Press, 1981).

34. Diane Ravitch, *National Standards in American Education* (Washington, DC: Brookings, 1995).

35. Denis P. Doyle and Terry W. Hartle, *Excellence in Education: The States Take Charge* (Washington, DC: American Enterprise Institute for Public Policy Research, 1985).

36. John F. Witte, "School Choice and Student Performance," in *Holding Schools Accountable: Performance-Based Reform in Education,* ed. Helen F. Ladd (Washington, DC: Brookings, 1996), 149–176.

37. Mike Allen, "Kennedy Says Budget Reneges on Promises; Public Focuses on War and Enron," *Washington Post,* March 3, 2002, A07.

38. Richard D. Strahan and L. Charles Turner, *The Courts and the Schools: The School Administrator and Legal Risk Management Today* (New York: Longman, 1987).

39. Perry A. Zirkel, Sharon Nalbone Richardson, and Steven S. Goldberg, *A Digest of Supreme Court Decisions Affecting Education,* 3rd ed. (Bloomington, IN: Phi Delta Kappa Educational Foundation, 1995).

40. Smith, *Courts and Public Policy.*

41. The CQ Researcher, *Issues in Social Policy* (Washington, DC: CQ Press, 2000).

42. Cochran et al., *American Public Policy.*

8

Transportation Policy

Transportation programs are an important area of expenditure for both the federal government and the states. On the federal level, transportation expenses accounted for about 3 percent of expenditure in 2001. As Figure 8.1 shows, that year the federal government spent $55.2 billion on transportation, while the states spent $91.1 billion, or 9 percent. Transportation programs were the third-largest single expenditure of the states. Nearly 29 percent of the monies spent by the states—$26 billion dollars of it—was sent to them by the federal government in the form of grants.[1] This transfer gives the federal government considerable influence over the states. When states do not comply with federal demands, Washington can threaten to withhold the monies.

Transportation expenses consume about 19 percent of the average household's income. As a whole, the transportation sector employed more than 10.5 million workers in 2000 and accounted for about 10.8 percent of the GDP.[2]

Transportation policy includes the development, maintenance, and use of all publicly provided passenger and freight or cargo transportation systems and infrastructure, including railways, roads, bridges, tunnels, inland and coastal waterways, and air transportation. Transportation policy is concerned with both qualitative and quantitative measures of transport performance: passenger safety and satisfaction as well as the volume and speed of traffic handled.[3] This chapter discusses a variety of transportation programs and issues that affect their implementation.

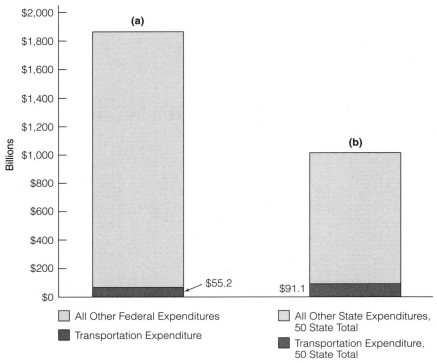

FIGURE 8.1 (a) Federal Expenditure for Transportation, FY 2001.
(b) Estimated 50 State Expenditure for Transportation, FY 2001.

SOURCES: (a) The Budget of the United States FY 2003, summary tables. [http://www.white-house.gov/omb/budget/index.html] (b) National Association of State Budget Officers, State Expenditure Report 2000, 2001.

THE EVOLUTION OF
TRANSPORTATION POLICY

The U.S. transportation system evolved with heavy reliance on the private sector. The primary impetus was commerce, and financing of many of the major forms of transportation came from the private sector, where profit motives dictated particular forms of geographic development. An important result of this reliance on the private sector was the growth of transportation with little regard for social equity.[4]

The American colonies were dependent on England for most goods and products, and access to trade was essential. During colonial times water was the preferred mode of transportation of goods. The roads that existed were in very poor condition, while water travel was both inexpensive and reliable. Population and commercial development were limited to regions with access to water transport.

Ships played an essential role in the development of commerce, as did ship-building. While most of the useful timber in Europe had been cut by the 1600s, the colonies had large virgin forests filled with timber. By the time of the American Revolution, the colonies were providing fully one-third of the ships that made up the British fleet.[5]

Development of the steamboat made river transportation much faster and more economical. Between 1825 and 1850 the states embarked on canal build-ing to take advantage of the steamboat, and certain areas along the canals became urbanized. The canals served as feeders to the rivers, creating new pas-sages for commerce. For instance, the Erie Canal connected New York City with the Great Lakes. From the Great Lakes, the Miami-Erie Canal connected to the Ohio and Mississippi Rivers. These canals thus made barge transport between New York and New Orleans possible[6] and led to the industrial devel-opment of the Great Lakes region.

Railroads began to be developed in the 1830s. The early rail routes were built to connect underserved areas with the waterways. As a result, commercial areas important to shipping maintained their importance even after shipping gave way to land transport. The railroads grew rapidly between 1870 and 1890. About half of railroad development money came from the government, and the rest came from private investors interested in developing new markets to increase profits. Railroad access ensured economic prosperity, and state and local land grants were used to entice railroad companies to particular locations. The federal government provided a grant of 131 million acres of public land with a right of way extending six miles on either side to encourage the devel-opment of the transcontinental railroad. These land grants were essential to the development of the railroads.[7]

Early road construction was financed either by state and local governments or by private investment. These private investments were paid for by tolls charged to users. Toll roads or turnpikes were constructed using a hardened surface called macadam that allowed them to carry heavy loads in all weather conditions.[8]

Prior to the availability of automobiles, trains and ships were generally used for travel between cities and for long distances. To travel within cities and towns people generally walked or took streetcars or horse-drawn taxicabs. This changed with the widespread application of the internal combustion engine to automo-biles.[9] With cars to transport them, people could live great distances from their work sites. The dispersion of population that resulted from the use of cars led to decreased reliance on fixed-line forms of public transportation. It also had enor-mous consequences for public health, safety, energy use, and pollution.

The network of roads in the United States consists of the interstate high-way system, state roads, and local roads. Urban road construction received fed-eral funding after the passage of the **Federal Highway Act of 1944.** The military played a critical role in the development of the **interstate highway system.** Interstate highways were built in response to an upsurge in automo-bile traffic. Advocates contended that the system would allow for faster and safer travel by alleviating congestion and bypassing urban areas by means of beltways. The system was built to serve as a primary network for both commerce and military transit.[10]

Urban transportation changed enormously with the advent of the automobile and the development of urban highways. The public transit systems that had been common in cities largely disappeared. Streetcars were replaced with a smaller system of buses in most cities, but in general the private automobile displaced earlier forms of urban mass transit. Large cities maintained their subways and overland rail systems, but most new urban transportation systems were dominated by the car.[11]

The air transportation industry developed as a result of federally funded research and development (R&D) as well as military use of aircraft during World War I. After the war the military sold surplus aircraft. The **Kelly Act of 1925** encouraged the growth of private airline companies by granting contracts for mail delivery to airlines that provided passenger services. The federal government did not become involved with civilian air transportation again until the passage of **Federal Airport Act of 1946,** which funded airport improvements. During World War II the federal government funded R&D to improve aircraft. These innovations were transferred to the private sector after the war and were the basis of the modern airlines that emerged at that time. In particular, the development of the jet engine revolutionized the industry by reducing flight time and increasing the number of flights available for civilian transportation.[12]

Three factors are important in understanding the evolution of air travel in the United States: airlines, airports, and government. The U.S. airline industry developed with enormous support from the government in terms of both R&D and market protection. Airline companies were private-sector corporations. They were completely regulated by the **Federal Aviation Administration (FAA)**. Routes, profits, and safety standards were all set by the government. Airports were constructed by local governments with the advice of the federal government. These three entities came together to produce a national airline system.

Regulation and Deregulation

As the transportation sector grew, the government slowly began to engage in regulation, starting with the railroads in the late 1880s. The **Interstate Commerce Commission (ICC)** was established for that purpose and set maximum rates to prevent the monopolistic railroads from charging excessive rates. The ICC also set minimum rates so that a railroad could not use below-cost pricing to drive other railroads out of business.[13]

Trucking and other forms of road transportation came under federal regulatory control in the 1930s. During the Great Depression there were drastic drops in demand for commodities, and as a result railroads and trucks competed for the small supply of available business. A demand for minimum rates and wages grew, and regulation became widespread. The **Motor Carrier Act of 1935** gave the ICC widespread regulatory power over interstate trucking, including control over entry into the market, rates, labor, and safety issues.

Airline regulation followed a similar pattern. During the Depression a group of independent airlines began to compete against the already established airlines, threatening their economic survival. The mature airlines sought protection from this competition. The result was the formation of the **Civil Aeronautics Board,** which was given regulatory power over entry into the airline business, routes, and prices.[14]

Beginning in the late 1970s transportation began to be deregulated. Air cargo was first to be deregulated, followed by trucking, passenger airlines, and busing. Deregulation resulted from the belief that regulation increased prices for transport while doing little to increase safety.[15] Deregulation permitted market forces to play leading roles in sectors of the economy in which the government had previously controlled industries.[16] During an economic downturn in the late 1970s and early 1980s, the promised increases in efficiency of a deregulated transport sector were attractive to politicians. In most cases, the industries themselves were content to stay under the protection of ICC regulation.[17] Deregulation reintroduced competition and the potential for economic failure.[18] However, regulation was seen as a cost to society, and it was generally held that benefits would accrue from opening transportation industries to competition.

Deregulation proceeded in the 1980s and 1990s. Airline deregulation, which was the most controversial and visible aspect of transportation deregulation, had mixed results. At first, a number of new "no frills" airlines, such as Valuejet and Southwest, provided low prices and served a wide range of locations. Concerns about safety arose, in large part because of a crash of one of Valuejet's flights, and insolvency resulted. Deregulation put greater pressure on all the airlines. For much of the 1990s none of the airlines was profitable.

Just as profits were returning in the early twenty-first century, Americans stopped flying in response to the September 11 terrorist attacks. All the major airlines found themselves losing money again and demanded a bailout from the federal government. That bailout came with the promise of direct subsidies to the airlines in 2001. Even with an infusion of additional funding, most of the airlines still struggle, and they need to fundamentally reform their business practices to return to profitability. By 2002 several major airlines had declared or were threatening to declare bankruptcy.

Organizations for Transportation Policy

The U.S. transportation system today is the most extensive network of highways, roads, air travel, and waterways in the industrialized world. Despite the importance of this huge system for economic prosperity and national defense, the United States lacks a centralized transportation policy and the organization to implement it.[19]

What centralized policy there is comes out of the **Department of Transportation (DOT).** The DOT was established by act of Congress in 1966 to coordinate policies to provide an efficient and economical national transportation system. Within the DOT are ten separate administrations, each of which is run by a presidential appointee. They are the Coast Guard, the Federal Aviation Administration (FAA), the Federal Highway Administration, the Federal Railroad Administration, the National Highway Traffic Safety Administration, the Federal Transit Administration, the Maritime Administration, the Saint Lawrence Seaway Development Corporation, the Research and Special Programs Administration, and the Bureau of Transportation Statistics.[20]

One form of organization commonly used in transportation policy is the **public corporation.** Public corporations (or authorities) are established by statute but operate independently of government controls, as do private corporations. Perhaps the most widely known example used in transportation is the New York and New Jersey Port Authority. There are tens of thousands of such semiautonomous entities, which are often classified as **special districts.** Many arose when government was experimenting with alternative ways to organize public utilities and other necessary services such as transportation during the 1930s. These public corporations currently exist on the federal, state, and local levels.[21]

CURRENT MODES OF TRANSPORTATION

The very large U.S. transportation system is comprised not only of the physical infrastructure but also of the vehicles and large workforce associated with it. Computers, telecommunications, and global positioning systems are increasingly being used. The system's more than 4 million miles of roads would circle the globe nearly 157 times if laid end to end. The rail lines would circle the globe another 7 times. The average American car covers a distance equivalent to nearly halfway around the globe every year.[22] Table 8.1 shows the major components of the U.S. transportation system, including the number of aircraft, vehicles, and vessels.

Most Americans travel by road in private vehicles. These are mostly cars, sport utility vehicles, light trucks, and vans. In 1999 only 9 percent of households were without cars, while 33 percent of households had one vehicle, 39 percent had two vehicles, and 19 percent had three or more vehicles.[23] There has been dramatic growth in the number of vehicles on the roads. From 1970 to 1989, for instance, the number increased by 73 percent. By 1997 there were 212 million vehicles on the roads, an increase of nearly 28 million in a ten-year period. Sport utility vehicles and light trucks made up 33 percent of the U.S. automobile fleet in 1997.[24] As Table 8.1 shows, by 2002 there were nearly 134 million passenger cars and another 79 million SUV-type vehicles on the road. The growth in the number of passenger miles traveled by each mode of carrier is shown in Figure 8.2.

Not only do Americans like to travel in private vehicles; they also like to travel alone. The average occupancy of an American automobile is 1.7 people, and the figure is even lower for people who use their cars to commute to their jobs. Eighty-five percent of commuters travel to work alone.

Table 8.1 The U.S. Transportation System, 2002

Infrastructure

Public highways	46,667 miles of interstate highways 114,511 miles of other national highway system roads 3,789,927 miles of other roads
Rail	120,022 class 1 freight miles 20,978 regional freight miles 28,937 local freight miles 22,741 passenger miles by Amtrak
Urban transit	160,506 bus miles serviced 469 trolley bus miles serviced 5,209 commuter rail miles serviced 1,558 heavy rail miles serviced 834 light rail miles serviced
Public-use airports	29 large hubs (72 airports) with 479 million enplaned passengers 31 medium hubs (53 airports) with 102 million enplaned passengers 54 small hubs (69 airports) with 40 million enplaned passengers 585 nonhubs (610 airports) with 18 million enplaned passengers
Water	26,000 miles of navigable waterways 276 locks 487 miles of ferry service

Vehicles

Aircraft	8,228 air carriers 219,464 general aviation carriers
Cars	133,621,420 passenger cars 4,346,068 motorcycles 79,084,979 other two-axle, four-tire vehicles
Trucks	5,926,030 single-unit trucks 2,096,619 combination trucks
Buses	746,125 buses
Railcars	1,894 Amtrak cars 378 Amtrak locomotives 4,883 commuter railcars and locomotives 11,603 transit cars 579,140 Class 1 freight cars 20,028 Class 1 locomotives 820,642 other freight cars
Ships and boats	447 oceangoing ships (1,000 gross tons and over) 12,782,143 recreational boats

SOURCES: United States Department of Transportation, Bureau of Transportation Statistics, *Pocket Guide to Transportation*, Washington, DC: Bureau of Transportation Statistics, February 2002.

Autos and light trucks account for the greatest number of all passenger-miles traveled. In 2000 cars, motorcycles, and light trucks traveled more than 4 trillion passenger-miles. Air transportation is the second most popular means of long-distance travel in the United States. In 2000 commercial air carriers flew more than 515 billion passenger-miles.[25]

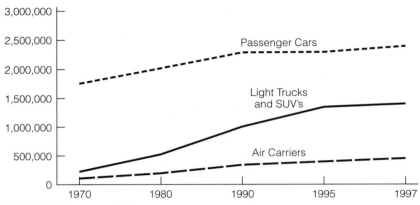

FIGURE 8.2 Passenger-Miles

SOURCE: United States Department of Transportation.

Only a modest number of the more than eight hundred airports in the United States account for the vast majority of air passengers. In 2002, for instance, seventy-two airports accounted for 479 million enplaned passengers.[26] Commercial passenger service, the flight service for general public use, is concentrated in a relatively few airports, and many airports may be used only by private planes or cargo planes.

Airlines operate **hub-and-spoke** systems in which passengers are collected by flights from many spoke cities and are flown to a hub airport. This hub airport is typically located at a centralized point in the airline's route system. Passengers arrive at the hub in a wave of flights at approximately the same time, then transfer to other airplanes that are going to their final destinations. All flights in the wave leave the hub to go to their spoke cities. This pattern is repeated multiple times a day to provide service at convenient frequencies.[27]

A large volume of freight is handled by the transportation system. The vast majority is shipped by truck. Rail and water carry about the same tonnage, but the value of freight shipped by rail is greater. Parcel post and courier services handle more valuable freight, as do the airlines.

Europe has a well-developed passenger rail system; the United States does not. The decline in passenger rail transportation in the United States began in the 1920s, at the same time as the growth in the use of automobiles. Year after year the number of passenger trains, the number of rail miles served, and passenger volume declined. By the 1960s the passenger rail corporations were reporting losses. A number of them, especially those in the Northeast, were facing bankruptcy because their passenger rail service was unprofitable. It seemed likely that America would have no passenger rail service at all after the 1960s.[28]

The possible disappearance of passenger trains concerned many people. Some worried about the environmental effects of relying only on cars. Others were troubled about increasing automobile congestion. Access to transportation by people who did not or could not afford to own cars was an equity issue. An effort was made to preserve passenger rail transport, and the semi-public corporation that came to be called **Amtrak** was created.[29]

Amtrak began with aging equipment gathered from the failing private passenger service lines. Track conditions were not conducive to fast trains. Providing high-quality service was difficult. Amtrak has struggled to improve service and attract customers, and its financial situation has remained fragile. Never producing a profit, it came to be seen as a failed enterprise. There were efforts to privatize it during the deregulation era of the 1970s and 1980s. Congress is still trying to decide what to do with the venture.

INFRASTRUCTURE FUNDING

The **Highway Trust Fund** was established in 1956 to ensure a dependable source of funds for highway programs. Federal transportation funding is heavily supplemented by the federal gasoline tax. Highway-based excise taxes are paid by highway users. These taxes differ in terms of type of user fee (tire, retail sale, vehicle-use tax) and type of fuel (gas, gasohol, diesel). The taxes are then distributed back to the states for the support of highway infrastructure, safety, and transit systems.

The process of collecting these taxes and redistributing them to the states is complex and a source of considerable contention.[30] The states collect some of the taxes when highway users purchase taxable items. The U.S. Treasury, however, collects most of them directly from large oil corporations and large distributors. Because these companies are unable to measure fuel use within each state, the Internal Revenue Service (IRS) is unable to correlate tax receipts with the location of the fuel use, and the states are required to report their fuel consumption to the federal government. The federal government uses the state-reported data and statistical models to determine the proportion of each state's motor fuel usage in comparison to the total for all fifty states. Distribution of the money in the Highway Trust Fund back to the states is determined by a formula set by legislation.[31]

State transportation expenditures are primarily funded through earmarked funds that are placed in a state transportation trust fund. The major source of revenue is the state gasoline tax, sometimes supplemented with general sales taxes. State gasoline taxes vary. In 2001 rates ranged from 7.5 percent in Georgia to 27 percent in Montana.[32]

With passage of the **Transportation Equity Act for the 21st Century (TEA-21)** in 1998, Congress greatly increased federal support for transit and highways. TEA-21 authorized $215 billion for highway, transit, research, and motor carrier programs between 1998 and 2003. This includes $175 billion for highway programs, $2.2 billion for highway safety, and $650 million for motor carrier safety grants. TEA-21 was a reform of the former Intermodal Surface Transportation and Efficiency Act of 1991 (ISTEA). Prior to TEA-21 transportation dollars were appropriated annually as part of the federal discretionary budget, and transportation highway taxes redistributed to the states were determined in an ad hoc manner. Some states collected more federal gas taxes than they received in federal transportation funding, while others received far more in federal funding than they helped collect in federal gas taxes. TEA-21 tried to address some of these inequities so that states would receive minimum level of funds directly tied to their collection of federal gas taxes.[33]

The **Transportation Infrastructure Finance and Innovation Act of 1998 (TIFIA)** was enacted the same year as TEA-21. TIFIA awards federal credit assistance in the form of secured loans, loan guarantees, and lines of credit to public and private sponsors of major transportation projects. State departments of transportation, private companies, local governments, and special districts are eligible for these funds. In 2000 TIFIA provided money for the Staten Island Ferries and Terminals in New York City, the Cooper River Bridge in Charleston, South Carolina, and the Tacoma Narrows Bridge in Washington. In 2001 a Texas turnpike project and a Reno, Nevada, rail corridor project were funded.[34]

In 2000 President Clinton signed the **Wendell H. Ford Aviation Investment and Reform Act for the 21st Century (AIR-21)** into law. This law increased money flowing to airport improvement projects by $10 billion, to a level of $40 billion, from 2001 to 2003. It authorized airports to charge passengers a tax for improvements, including noise mitigation, security, safety, and terminal maintenance and construction.[35] The need to improve the infrastructure for the airlines was in part a result of the 50 percent increase in the number of enplaned passengers between 1991 and 2000.[36]

A controversial issue in the use of transportation funds is the application of **crossover sanctions** to force state and local compliance with federal requirements. In particular, the federal government can withhold funds meant for one program because of failure to comply with another program. This power was first used in 1958 when the federal government wanted to force states to remove billboards from major highways. The federal government began by offering additional highway funds to states willing to regulate billboards in accord with federal desires. When the Johnson administration undertook the passage of the Highway Beautification Act of 1965, only half the states had taken advantage of the bonus, and Congress replaced it with the threat of withholding 10 percent of highway construction funds of states that did not comply with federal billboard requirements. Despite the lobbying and opposition of the billboard industry, all the states eventually passed billboard control restrictions.[37]

Crossover sanctions were effective in a variety of instances. For example, the Emergency Highway Energy Conservation Act of 1974, passed to deal with soaring gas prices and short supplies resulting from the OPEC oil embargo of 1973, prohibited the secretary of transportation from approving any highway construction projects in states with speed limits over fifty-five miles per hour. All states lowered their speed limits within two months of the passage of the act.[38] Similarly, the Clean Air Act of 1970 prohibits the Environmental Protection Agency (EPA) and the Department of Transportation from providing federal grants to any locality or region that has not attained mandated air quality standards and that does not have an adequate transportation control plan.[39] Given the importance of federal highway money to the states, this law gives the EPA a very large stick with which to enforce compliance.

CURRENT ISSUES

The use of transportation presents some serious issues for the government and the public. Transportation safety is one of them. While road accidents have long been a concern, securing the airlines in the aftermath of the terrorist attacks of September 11, 2001, has become urgent. Increasing use of different modes of transportation—motor vehicles and airplanes in particular—has resulted in congestion. Increased use of transportation has also resulted in increased pollution and negative impacts on the environment.

Safety

We pay a high price for mobility. Transportation-related deaths account for roughly half of accidental deaths in the United States. The automobile is by far the most dangerous mode of transportation. About 95 percent of all transportation fatalities occur on the roads. As Table 8.2 shows, nearly 42,000 people were killed in traffic accidents on the nation's highways in 2000. This number is fairly constant from year to year. Travel also results in a number of injuries. Injuries are often not considered carefully enough when estimating the costs of transportation. They can result in temporary or permanent incapacity and inability to work.

Water, rail, and air travel are far safer than automobile travel, although deaths and injuries occur there also. In 2000 small personal planes (general aviation) accounted for 592 deaths, recreational boating claimed 701 lives, large commercial airline accidents resulted in 92 deaths, and 512 railroad passengers were killed.

Airline safety has been a major issue since the September 11, 2001, terrorist attacks. Having gone more than a decade with no airline hijackings, the airline industry and passengers alike were shocked when terrorists commandeered four commercial jetliners to use as weapons. Previous hijackers had merely wanted to divert planes to other locations, and crews were required to comply passively with hijackers' requests. The events of September 11 forced the rethinking of safety procedures at airports and on airplanes.

On November 19, 2001, Congress passed the **Aviation and Transportation Security Act,** which took responsibility for airline safety out of the hands of the airline industry and gave the job to the federal government. The act created the Transportation Security Administration within the Department of Transportation (later moved to the Department of Homeland Security) and gave it responsibility for ongoing federal security screening operations for passenger air transportation and all intrastate air cargo transportation.

Table 8.2 Injuries and Fatalities by Transportation Mode, 2000

Mode	Injuries	Fatalities
Large Air Carrier	26	92
General Aviation	329	592
Highway	3,189,000	41,821
Railroad	10,424	512
Recreational Boating	4,355	701

SOURCE: United States Department of Transportation, Bureau of Transportation Statistics, *Pocket Guide to Transportation,* Washington, DC: Bureau of Transportation Statistics, February 2002.

The Transportation Security Administration was instructed to develop standards for the hiring and retention of security screening personnel, to train and test them, and to hire them at all airports in the United States. It was given authority to

receive, assess, and distribute intelligence information related to transportation security; assess threats to transportation; develop policies, strategies, and plans for dealing with threats to transportation security; make other plans related to transportation security, including coordinating counter-measures with appropriate departments, agencies, and instrumentalities of the United States Government; serve as the primary liaison for transportation security to the intelligence and law enforcement communities.

The act required the Transportation Security Administration to

inspect, maintain, and test security facilities, equipment, and systems; ensure the adequacy of security measures for the transportation of cargo; oversee the implementation, and ensure the adequacy, of security measures at airports and other transportation facilities; require background checks for airport security screening personnel, individuals with access to secure areas of airports, and other transportation security personnel; work in conjunction with the Administrator of the Federal Aviation Administration with respect to any actions or activities that may affect aviation safety or air carrier operations; and to work with the International Civil Aviation Organization and appropriate aeronautic authorities of foreign governments . . . to address security concerns on passenger flights by foreign air carriers in foreign air transportation.

During times of national emergency, the Transportation Security Administration is responsible for coordinating all domestic transportation (aviation, rail, automobile, and maritime) and overseeing the transportation–related responsibilities of other departments and agencies of the federal government (excluding the Department of Defense and the military departments). In addition, the Transportation Security Administration has the authority to coordinate and provide notice to other departments and agencies of federal, state, and local governments (including departments and agencies for transportation, law enforcement, and border control) about threats to transportation.

The first new safety measures to be put into place included baggage matching, limitations on the number of carry-on bags, increased training for airline security personnel, strict control of secure areas in airports, and cockpit door fortifications.[40] Bag matching, a procedure that involves matching all bags aboard a plane with the passengers flying on the plane, presumably eliminates the possibility of a terrorist's purchasing a ticket, checking a bag containing explosives, and not boarding the plane. The assumption, of course, is that the terrorist would want to live. As the events of September 11 showed, this is not always a valid assumption. On that day the terrorist hijackers of the four planes chose to sacrifice their lives as part of their terrorist attack.

Increased training of airline security personnel was instituted directly after the events of September 11. The airlines had been using extremely low-paid workers to provide security screening and had inadequately supervised and trained them. It was believed that well-trained, better-paid federal workers would do a better job of ensuring passenger safety. Secure areas in the airports were more closely watched and controlled, and several states activated the National Guard to secure airports. Cockpit doors have been strengthened to ensure that intruders will not gain entrance., and several airlines are equipping cockpit crews with stun guns in case an intruder does manage to break through to the cockpit. By September 2002 both the House and Senate had passed resolutions calling for arming airline pilots.

Long-term security for airlines will require the eventual installation of scanning machines that will be able to detect explosives, guns, chemical agents, and nuclear weapons. These machines are expensive, and their installation in existing airports may necessitate physical reorganization or expansion of facilities.

A controversial issue in the implementation of new security measures has been the use of **profiling,** in which persons of Middle Eastern origin or ancestry are more carefully screened than are other individuals. The controversy over the use of profiling to assist in airline security is rooted in the potential for humiliation, violations of personal privacy, and discrimination. The issue received a great deal of scrutiny when a member of President Bush's Secret Service, who was of Middle Eastern ancestry, was denied passage on a commercial flight.

Congestion

Congestion on the streets, highways, and airports is bad and is getting worse. Congestion wastes time and energy, creates extra pollution, harms human health, and damages the economy.[41] In most urban areas, congestion has increased rapidly in the past several years, and gridlock is becoming all too common.

Part of the reason for road congestion is that jobs are not located near where people live. Long drives from homes to employment centers in the morning and back to homes at night result in considerable traffic. Long commutes in heavy traffic can strain tempers, as the incidence of events of "road rage" show.

Between 1991 and 2000 a 50 percent increase in the number of airline passengers helped cause airline congestion and strained the airport and airline infrastructure.[42] A decline in the number of airline passengers resulting from the terrorist attacks reduced congestion to an extent (but created severe economic problems for the airlines). If more people resume flying, airline and airport congestion will again become a significant issue.

Transportation planners have suggested adopting policies such as **congestion pricing** to charge motorists for the overcrowding they cause. People who wish to use the roads during peak times would have to pay higher road fees than those who stay off the roads at those times. Such schemes have not been widely adopted. Public policy generally addresses congestion by expanding infrastructure capacity—that is, by building more roads, running more buses, and installing more railroad track.[43] Electronic toll collection systems as well as electronic fare collection systems have been adopted to increase the efficiency of traffic management and improve transportation flows.[44]

Energy Consumption and the Environment

Transportation consumes about 63 percent of the energy used in America.[45] For transportation, the primary fuel is petroleum, which has been abundant and cheap since the 1980s. As a consequence of the availability of and the relatively low taxes on gasoline, Americans consume more petroleum than the nation produces, contributing heavily to U.S. dependence on foreign oil.

The energy used for transportation is one of the leading causes of air pollution. Vehicles emit carbon monoxide, volatile organic compounds, nitrogen oxides, and airborne particulates. Auto emissions are a cause of high ozone levels (smog) in most major American cities. Figure 8.3 compares the carbon dioxide emissions from the transportation sector with emissions from other sectors from 1980 to 1998.

Transportation causes other kinds of pollution as well. For instance, transporting oil to refineries, where it is processed into gasoline, results in frequent oil spills. Much oil is transported over the oceans, and spills can be devastating to coastlines as well as to marine animal populations. Underground storage tanks at gas stations can leak gasoline into the groundwater. Motor oil is frequently not disposed of properly, resulting in serious environmental damage. Highway runoff comprised of oil, fuel, and other chemicals washes into the groundwater and surface water. Used vehicles and their tires are a considerable source of solid waste.[46]

The United States has tried several policies to reduce fuel consumption and its associated pollution. For a brief time following the OPEC oil embargo of 1973, the states enforced a speed limit of fifty-five miles per hour to reduce gasoline consumption, since cars burn far less fuel at that speed than at higher speeds.

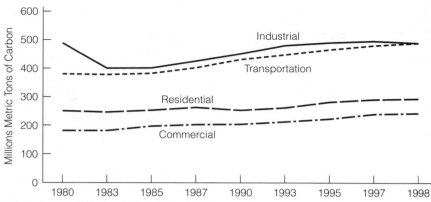

FIGURE 8.3 Carbon Dioxide Emissions from Energy Consumption, 1980–1998

SOURCE: United States Department of Energy, Emissions of Greenhouse Gasses in the United States, 1998.

The law was quite unpopular, especially in western states where the distances are vast, and among the truckers who transport most freight in the United States. The limits were eliminated after the election of Ronald Reagan in 1980.

Another policy put in place during the energy crisis of the 1970s was corporate average fuel efficiency (CAFE) standards requiring automobile manufacturers to design and manufacture cars that achieved greater fuel efficiency. When the deregulation movement took strong hold in the 1980s, there was a glut of oil on the markets and prices were falling, so there was less interest in improving fuel efficiency. CAFE standards did not increase over the years, and the popularity of gas-guzzling sport utility vehicles has further exacerbated the problem.

SUMMARY

Transportation policy includes the development, maintenance, and use of all publicly provided transportation systems and infrastructure. These modes of transportation include railways, roads, bridges, tunnels, inland and coastal waterways, and air transportation. Transportation is one of the largest areas of public policy. In 2001 the federal government spent $55.2 billion on transportation and the states spent $91.1 billion, making it the third highest funded area of state policy. Transportation expenses consume about 19 percent of the average household's income.

The U.S. transportation system evolved primarily to serve commerce. During colonial times water was most commonly used for the transportation of goods. Ships played an essential role in the development of commerce in the country. Development of the steamboat made river transportation much faster and more economical, and the states embarked on canal building efforts to take advantage of steamboats.

Railroad development began in the 1830s. The early rail routes were built to connect underserved areas to the waterways. The railroads grew rapidly between 1870 and 1890.

Early road construction was financed by state and local governments and by private investment. Private investments were paid for by tolls charged to users. With cars to transport them and good roads to drive on, the population spread outside of the cities, with consequences for public health, safety, energy use, and pollution.

The air transportation industry developed as a result of federally funded research and development (R&D) as well as military uses of aircraft. These innovations were transferred to private-sector industry and provided the basis for the modern airlines. In particular, the development of the jet engine revolutionized the industry by reducing flight time and increasing the number of flights available for civilian transportation.

As the U.S. transportation sector grew, the government slowly began to engage in regulation. Interstate Commerce Commission regulation began with the railroads in the late 1880s. Trucking and other forms of road transportation came under federal regulatory control in the 1930s. Airline regulation under the Civil Aeronautics Board followed a similar pattern. Beginning in the late 1970s transportation began to be deregulated, permitting market forces to take over from government intervention and control.

The U.S. transportation system is the most extensive network of highways, roads, air travel, and waterways in the industrialized world. National policy is the responsibility of the Department of Transportation (DOT), which includes the Coast Guard, the Federal Aviation Administration (FAA), the Federal Highway Administration, the Federal Railroad Administration, the National Highway Traffic Safety Administration, the Federal Transit Administration, the Maritime Administration, the Saint Lawrence Seaway Development Corporation, the Research and Special Programs Administration, and the Bureau of Transportation Statistics. Public corporations (or authorities), which are common in transportation policy, are established by statute and operate independently of government controls.

The U.S. transportation system is very large. It is comprised of not only a physical infrastructure but also of vehicles and a large workforce. Most Americans travel in private vehicles, mostly cars, sport utility vehicles, other light trucks, and vans. Air transportation is the second most popular means of long-distance travel. A large volume of freight is handled by the transportation system. Most is shipped by truck. Rail and water carry about the same tonnage, but the value of freight shipped by rail is greater. Parcel post and courier services handle more valuable freight, as do the airlines.

Safety is a critical issue for transportation policy. Transportation-related deaths account for roughly half the accidental deaths in the United States, mostly on the roads. Water, rail, and air travel are far safer. The events of September 11 caused serious reconsideration of air travel. Reforms of airline security have contributed to a new environment for air travel.

Congestion of the streets, highways, and airports wastes time and energy, creates extra pollution, harms human health, and damages the economy. Transportation consumes about 63 percent of the energy used in America. The energy used for transportation is one of the leading causes of air pollution. Auto emissions are a cause of high ozone levels in most major American cities.

KEY TERMS

Amtrak

Aviation and Transportation Security Act (2001)

Civil Aeronautics Board

congestion pricing

crossover sanctions

Department of Transportation (DOT)

Federal Airport Act of 1946

Federal Aviation Administration (FAA)

Federal Highway Act of 1944

Highway Trust Fund

hub-and-spoke

Interstate Commerce Commission (ICC)

interstate highway system

Kelly Act of 1925

Motor Carrier Act of 1935

profiling

public corporations

special districts

Transportation Equity Act for the 21st Century (TEA-21)

Transportation Infrastructure Finance and Innovation Act of 1998 (TIFIA)

Wendell H. Ford Aviation Investment and Reform Act for the 21st Century (AIR-21)

WEB SITES

http://www.dot.gov/
The home page of the Department of Transportation has information about DOT's budget, airlines, flight delays, and airport congestion, along with interesting news stories about current issues. The site provides access to transportation safety organizations and programs, including the DOT Safety Council, which coordinates DOT safety policy; the National Response Center, which is the federal point of contact for reporting oil and chemical spills; the Transportation Safety Institute, which is responsible for assessing enforcement and compliance with DOT safety standards; the Office of Drug and Alcohol Policy and Compliance, which provides advice to industry representatives on implementation of controlled substance and alcohol testing rules; and the Hazardous Materials Safety Office, which is responsible for

coordinating a national safety program for the transportation of hazardous materials. It also contains links to specific programs for air, land, and water travel.

http://www.bts.gov/
The site of the Bureau of Transportation Statistics provides excellent access to information and databases for research. The National Transportation Library, which is accessible from this site, is a repository of materials about transportation from public and private organizations around the country. TRIS Online (http://ntl.bts.gov/tris/) is a comprehensive source of information on published transportation research. The site also provides access to the *Journal of Transportation and Statistics*.

http://www.faa.gov/
The home page of the Federal Aviation Administration provides information on aviation rules and regulations, travel, safety and security, and jobs in aviation.

http://www.piperinfo.com/state/index.cfm
This URL will take you to an indexed listing of all the states. Click on a state, then go to its Department of Transportation.

DISCUSSION QUESTIONS

1. What were the incentives for the government to begin regulating the transportation sector, and why was the sector eventually deregulated?
2. What is the government's policy on traffic congestion? Do you feel that it will reduce or increase congestion?
3. What are crossover sanctions, and how are they used? If you were a state official, how would you feel about the use of these sanctions?
4. Do you think the government should support Amtrak?

WEB QUESTIONS

1. Identify the administrations within the Department of Transportation (www.dot.gov/chart.html).
2. The Bureau of Transportation Statistics (BTS) was established in 1991 by the Intermodal Surface Transportation Efficiency Act (ISTEA). What are the responsibilities of BTS (www.bts.gov/aboutbts.html)? Briefly discuss the findings of an article in the *Journal of Transportation Statistics* (www.bts.gov/jts/).
3. Explain a recent rule that has been established by the Federal Aviation Administration (www.faa.gov/avr/nprm.htm).

NOTES

1. National Association of State Budget Officers, *State Expenditure Report 2000* (Washington, DC: National Association of State Budget Officers, 2001).

2. United States Department of Transportation, Bureau of Transportation Statistics, *Pocket Guide to Transportation* (Washington, DC: Bureau of Transportation Statistics, 2002).

3. Tsuneo Akaha, "Introduction," in *International Handbook of Transportation Policy,* ed. Tsuneo Akaha (Westport, CT: Greenwood Press, 1990), 1–15.

4. Frank McKenna and David Anderson, "United States," in *International Handbook of Transportation Policy,* ed. Tsuneo Akaha (Westport, CT: Greenwood Press, 1990), 269–296.

5. H. David Bess and Martin T. Farris, *U.S. Maritime Policy: History and Prospects* (New York: Praeger, 1981).

6. McKenna and Anderson, "United States."

7. Ibid.

8. Ibid.

9. David J. St. Clair, *The Motorization of American Cities* (New York: Praeger, 1986).

10. Deborah Gordon, *Steering a New Course: Transportation, Energy, and the Environment* (Washington, DC: Island Press, 1999).

11. St. Clair, *The Motorization of American Cities.*

12. McKenna and Anderson, "United States."

13. Paul Teske, Samuel Best, and Michael Mintrom, *Deregulating Freight Transportation: Delivering the Goods* (Washington, DC: The AEI Press, 1995).

14. Dorothy Robyn, *Braking the Special Interests: Trucking Deregulation and the Politics of Policy Reform* (Chicago: University of Chicago Press, 1987).

15. Lucile Sheppard Keyes, *Regulatory Reform in Air Cargo Transportation* (Washington, DC: American Enterprise Institute, 1980).

16. Kenneth Burton, "Regulatory Reform," in *Transport Deregulation: An International Movement,* ed. Kenneth Burton and David Pitfield (New York: St. Martin's Press, 1991).

17. American Trucking Association, *The Case Against Deregulation* (Washington, DC: American Trucking Associations, 1972).

18. John Richard Felton and Dale G. Anderson, *Regulation and Deregulation of the Motor Carrier Industry* (Ames, IA: Iowa State University Press, 1989).

19. McKenna and Anderson, "United States."

20. R. Dale Grinder, "Department of Transportation," in *A Historical Guide to the U.S. Government,* ed. George T. Kurian (New York: Oxford University Press, 1998), 573–579.

21. Robert G. Smith, *Ad Hoc Governments: Special Purpose Transportation Authorities in Britain and the United States* (Beverly Hills, CA: Sage Publications, 1974).

22. Bureau of Transportation Statistics, *Transportation in the United States* (Washington, DC: U.S. Department of Transportation, 1997).

23. U.S. Department of Transportation, Bureau of Transportation Statistics, *Pocket Guide to Transportation.*

24. Bureau of Transportation Statistics, *Transportation Statistics Annual Report, 1999* (Washington, DC: U.S. Department of Transportation, 1999).

25. U.S. Department of Transportation, Bureau of Transportation Statistics, *Pocket Guide to Transportation.*

26. Ibid.

27. Michael S. Nolan, "Airport," Microsoft Encarta Online Encyclopedia 2001. http://encarta.msn.com (4/13/01).

28. David C. Nice, "Amtrak," in *A Historical Guide to the U.S. Government,* ed. George T. Kurian (New York: Oxford University Press, 1998).

29. Ibid.

30. U.S. Department of Transportation, Federal Highway Administration, *Attribution and Apportionment of Federal Highway Tax Revenues: Process Refinements* (Washington, DC: Federal Highway Administration, 2002).

31. Ibid.

32. National Association of State Budget Officers, *State Expenditure Report 2000.*

33. Ibid.

34. Ibid.

35. Ibid.

36. Transportation Research Board, National Research Council, *Aviation Gridlock* (Washington, DC: Transportation Research Board, 2001).

37. U.S. Advisory Commission on Intergovernmental Relations, "The Techniques of Intergovernmental Regulation," in *American Intergovernmental Relations,* ed. Laurence J. O'Toole, Jr. (Washington, DC: CQ Press, 2000), 278–284.

38. Ibid.

39. Ibid.

40. American Civil Liberties Union, *Safe and Free in Times of Crisis.* http://www.aclu.org/safeand free/index.html (03/04/2002).

41. Gordon, *Steering a New Course.*

42. Transportation Research Board, National Research Council, *Aviation Gridlock.*

43. Clifford Winston, "Government Failure in Urban Transportation," *Fiscal Studies* 21 (4): 403–425.

44. Paul F. Rothberg, Frederick W. Ducca, and Brad A. Trullinger, "Intelligent Transportation Systems Program: Importance, Status, and Options for Reauthorization," Congressional Research Service Report to Congress, 1997.

45. Gordon, *Steering a New Course.*

46. Bureau of Transportation Statistics, *Transportation in the United States.*

9

Environmental Policy

One of the largest areas of national expense is environmental and natural resources policy. This expense is incurred both through direct government expenditure and through government regulation that requires companies to comply with pollution abatement standards. Just how much the country spends on environmental policies is a matter of debate.

As shown in Figure 9.1, direct federal government spending in 2001 for environmental, natural resources, and energy policy amounted to slightly more than $26 billion, or less than 1.4 percent of all federal spending. Direct state spending in 2001 was estimated at about $25 billion, or approximately 2.5 percent of total state budgetary expenditure. These numbers show only a small percentage of overall national spending on the environment. Most environmental policy is regulatory—that is, the government requires the private sector to comply with federal and state regulations and to pay the price for that compliance. Regulation is expensive. In 1999 the Office of Management and Budget (OMB) reported that the annual costs of all social regulation amounted to somewhere in the range of $146 billion to $229 billion. These costs were primarily associated with regulating the environment, transportation, and labor. Environmental regulation was the most costly, amounting to between an estimated $96 billion and $170 billion.[1] Other estimates of private-sector costs of regulation are higher. Thomas Hopkins of the Rochester Institute of Technology estimates that regulatory costs associated with environmental and risk reduction totaled $267 billion in 2000, nearly twice as much as OMB estimated.[2] No matter which estimate is used, it is clear that we spend a

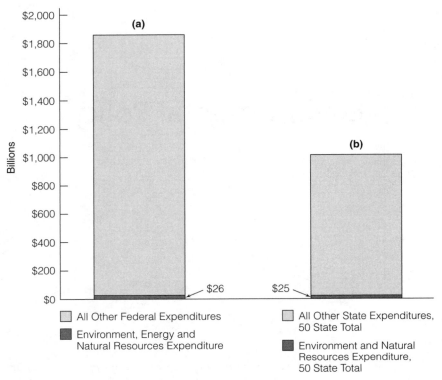

FIGURE 9.1 (a) Federal Expenditure for Environment, Natural Resources and Energy, FY 2001. **(b)** 50 State Expenditure for Environment and Natural Resources, FY 2001.

SOURCES: (a) Executive Office of the President, The Budget of the United States Government, Historical Tables, FY 2003. (b) National Association of State Budget Officers, State Environmental Expenditures and Innovations; May 2000, National Association of State Budget Officers, State Expenditure Report 2000, 2001; Author's Calculations.

considerable amount of money on environmental policy. It is also clear from Figure 9.2 that while other regulatory costs (price and entry controls) have been declining over time, environmental regulatory costs are increasing substantially.

EVOLUTION OF ENVIRONMENTAL POLICY

What we refer to as environmental policy is really a mix of three distinct but overlapping policy areas. Natural resources policy typically centers on land use. The main issues in natural resources policy concern the protection or use of the land for development and other purposes. Energy policy is important because a great deal of the pollution that affects our world is a direct result of

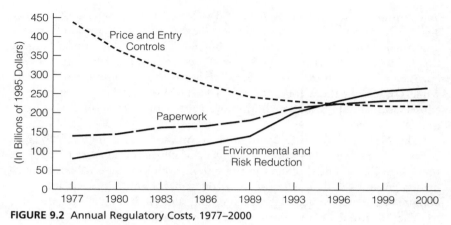

FIGURE 9.2 Annual Regulatory Costs, 1977–2000

SOURCE: Thomas D. Hopkins, Center for the Study of American Business.

fossil fuel use. Finally, environmental policy focuses on clean air, clean water, and disposal of solid and hazardous waste. Environmental policy also includes international issues, including treaties for global climate protection and the maintenance of biodiversity.

Natural Resources Policy

Natural resources policy is older than environmental policy, dating to the very beginnings of the nation. One of America's primary resources was land, and when the nation was formed, colonies with claims to western lands were required to release those lands to the federal government. As a result, the federal government became the holder of vast acres of lands. When the Jefferson administration purchased the Louisiana Territory in 1803, the size of the country doubled. As settlers moved west, more and more land was added to the national domain.

Congress used much of this land to lure development to the west. The **Homestead Act of 1862,** which gave 160 acres of public land to anyone willing to farm it, eventually converted 250 million acres of public lands to private farms. The federal government encouraged the development of railroads by giving land to railroad corporations in exchange for miles of track laid. The federal government also provided incentives for westward expansion and development by providing mineral and grazing rights on public lands. The **Mining Law of 1872,** for instance, gave miners free access to mineral deposits on public lands. In like fashion, ranchers were allowed to graze their herds on public lands.[3]

By the time of the Civil War, a movement had begun to preserve some wilderness lands for future generations. This movement was spearheaded by John Muir, founder of the Sierra Club, who was able to secure the protection of Yosemite Valley from economic development in 1864. Congress set aside

Yellowstone National Park in 1872 and followed with other national parks. This early preservationist movement was countered by the conservationist movement championed by Gifford Pinchot, who became head of what is today the U.S. Forest Service in Theodore Roosevelt's administration. Pinchot encouraged the managed use of forest resources for economic development while conserving them for sustained yield. Despite the differences between conservation and preservation, both movements achieved considerable success in the early 1900s.

The **National Wildlife Refuge System** was created in 1903. Today it contains 91 million acres, about 85 percent of which are in Alaska. There are more than five hundred refuges in the system, which provide habitat for animals, as well 18 million acres of forest on which limited logging and other commercial activities such as grazing, mining, and oil drilling are permitted.

The **National Forest System,** which was created in 1905, includes 187 million acres of land in 156 units, mostly in Alaska, the far West, and the Southeast. Fifty national forests located in eastern states are chiefly managed by the National Forest Service.

The **National Park System** was established in 1916.[4] Today it covers more than 80 million acres and contains more than 360 parks. Fifty of them are national parks. The National Park System also contains 300 national monuments, battlefields, memorials, historic sites, and recreational areas.[5]

The second great wave of natural resources policy came in the 1930s. During President Franklin Roosevelt's twelve years in office, much was done to promote flood control and soil conservation in response to the drought that resulted in the Dust Bowl. The Civilian Conservation Corps and the Soil Conservation Service were established to help repair environmental damage. Controls on overgrazing were instituted through the **Taylor Grazing Act of 1934.** Congress created the **Bureau of Land Management** within the Department of Interior in 1946 and ended the practice of selling or giving away public lands.[6]

Attention once again turned to conservation and preservation in the 1960s. The **National Wilderness Preservation System** was created in 1964. It contains millions of acres without any roads, permanent improvements, or sustained human habitation. In 1968 Congress created the **National Wild and Scenic River System,** which today protects 10,500 miles of free-flowing rivers and shorelines from development. In the early 1970s additional land was given protected status in **National Marine Sanctuaries** and **National Estuarine Research Reserves,** which contain thirteen marine units of 9,000 square nautical miles. These were ordered to be protected by the National Oceanic and Atmospheric Administration (NOAA) under the **Coastal Zone Management Act of 1972.**

Membership in older established conservation societies grew rapidly in the 1960s, and new environmental groups were established. Differences among these interest groups emerged. The mainstream groups, including the Sierra Club and the National Wildlife Federation, devoted their efforts to national public policy. The "Greens," including Greenpeace and Earth First! focused mainly on local issues; emphasized public education, direct action, and social change; and worked to mobilize the grassroots. Policy analysis and research-based interest groups such as Resources for the Future, Union of Concerned Scientists, the Worldwatch Institute, and the World Resources Institute gained popularity. Private land conservation groups like the Nature Conservancy also emerged.

Energy Policy

We need energy to light, heat, and cool our homes and workplaces, to run our machines, and to fuel our cars, planes, and trains. Without energy, everything stops. Products cannot be manufactured; computers cannot run; and transport ceases. An advanced industrial economy such as ours is totally dependent on an uninterrupted supply of affordable energy.

Unfortunately, energy use results in pollution. Fossil fuel use is the number-one cause of air pollution. The emissions from automobiles and from power plants that burn fossil fuel put millions of tons of sulfur dioxide and nitrogen dioxide into the air. These chemicals combine with water to form acid precipitation. Power plants and autos emit particulates (small solid particles) that are known to cause cancer. Fossil fuel use also results in the production of carbon dioxide, the main cause of global climate change.

To avoid the potential consequences of global climate change (for example, rising sea levels, habitat destruction, species extinction, and increasing number and strength of disastrous storms), carbon dioxide emissions—and thus fossil fuel use—must be reduced. However, global demand for energy has tripled in the past fifty years and is likely to triple again in the next thirty. In the past the increasing demand for energy came from industrialized countries; in the future it is likely to come from developing nations.[7] Finding substitutes for fossil fuels while still providing energy for growth and development is one of the largest challenges confronting society today.

Nuclear power also presents environmental challenges. Accidents at nuclear power plants (such as the meltdown at Pennsylvania's Three Mile Island and the far more catastrophic massive radioactive release at Chernobyl in Soviet Ukraine) have drawn attention to the dangers of nuclear power. Another major problem is the failure of a fully developed system to deal with nuclear waste, an unfortunate but significant by-product of nuclear power.

The United States has abundant domestic coal and natural gas, but imports the majority of oil that is used, largely from the Arab nations of the Middle East. Keeping the oil flowing is a national security issue. In 1991 the Gulf War was in large part fought to keep friendly oil-rich nations from succumbing to regional powers unfriendly to the West. Our energy dependency also has a massive impact on our economy due to the ability of the Organization of Petroleum Exporting Countries (OPEC) to control supply and prices. OPEC's withholding of oil, which increased prices in 1973 and in 1979, created "oil shocks" that profoundly affected our economy.[8]

Before the energy crisis of 1973, the federal government acted more as a broker among diversified interests than as a master planner. With the exception of supporting the development of nuclear energy, long-range energy planning was largely left to the private sector, and government energy policy was little more than reliance on the private sector to provide cheap and abundant energy, primarily from fossil fuels supplemented with government-subsidized nuclear power. When the government did intervene, it was only to stabilize prices and encourage consumption. There was little concern with conservation, energy efficiency, or international dependency.[9]

As a result of the 1973 Yom Kippur War with Israel, the Arab states implemented a 5 percent reduction in exports to nations that supported Israel, resulting in a rapid increase in cost of oil. The United States responded by shifting to non–Persian Gulf sources for imported oil, legislating a fifty-five-mile-per-hour speed limit to save gas, and building the Alaskan oil pipeline. We also reacted by restructuring the government. The **Energy Reorganization Act of 1974** replaced the Atomic Energy Commission (AEC) with the **Nuclear Regulatory Commission (NRC)** and the Energy Research and Development Agency (ERDA). NRC was given the responsibility of licensing and regulating private nuclear facilities, and ERDA was responsible for centralizing federal research programs and running AEC's national labs and nuclear weapon production facilities.[10]

Further efforts to reorganize the nation's energy agencies came during the Carter administration. In 1977 President Jimmy Carter established the **Department of Energy (DOE)** as a cabinet-level department. The centerpiece of Carter's national energy policy, DOE was created from ERDA and several other agencies and was responsible for coordinating national energy policy and managing federal energy programs, including production, distribution, research, regulation, pricing, and conservation. The Carter administration also deregulated natural gas to encourage production, provided incentives to convert from oil to coal, instituted research into clean coal technologies, established tax credits to encourage use of renewables (sources of energy such as solar power and wind power), imposed a gas-guzzler tax on large cars, and introduced **corporate average fuel efficiency (CAFE)** standards to promote automobile energy efficiency.

In 1980 the incoming Reagan administration rejected the idea that fossil fuels could not be relied upon. Instead of continuing Carter's reliance on conservation and government programs to strategically manage energy policy, there was a return to full reliance on the private sector to deliver cheap energy. The Reagan administration sought to boost supply by opening federal lands to gas and oil exploration and by the further development of nuclear power. Renewable energy technologies were not given much government support. These policies have continued without major modification to today. The administration of George W. Bush relies on the private sector to generate cheap and abundant energy and denigrates conservation as a solution for the nation's energy problems. The administration favors the revitalization of the moribund nuclear energy industry as well as removal of environmental protections so that drilling for oil and gas may begin in areas previously designated as protected.[11]

Environmental Policy

In 1962 Rachel Carson's influential book, *Silent Spring,* raised the issue of the potential effects of chemicals on the environment. In 1965 President Lyndon Johnson's State of the Union Address spoke of the population explosion and its potential effects on the capacity of Earth to provide for humanity. A new consciousness brought together issues of conservation, public health, natural resources, energy use, population growth, urbanization, and consumer protection and created demand for environmental legislation.

The first areas to receive attention in the 1970s were clean air and clean water. By 1980 the problems of hazardous and toxic waste were added to the list of environmental issues needing government action. The 1990s focused on the destruction of ecologically critical lands and forests along with the loss of wilderness and wildlife. The 1990s also saw the emergence of global environmental issues, including climate change, ozone depletion, loss of biodiversity, deterioration of quality of life in urban areas, and sustainable development.

The first wave of environmental policy focused on the air and water. A series of laws with a primarily goal of protecting human health and a secondary goal of protecting the environment were drafted. These laws generally relied on national environmental standards and national regulatory mechanisms, primarily implemented by the Environmental Protection Agency (EPA) in cooperation with the states.

The first law was amendment of the **Clean Air Act (CAA).** The Clean Air Act of 1963 had modestly initiated federal air pollution control by supporting research and development and assisting the states to implement their own policies. It was generally unsuccessful, because it relied on voluntary compliance and independent state standards.[12] The 1970 CAA amendments were a fairly radical change in policy. They established **National Ambient Air Quality Standards (NAAQS)** to be enforced by the EPA and the states. The primary standards were designed to protect human health, and secondary standards were included to protect buildings, forests, water, and crops from damage due to air pollution. EPA set the NAAQS for the six major "criteria" pollutants (sulfur dioxide, nitrogen dioxide, lead, ozone, carbon monoxide, and particulates) to provide an "adequate margin of safety." An "ample margin of safety" was mandated for toxic pollutants including arsenic, chromium, hydrogen chloride, zinc, pesticides, and radioactive substances. The law required setting the NAAQSs without consideration of cost of attainment. If control technologies were not available to meet the standards, Congress expected such technologies to be developed by fixed deadlines.

The 1970 CAA amendments also set national emission standards for mobile sources of air pollution (cars, buses, and trucks). They were set to promote 90 percent hydrocarbon emission reduction in 1975 vehicles and 90 percent nitrogen oxide reductions in 1976 vehicles. The amendments also set tough emission standards for such stationary sources as refineries, chemical companies, and other industrial facilities. New sources of pollution were held to **New Source Performance Standards** to be set by industry, enforced by the states, and based on the best available technology, while existing sources of pollution were held to lower standards set by the states according to a **State Implementation Plan (SIP).** The nation was divided into 247 air quality control regions, for which the states were responsible. SIPs were to determine how much of the total pollution load within a region was the responsibility of each polluter and how much emission control that polluter must achieve.[13]

In 1977 CAA was amended again. This amendment eased compliance dates but strengthened the rules for nonattainment areas (areas that had been unsuccessful in reducing pollution to acceptable levels to protect human health) and added provisions for prevention of significant deterioration (PSD) in areas that were already cleaner than national standards. The nation was divided into classes, and Class I areas such as national parks were protected against further deterioration of air quality. Congress provided for protection of visibility in national parks and wilderness areas that were affected by haze and smog. The 1977 amendments also called for the use of scrubbers to remove sulfur dioxide emissions from new fossil-fuel-burning power plants.[14]

Significant changes were ushered in with the 1990 CAA amendments. These amendments extended the act to control acid rain (sulfur dioxide and nitrogen oxides) emitted primarily by coal-burning power plants and to control CFCs (chlorofluorocarbons) that affect the ozone layer. They called for 35 to 60 percent reductions in auto emissions between 1994 and 1996 and for the development of cleaner fuels for use in nonattainment areas. The 1990 amendments established a plan to bring urban areas into compliance within twenty years, required the EPA to set emissions levels for toxic air pollutants, and listed 189 toxic chemicals that the EPA was to regulate. Title V required major stationary sources of air pollution to get EPA-issued operating permits that specify allowable emissions and necessary control measures (commonly called Title V permits).[15]

One of the more innovative and controversial aspects of the 1990 amendments was the introduction of **emissions trading.** This policy was made part of the 1990 amendments after the success of experiments conducted by EPA to change its traditional command and control (standards and enforcement) posture. In command and control the federal government sets standards of acceptable pollution levels, prescribes pollution control technology, licenses and monitors polluters, and identifies and punishes violators. The experiments substituted the market incentives of netting, offsets, and bubbling for traditional command and control. In netting, firms creating new emissions sources within the same plant could reduce emissions from other plant sources so that net emissions did not significantly increase. For offsets, the EPA allowed new pollution sources to locate within a nonattainment area if they could offset new pollution emissions by reducing emissions from other sources in that area. Firms could buy pollution allowances from other local firms to accomplish this. Bubbling allowed firms operating within a "bubble" (a locally designated air shed such as the Los Angeles area) to decide on the most cost-effective methods for obtaining overall bubble compliance and allowed banking or selling of unused pollution credits.[16]

The CAA amendments formalized these experiments in the Title IV emissions trading provisions. Title IV required the EPA to give each major coal-fired electric utility an allowance for each ton of sulfur dioxide emission permitted and to limit utility emissions to the total allowances issued. The allowances can be bought, sold, or traded by other companies or people, including by environmentalists who might want to take them out of circulation. The purpose of the program is to replace command and control with more efficient mechanisms of pollution reduction.[17]

The regulation of water pollution followed a similar path. The first law, the **Water Pollution Control Act of 1948,** emphasized research on clean water issues, but the federal government had no authority over water quality and no standards were set. Some strengthening occurred in the 1965 Water Quality Act, which required the states to establish water quality standards and limit pollution discharges into interstate bodies of water.

The **Clean Water Act (CWA)** of 1972 changed things dramatically. It established national policy and deadlines for eliminating the discharge of wastes into navigable waters. It was very vague, however, stating only that all waters were to be "fishable and swimable" by 1983, which meant that the EPA had to determine what constituted fishable and swimable water. It made the discharge of toxic amounts of pollutants illegal. The CWA amendments of 1977 and 1987 generally strengthened water protection but postponed several deadlines for compliance.[18]

Like the Clean Air Act, the CWA gives the states primary responsibility for implementation as long as they follow federal standards and guidelines. Discharges into navigable waters must meet federal standards, and a discharger must get a permit that specifies the type and quantity of discharge allowed. The EPA has granted authority to most states to issue **National Pollution Discharge Elimination System (NPDES)** permits. These permits apply to municipal facilities as well as to industry. Compliance is determined by self-reported discharge data and on-site state inspections. The states apply **water quality criteria (WQC)** that define the maximum allowable concentration of pollutants in surface waters. EPA effluent limitations specify how much pollution a discharger may emit into the water and the specific treatment technologies to be used prior to discharge.[19]

The CWA gave local governments federal money to build municipal wastewater treatment facilities. The subsidies were significant: in the 1970s the federal government assumed 75 percent of the capital costs, amounts in excess of $7 billion a year. These federal subsidies were reduced in the 1980s to about $2.5 billion a year.[20]

As its name suggests, the 1974 **Safe Drinking Water Act (SDWA)** focused on tap water. The law required the EPA to set National Primary Drinking Water Standards for chemical and microbiological contamination of tap water and to regularly monitor the nation's tap water supplies. The EPA made slow progress, setting only twenty-two standards for eighteen substances by the mid-1980s. In 1986 the law was amended, and the EPA was required to set maximum contamination level standards for eighty-three specific chemicals by 1989, for twenty-five more by 1991, and for twenty-five more every three years. The states were given primary authority for enforcing standards and monitoring levels, using the best available technology to remove pollutants. Many states see this law as an unfunded mandate in that they receive only about half the funding they need. Funding issues are crucial for small water systems that cannot afford new water-treatment technologies. In 2000 small systems were paying more than $3 billion to comply with standards and another $20 billion to repair, replace, and expand systems.[21]

Hazardous and toxic waste policy is another critical area. As with air and water policy, legislation passed prior to the 1970s, such as the 1965 Solid Waste Disposal Act, was weak, relying on the states for standards and expecting voluntary compliance by polluters. The **Resource Conservation and Recovery Act (RCRA)** was a 1970 amendment to the Solid Waste Disposal Act. Its purpose was to regulate hazardous waste disposal sites and practices and to promote conservation and recovery of resources through the management of solid waste.

RCRA required the EPA to identify and characterize hazardous wastes and develop criteria for safe waste disposal. The Department of Commerce was responsible for promoting waste recovery technologies. The EPA was to develop a cradle-to-grave system of regulation to monitor and control production, storage, transportation, and disposal of hazardous waste. The agency subsequently developed specific measures of toxicity, ignitability, corrosivity, and chemical reactivity. A substance that tests positive on any one of these indicators is governed by RCRA. A substance may also be specifically listed by the EPA as hazardous and thus fall under RCRA control. In an effort to eliminate midnight dumping, illegal secret dumping of wastes on public or private lands, the EPA established the **National Manifest System** to keep track of the generation and transportation of hazardous wastes.

Implementation of RCRA was slow. The EPA took four years to issue the first major regulations and six years to issue standards for incinerators, landfills, and surface storage tanks. Upset about the amount of time implementation was taking, Congress strictly limited the EPA's administrative discretion when it passed the **1984 Hazardous and Solid Waste Water Amendment Acts (HSWA).** One of the most detailed and restrictive environmental laws ever written, HSWA contains seventy-six statutory deadlines, eight of which had provisions that would take effect if the EPA failed to meet a deadline. HSWA sought to phase out disposal of most hazardous wastes in landfills by establishing demanding safety standards; covering more wastes, small sources previously omitted, and leaking underground storage tanks; and establishing a specific timetable. HSWA made handling hazardous waste very costly, and the law introduced strong economic incentives for companies to adopt nonpolluting alternatives.

The **Toxic Substances Control Act (TSCA) of 1976** gave the EPA authority to identify, evaluate, and regulate risks associated with commercial chemicals. The EPA was required to produce an inventory of chemicals in commerce and to regulate their manufacture, processing, use, disposition, and disposal. The agency was given the power to ban chemicals or to require special labeling. Under TSCA the manufacturer of a new chemical must notify the EPA and supply test data ninety days before putting the chemical on the market. TSCA was amended by the 1986 Asbestos Hazard Emergency Response Act and the 1992 Residential Lead-Based Paint Hazard Reduction Act, which added asbestos and lead-based paint to the list of toxic substances.

Implementation of TSCA has not gone smoothly. There was business opposition to the law. Because the EPA has to prove that a chemical is unsafe before banning it, only a few chemicals have been banned. The dependence of the EPA on the regulated community for data is also considered problematic.[22]

The **Federal Insecticide, Fungicide, and Rodenticide Act (FIFRA)** of 1947 originally dealt with labeling requirements for pesticides and was implemented through the Department of Agriculture. FIFRA was amended in 1964, 1972, and again in 1978 as a result of increasing public awareness of the dangers of pesticides. Implementation was placed under the EPA in 1970. Today FIFRA allows commercial use of only those pesticides registered with the EPA. Less stringent than other environmental laws passed during the 1970s, FIFRA clearly requires the EPA to take cost into account. EPA must prove an existing pesticide harmful before suspending registration, but the manufacturer must demonstrate the safety of new pesticide.

The **Comprehensive Environmental Response, Compensation, and Liability Act of 1980 (CERCLA,** which is called **Superfund)** was passed as a response to the discovery of toxic waste in Love Canal, a dry canal that was not connected to upstate New York's wider canal system and that was used by the Hooker Chemical Corporation as a disposal site. Discovery of the chemicals that had leaked into the basements of houses surrounding Love Canal led to the passage of the law. While RCRA deals with active sites (sites with current waste generation and disposal), Superfund deals with abandoned or uncontrolled waste sites. Congress initially gave the EPA $1.6 billion to identify, characterize, and clean these abandoned sites. The EPA was expected to track down the original polluters and make them pay for the final cleanup. This emphasis resulted in a great deal of litigation, and Superfund is a very controversial law not only because of liability issues but also because cleanup has been slow and the program has been expensive.[23]

In 1986 Superfund was amended by the **Superfund Amendments and Reauthorization Act (SARA),** which added $8.5 billion to the fund. Because of a 1984 accident at Bhopal, India, in which a release of toxic gas killed five thousand people, SARA initiated the **Toxic Release Inventory (TRI)** under the **Community Planning and Right-to-Know** section of the law.[24] Table 9.1 shows the releases to the land, air, surface waters, and underground water for each of the states in 2000.

Debate about global environmental issues began in the 1980s and grew more urgent thereafter. For more than eighty years the United States has been a participant in international environmental agreements. The scope and pace of such agreements have increased in the last thirty years, and during that period the United States has adopted 97 multilateral environmental treaties, bringing the total to 152. Prior to the 1980s most dealt with access to common global

Table 9.1 TRI Reported Releases for All Industries and All Chemicals by State, 2000 (in Pounds)

State	Air	Water	Underground	Land	Total Releases
Alabama	81,165,605	6,858,252	154,024	47,000,566	150,636,704
Alaska	2,853,383	103,653	36,790,623	495,737,280	535,489,271
Arizona	5,189,155	9,238	0	737,242,453	744,720,144
Arkansas	26,293,694	2,289,707	1,464,573	6,824,038	51,434,462
California	23,838,745	6,094,176	58,794	34,411,538	75,609,346
Colorado	3,831,194	3,171,556	.	17,754,944	30,600,506
Connecticut	5,562,407	815,903	.	49,441	8,746,602
Delaware	7,805,938	866,313	.	1,105,457	13,601,006
Florida	87,762,359	1,797,794	34,849,655	14,631,534	143,572,617
Georgia	96,124,645	6,504,826	0	14,860,845	122,208,791
Hawaii	1,057,085	1,224	7,284	31,833	1,273,971
Idaho	5,540,160	6,221,090	.	64,430,860	76,668,144
Illinois	68,048,374	6,856,204	500	44,712,893	150,340,904
Indiana	89,664,614	17,951,843	1,026,106	32,735,290	204,096,781
Iowa	23,780,019	5,597,894	0	6,410,943	43,425,537
Kansas	16,991,536	1,248,496	487,909	8,604,056	38,347,383
Kentucky	68,547,481	3,467,850	3,092	21,296,114	101,430,933
Louisiana	70,357,963	12,868,235	51,703,983	14,542,019	154,522,636
Maine	6,394,817	2,149,436	.	899,300	10,597,403
Maryland	36,062,563	3,564,265	54,434	3,925,048	45,194,293
Massachusetts	9,285,816	199,958	.	370,712	12,996,573
Michigan	71,196,133	1,134,854	2,057,816	33,039,616	140,189,990
Minnesota	15,167,302	1,361,628	.	9,841,615	33,003,217
Mississippi	45,030,203	13,541,571	12,591,718	8,217,749	81,083,440
Missouri	38,376,910	1,946,686	2	84,687,284	130,957,247
Montana	6,275,207	47,461	.	110,675,133	122,149,439

resources. Since then most have dealt with transboundary issues including acid precipitation, ozone depletion, and global warming. Meetings have been held in Stockholm, Montreal, Rio de Janeiro, and Kyoto to determine a multinational response to these environmental challenges.

The theme of the 1972 Stockholm meeting was Only One Earth. The first truly international meeting on environmental issues, it was attended by 113 countries and 19 representatives from international organizations. A key outcome was the **Stockholm Declaration,** which stated that nations have the sovereign right to exploit their own resources in accord with their own environmental policies and that nations have the obligation to ensure that activities within their jurisdiction or control do not damage the environment of other nations or areas.

The outcome of the Montreal meeting was the **1987 Montreal Protocol on Substances That Deplete the Ozone Layer.** This protocol limited domestic production and consumption of CFCs and other chemicals that were destroying the ozone layer, which blocks harmful ultraviolet radiation twenty to thirty miles above Earth. It was signed by the United States and forty-six other

Table 9.1 *(continued)*

State	Air	Water	Underground	Land	Total Releases
North Carolina	125,660,985	9,165,369	0	11,280,855	157,279,810
North Dakota	3,287,328	125,839	.	10,676,965	24,200,419
Nebraska	8,368,905	10,830,967	.	5,543,497	30,061,384
Nevada	3,320,975	121,808	1,050	1,002,437,400	1,008,269,713
New Hampshire	5,411,035	95,776	.	64,866	6,160,861
New Jersey	17,164,803	5,547,375	4	195,513	29,010,100
New Mexico	1,260,869	45,398	895	121,181,868	125,209,213
New York	33,325,291	8,992,560	250	8,329,309	60,536,268
Ohio	144,849,286	7,670,188	30,288,567	46,810,886	283,019,996
Oklahoma	18,725,373	2,518,989	2,460,937	5,340,409	33,002,867
Oregon	16,429,071	3,607,695	0	55,402,779	82,159,662
Pennsylvania	96,898,649	43,260,726	0	14,787,090	225,912,778
Rhode Island	992,815	1,348	0	26	1,275,550
South Carolina	55,743,081	2,962,485	0	5,126,299	79,368,824
South Dakota	2,049,646	2,316,585	822,600	4,294,224	9,605,753
Tennessee	104,129,125	3,271,969	5	46,980,819	162,855,882
Texas	103,203,480	33,064,455	94,832,009	40,519,292	301,518,708
Utah	49,323,729	999,338	0	903,988,120	955,941,798
Vermont	120,566	178,519	.	255	401,956
Virginia	59,217,794	8,212,342	.	6,215,803	82,194,202
Washington	19,902,669	2,777,130	.	4,235,025	31,707,875
West Virginia	73,373,396	4,667,332	14,409	13,494,319	97,713,603
Wisconsin	29,027,896	3,563,174	0	1,918,981	49,678,719
Wyoming	2,040,886	24,521	9,365,405	8,466,185	21,131,448
Total	**1,904,405,335**	**260,882,380**	**279,036,646**	**4,131,361,986**	**7,100,730,829**

SOURCE: U.S. EPA, Toxic Release Inventory Data, 2000.

nations. Subsequent conferences in London in 1990 and Copenhagen in 1992 accelerated the pace of CFC reduction. The success of the protocol was due in large part to broad scientific consensus on ozone depletion as well as the development of alternatives to CFCs.

In 1992 the Conference on Environment and Development, or Earth Summit, was held in Rio de Janeiro and was attended by 179 countries. It emphasized the growing urgency of environmental problems and focused on issues faced by developing nations. The outcome was the twenty-eight guiding principles of the **Rio Declaration on Environment and Development.** Principle 16 stated that the polluter should bear the cost of cleaning up pollution. The Rio Declaration also supported the "precautionary principle," which indicated that nations should take action to abate potentially harmful pollutants even in the absence of scientific certainty about their effects.[25]

In 1988 NASA's James Hansen testified before Congress on the reliability of scientific evidence of global climate change trends. Hansen's testimony brought scientific credibility to the issue. Much global climate change results from fossil fuels that release carbon dioxide, the major greenhouse gas. The United States is a major producer of greenhouse gases. The **Kyoto Protocol** that emerged from the 1997 environmental meeting raised the visibility of this issue, and President William Clinton pledged to abide by a compulsory target and timetable agreement to limit U.S. emissions of greenhouse gases to 1990 levels.

There is considerable partisan disagreement about reducing the emission of greenhouse gases, and some groups are unwilling to implement policies that would result in reductions. Congress warned President Clinton that it would not ratify the Kyoto Protocol if he submitted it to them, so he did not, and in 2001, announcing that his administration would not honor the Clinton pledges, President George W. Bush fully withdrew the United States from the agreement. Figure 9.3 shows U.S. carbon dioxide emissions by economic sector.

POLICY OPERATION

The agency most thought of as having national control over environmental policy is the **Environmental Protection Agency (EPA).** The EPA was created in December 1970 as part of President Richard Nixon's general reorganization of the executive branch. The goal was to combine health and regulatory responsibilities from across the government into one agency.[26] The EPA was patched together from pieces of Health, Education and Welfare (air quality, solid waste, and drinking water), the Department of Interior (water quality and pesticide research), the Department of Agriculture (pesticide regulation), and other agencies such as the Food and Drug Administration and the Atomic Energy Commission.[27] As a result, the EPA began as an agency that lacked full integration.[28]

The creation of the EPA was vigorously opposed by several key members of the Nixon administration, including the secretaries of the Departments of Interior; Health, Education and Welfare; and Agriculture. The opposition from the Interior Department was largely due to the fact that Interior wanted to take over all environmental regulatory functions. The other agencies did not want to lose power to the newly created agency. The business community generally favored the creation of the EPA, believing that a single regulatory agency was preferable to multiple state-based regulatory standards.[29]

The EPA is the largest of the environmental agencies. Its mission is to protect human health and to safeguard the natural environment, and its focus is on air, water, and land.[30] Congress passed a series of environmental laws over time, each responding to a different environmental problem, and gave the EPA responsibility for implementing them. The agency was granted regulatory authority over air pollution in 1970, surface water pollution in 1972, drinking water quality in 1974, generation and disposal of hazardous wastes and manufacture and marketing of chemicals in 1976, and cleanup of abandoned waste sites in 1980. Fragmentation of its legal authority affects the EPA and the operation of its programs. For most programs, the EPA shares implementation authority with state and local governments. States and localities exercise various amounts of discretion, depending on the law and the willingness of the state or locality to take lead action for enforcement.[31]

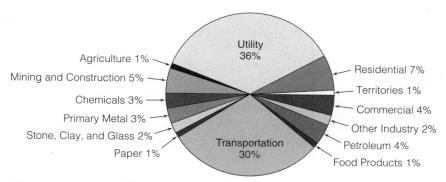

FIGURE 9.3 U.S. Carbon Dioxide Emissions by Sector, 1994

SOURCE: United States Environmental Protection Agency.

The EPA is organized under a central administrator, a deputy administrator, ten assistant administrators, and ten regional administrators who are appointed by the president and confirmed by the Senate. These appointed officials set policy for the agency. They serve at the pleasure of the president and are almost always replaced by new presidential administrations.

An assistant administrator leads each of the main operating units, which include the offices of air and radiation; water; solid waste and emergency response; and prevention, pesticides, and toxic substances. Other assistant administrators lead offices with functional responsibilities, including the offices of administration and resources management; research and development; enforcement and compliance assurance; and the office of the general counsel.[32]

The agency has a few staff positions filled by non–civil service employees, but most of the EPA is staffed by highly professional career civil servants. In 1996 career staff numbered about 17,000. About two-thirds have college degrees and one-third graduate degrees. Their training is largely in engineering, law, health, agriculture, biological science, physical and environmental sciences, and social sciences. Agency staffing fell from 13,000 at the start of the Reagan administration to 11,000 in 1983, then peaked at 18,000 in 1995.[33]

While EPA is the largest federal environmental policy agency, a number of other agencies are also involved with the environment. The National Aeronautics and Space Administration (NASA) collects data to support climate research and to describe and measure energy and environmental phenomena that may contribute to climate variation and change. NASA's mission to Planet Earth program plays a central role in this environmental mission. The National Oceanic and Atmospheric Administration (NOAA) gathers worldwide environmental data about the oceans, land, air, space, and the sun. NOAA also maintains a national environmental database that combines its own data with environmental information collected by other agencies. The United States Geological Survey (USGS) collects and maintains data on streams, groundwater, erosion, flooding, water contamination, and sedimentation.[34]

EPA is not in charge of natural resources policy, most of which falls to the Department of Interior. Within the Department of Interior, the Bureau of

Land Management (BLM) controls most lands in the national domain. The BLM is responsible for 270 million acres of public lands, located primarily in twelve western states.[35] The National Park Service is charged with managing nearly 81 million acres of parks, national monuments, battlefields, memorials, historic sites, recreational areas, scenic parkways and trails, near-wilderness, seashores, and lakeshores. The Park Service also gathers, compiles, and issues public-use data to forecast future demands and needs.[36] The Fish and Wildlife Service is responsible for another 91 million acres of the public domain. It conducts annual surveys to monitor fish and migratory bird populations, track diseases of cultured and wild fish, measure the changing status of waterfowl and game bird populations, and evaluate harvests by fishermen and hunters. The Interior Department also contains the Office of Surface Mining and the Bureau of Indian Affairs.

The Department of Interior contains one science agency—the U.S. Geological Survey. Its role is to help resolve complex national and international natural resources problems.[37] The USGS Biological Resources Division collects and analyzes data on birds and fish to determine trends in environmental contamination and tracks species and their habitats. Data from its annual breeding bird survey identify species whose populations are declining and that may eventually become candidates for listing under the Endangered Species Act.[38]

Another agency responsible for a large part of the national domain is the U.S. Forest Service. Located within the Department of Agriculture, the Forest Service manages the nation's 191 million acres of forest.[39] The Natural Resources Conservation Service (NRCS), also within the Department of Agriculture, maintains a database containing physical land facts and monitors water and snow supply to forecast water availability.[40] The National Marine Fisheries Service, located within the National Oceanic and Atmospheric Administration, monitors domestic commercial and recreational fisheries and provides data on how much fishing is done and the status of the remaining stocks.[41]

Even though energy use and production are intimately tied to environmental quality, the EPA does not have the authority to regulate energy. Instead, use and production of energy are controlled by the Department of Energy (DOE). When DOE was formed in 1977, it took over the responsibilities of the Federal Energy Administration, the Energy Research and Development Administration, the Federal Power Commission, and parts and programs of several other agencies. The primary responsibility of DOE is to administer the nation's nuclear weapons. It also conducts some research and development of energy technology, is involved in energy conservation and energy regulatory programs, and has a central energy data collection and analysis program.[42]

CURRENT ISSUES

A group of key environmental and natural resource issues are controversial. Among them are regulatory reform, the organizational capacity of the EPA to carry out its mission, and the appropriate way to manage the national domain.

Regulatory Reform

Perhaps no area of environmental policy is in more conflict that that of trying to evaluate the relative success or failure of environmental policy. There is a widespread belief that environmental policy has not worked well, and there have been calls for "comprehensive" reform and reinvention of laws, institutions, and procedures. There are disputes over the causes of environmental problems. Some critics suggest that environmental policy is based on insufficient science and technology. Others argue that traditional command and control structures do not provide adequate economic incentives. There are a large number of questions about the efficiency, effectiveness, and economy of programs.

With the election of Ronald Reagan in 1980, regulatory reform was catapulted to the forefront of national priorities. President Reagan was determined to slow the pace of regulation making.[43] His first effort, Executive Order 12291 in 1981, established the **Office of Information and Regulatory Affairs (OIRA)** within the Office of Management and Budget (OMB) and required a formal **cost-benefit analysis,** or **Regulatory Impact Analysis,** prior to proposal of a major regulation with an annual economic impact of at least $100 million. A few years later Executive Order 12498 required the EPA and other federal agencies to develop an annual regulatory agenda for submission to OMB and to indicate how their programs were consistent with the president's agenda. President George H. W. Bush retained these executive orders and established the Council on Competitiveness, which was used by unhappy industries to complain about regulation. When President Clinton assumed office, he terminated the Council on Competitiveness and replaced Reagan's two executive orders with Executive Order 12866, which required timely review of proposed regulations by OIRA and a written explanation of all requested changes in regulatory action. Cost-benefit analysis remained in place, but it was no longer the only basis of policy decision making.

Cost-benefit analysis is controversial. It is often easy to change the outcome of a cost-benefit analysis by making small changes to critical parts of the analysis, such as the discount rate. A simple switch of a discount rate could change a proposed project or regulation from cost-effective to cost-ineffective. Even more controversial is setting the value of items that do not have market value, such as the value of human life.[44] Some critics argue that it is inappropriate to put a dollar value on human life, but if cost-benefit analysis is to be used in environmental decision making, it is necessary to do so.

Organizational Issues at EPA

Does the EPA have the ability to carry out the tasks expected of it? Both detractors and supporters of the agency have claimed that it does not. The formation of the agency from the remnants of other agencies is said to have created organizational confusion, if not dysfunction. These rocky beginnings were magnified by the Reagan administration's operation of the agency. President Reagan was openly hostile to the EPA, and while he was unable to eliminate the agency, he did cut its budget and staff and appointed managers who were equally opposed to its mission. This led to congressional micromanagement of the agency. Congress passed a series of extremely detailed and rigid laws to compel strict administrative compliance. Congress also enacted complex and ambitious new environmental laws, but EPA's budget and staffing did not increase proportional to the new tasks.

By the mid-1990s EPA found itself in a highly charged political setting. Mounting dissatisfaction with its programs, from both supporters and detractors, ended in calls for reform. The 1994 elections brought to office a group of Republicans determined to lead the country down another road of regulatory reform. Congress focused on detailed scientific risk assessment, cost-benefit analysis, challenging existing rules, and finding ways to devolve authority to the states whenever possible. Threats of budget cuts also loomed. The Clinton administration's response was general agreement that the EPA needed reform.

Internal administrative reforms were undertaken under Vice President Al Gore's National Performance Review. These reforms included identification of obsolete and burdensome regulations that needed revision or elimination. There was general nonpartisan agreement about the need for a coherent mission statement to set agency priorities, an adequate budget for research and development that permits creation and defense of risk assessments, a more integrated approach to pollution management, a different way of working with the states, and elimination of the quagmire of congressional oversight by six Senate committees, seven House committees, and thirty-one subcommittees. The administration and Congress disagreed about which reforms would improve the EPA's performance and which were attempts to dismantle the agency and its programs.

George W. Bush's administration has made further attempts to weaken the agency. Not unlike Ronald Reagan, Bush is hostile to the EPA and its regulatory agenda. Early in his term of office he attempted to reduce environmental protections put in place by former administrations. For instance, he called for increasing the allowable level of arsenic in water. Public concern forced the administration to abandon the plan. Bush's energy policy statements called for drilling for oil in previously protected areas of the Alaskan wilderness. Over the course of two years, Congress failed to act to allow this. Additional controversies stem from the administration's attempt to roll back clean air standards so that coal-burning electric generating plants might continue to produce electricity unhindered by air-quality standards.

Conflict over Wilderness

There have been conflicts over the management of federal lands since the nation's beginning. The agency at the center of this debate is the Bureau of Land Management (BLM), which oversees more land than any other government agency. As a result of the Alaska Land Act of 1980, BLM controls large areas of wilderness; these now constitute about half of BLM lands. The agency is also in charge of federal mineral leases. In 1976 the Federal Land Policy Act formally ended the practice of disposing of the national domain and gave BLM control of the remaining national domain. BLM has been moving slowly toward a policy of sustainable resource management.

As part of a review of land use in the 1970s, the Forest Service undertook an inventory of roadless land within the national forest system for possible inclusion in the protected wilderness system. **RARE I** (Roadless Area Review and Evaluation) was completed in 1976 and **RARE II** in 1979. The Reagan administration was not sympathetic to the idea of wilderness preservation, and Interior Secretary James Watt proposed opening wilderness areas to mineral development. Congress designated lands as protected wilderness despite Reagan administration opposition. When President Reagan and Secretary Watt tried to withdraw millions of acres from possible wilderness designation, Congress demurred. In 1990 Congress refused to allow logging on more than 1 million acres in southeast Alaska.

In its last days, the Clinton administration issued final regulations banning road construction and most logging in 60 million acres of federal land, or about one-third of the federal forests. President George W. Bush opposed the designation of land as wilderness, but decided to let it stand with some modifications. The Bush administration intends to let local officials modify the ban on a case-by-case basis and allow logging, mining, and drilling. According to the Bush administration, these changes address federal lawsuits brought by Idaho and Boise Cascade. Environmentalists argue that the changes will damage the protections intended by the regulation.[45] The battle continues.

SUMMARY

Environmental policy is a mix of three distinct but overlapping policy areas. Natural resources policy typically centers on land use. The main issues in natural resources policy concern the protection or use of the land for development and other purposes. Energy policy is important because a great deal of the pollution that affects our world is a direct result of fossil fuel use. Environmental policy focuses on clean air, clean water, and the disposal of solid and hazardous waste.

Environmental policy and natural resources policy are one of the largest areas of national expense (through direct government expenditure and regulation). There have been three great waves of natural resources policy. The first dates to the beginnings of the nation when the federal government used its vast acres of western lands to lure settlers to the west. By the time of the Civil War, a movement had begun to preserve wilderness lands for future generations. This early preservationist movement was countered by a conservationist movement that encouraged the managed use of forest resources for economic development while conserving them for sustained yield. The second great wave of natural resources policy came in the 1930s when the center of attention was flood control and soil conservation. The third wave began when attention turned once again to conservation and preservation in the 1960s.

Energy policy is key to a cleaner environment. Fossil fuel use creates air pollution, acid precipitation, particulates that are known to cause cancer, and carbon dioxide (the leading climate change gas). Finding substitutes for fossil fuels while still increasing the amount of available energy for growth and development is one of the largest challenges confronting society today.

Environmental policy burst on the national scene in the 1960s. The first areas to receive attention in the 1970s were clean air and clean water. By 1980 hazardous waste and toxic waste were added to the list of environmental issues needing government action. The 1990s focused on the destruction of ecologically critical lands and forests, climate change, ozone depletion, loss of biodiversity, deterioration of urban quality of life, and sustainable development.

Environmental policy involves several governmental agencies. The largest agency is the EPA, which has the mission of protecting human health and safeguarding the natural environment. Its focus is on air, water, and land. The EPA typically shares implementation authority with state and local governments. Other government agencies share some part of the natural resources and environmental policy role. Even though much of the nation's pollution is the result of energy use and production, EPA does not have authority to regulate energy.

Many issues in the arena of environmental and natural resources policy are controversial. Among the most important are regulatory reform, institutional capacity of the EPA, and use of public lands.

KEY TERMS

Bureau of Land Management (BLM)

Clean Air Act (CAA)

Clean Water Act (CWA)

Coastal Zone Management Act of 1972

Community Planning and Right-to-Know

Comprehensive Environmental Response, Compensation, and Liability Act (CERCLA, Superfund)

corporate average fuel efficiency (CAFE)

cost-benefit analysis

Department of Energy (DOE)

emissions trading

Energy Reorganization Act of 1974

Environmental Protection Agency (EPA)

Federal Insecticide, Fungicide, and Rodenticide Act (FIFRA)

Hazardous and Solid Waste Water Amendment Acts of 1984 (HSWA)

Homestead Act of 1862

Kyoto Protocol

Mining Law of 1872

Montreal Protocol on Substances That Deplete the Ozone Layer of 1987

National Ambient Air Quality Standards (NAAQS)

National Estuarine Research Reserves

National Forest System

National Manifest System

National Marine Sanctuaries

National Park System

National Pollution Discharge Elimination System (NPDES)

National Wild and Scenic River System

National Wildlife Refuge System

Natural Wilderness Preservation System

New Source Performance Standards

Nuclear Regulatory Commission (NRC)

Office of Information and Regulatory Affairs (OIRA)

RARE I

RARE II

Regulatory Impact Analysis

Resource Conservation and Recovery Act (RCRA)

Rio Declaration on Environment and Development

Safe Drinking Water Act (SDWA)

State Implementation Plan (SIP)

Stockholm Declaration

Superfund Amendments and Reauthorization Act (SARA)

Taylor Grazing Act of 1934

Toxic Release Inventory (TRI)

Toxic Substances Control Act (TSCA) of 1976

Water Pollution Control Act of 1948

water quality criteria (WQC)

WEB SITES

http://www.doi.gov
The home page for the Department of the Interior contains links to each of the department's bureaus, including the National Park Service, the U.S. Fish and Wildlife Service, the Bureau of Indian Affairs, the Bureau of Land Management, the Office of Surface Mining, the Minerals Management Service, the U.S. Geological Survey, and the Bureau of Reclamation. If you prefer, you can access these independently.

http://www.nps.gov/
The National Parks Service home page, where you can find information on each of the national parks and monuments maintained by the service. It also provides interesting information on the history of the park system. A fine aspect of this site, Nature Net, provides a host of information about biology and ecology associated with National Park Service sites.

http://www.fws.gov/
The Fish and Wildlife Service home page provides interesting information on conserving wildlife and habitats. This site also has useful information on education for conservation.

http://www.blm.gov/nhp/index.htm
The main page of the Bureau of Land Management has interesting maps that show in detail the land that is under the authority of the BLM. The What We Do button provides access to details about a wide variety of activities, including boundaries, buildings, and land title information; commercial activities; customer service; economic and technical assistance; environmental education; geospatial information systems; land and mineral records; lands and realty; planning, assessment, and community support; national landscape conservation; national and cultural heritage; recreation; reducing threats to public

health, safety, and property; regulatory responsibilities; restoring and maintaining the health of the land; volunteers; and wild horses and burros.

http://www.usgs.gov/
The home page of the U.S. Geological Survey with information by state and general U.S. information. It covers earthquakes, floods, hurricanes, and volcanoes and provides links to information on natural disasters. One of the interesting items is access to maps, including topographical maps.

http://www.epa.gov/
The home page of the Environmental Protection Agency has links to the regions and provides information on laws and regulations, which is helpfully arranged into major laws, laws currently under consideration, U.S. Code of Federal Regulations, and proposed regulations currently under consideration. There are details on acid rain, global warming, toxic waste cleanups, brownfields, Superfund, compliance and enforcement, cost-benefit analysis, wetlands, watersheds, endangered species, oil spills and accidents, human health, risk assessment, business permits and pollution reporting, pesticide and insecticide registration, pollutants, pollution prevention, hazardous wastes, landfills, wastewater, drinking water, and groundwater. The site also has links to data on pollution releases and emissions.

DISCUSSION QUESTIONS

1. Discuss the policy difference between conservation and preservation. Identify policies or government actions that encompass each ideology.
2. Describe the market-based policies for pollution reduction in the 1990 Clean Air Act.
3. States were given primary responsibility for implementing the CAA and CWA. List and describe EPA-mandated strategies for pollution reduction that were implemented by the states.
4. Describe the major provisions of two of the following pieces of legislation: CAA, CWA, SDWA, RCRA, CERCLA, SARA.
5. What is EPA's mission, and for what environmental problems is EPA responsible? What other agencies are responsible for environmental issues?

WEB QUESTIONS

1. Briefly explain the EnergyStar program (www.energystar.gov) administered by the EPA and the DOE and some of the services it provides.
2. Locate toxic release inventory data for your or another neighborhood at www.epa.gov/tri, and print a map.

3. What are some of the current environmental legislative issues facing Congress (www.epa.gov/epahome/rules.html#legislation)?

4. What is the EPA Office of Policy, Economics and Innovation (www.epa.gov/opei)? Discuss some of its roles and responsibilities.

NOTES

1. Office of Management and Budget, *Report to Congress on the Costs and Benefits of Federal Regulations* (Washington, DC: Office of Management and Budget, 2000).

2. Thomas D. Hopkins, *Regulatory Costs in Profile* (Center for the Study of American Business, Policy Study Number 132, August 1996).

3. Michael E. Kraft, *Environmental Policy and Politics* (New York: HarperCollins College Publishers, 1996).

4. National Park Service, *Legacy and Timeline*. http://www.nps.gov/legacy/legacy.html (4/25/01).

5. Kraft, *Environmental Policy and Politics*.

6. Ibid.

7. Roger A. Hinrichs and Merlin Kleinbach, *Energy: Its Use and the Environment*, 3rd ed. (Fort Worth, TX: Harcourt College Publishers, 2002).

8. Walter A. Rosenbaum, *Environmental Politics and Policy*, 4th ed. (Washington, DC: CQ Press, 1998).

9. Ibid.

10. Clarke E. Cochran, Lawrence C. Mayer, T. R. Carr, and N. Joseph Cayer, *American Public Policy: An Introduction*, 6th ed. (Boston: St. Martin's, 1999).

11. B. Guy Peters, *American Public Policy: Promise and Performance*, 5th ed. (New York: Seven Bridges Press, 1998).

12. Robert F. Durant, *When Government Regulates Itself: EPA, TVA, and Pollution Control in the 1970s* (Knoxville, TN: University of Tennessee Press, 1985).

13. Rosenbaum, *Environmental Politics and Policy*.

14. Richard A. Liroff, *Reforming Air Pollution Regulation: The Toil and Trouble of EPA's Bubble* (Washington, DC: The Conservation Foundation, 1986).

15. Gary C. Bryner, *Blue Skies, Green Politics: The Clean Air Act of 1990 and Its Implementation*, 2nd ed. (Washington, DC: CQ Press, 1995).

16. Rosenbaum, *Environmental Politics and Policy*.

17. Brian J. Cook, *Bureaucratic Politics and Regulatory Reform: The EPA and Emissions Trading* (New York: Greenwood Press, 1988).

18. Kraft, *Environmental Policy and Politics*.

19. Margaret C. Jasper, *Environmental Law* (Dobbs Ferry, NY: Oceana Publications, 1997).

20. Kraft, *Environmental Policy and Politics*.

21. Ibid.

22. National Research Council, *Decision Making in the Environmental Protection Agency* (Washington, DC: National Academy of Sciences, 1977).

23. Dianne Rahm, "Controversial Cleanup: Superfund and the Implementation of U.S. Hazardous Waste Policy," *Policy Studies Journal* 26 (4): 719–734; and Joel A. Mintz, *Enforcement at the EPA: High Stakes and Hard Choices* (Austin, TX: University of Texas Press, 1995).

24. Rosenbaum, *Environmental Politics and Policy*.

25. Ibid.

26. John Quarles, *Cleaning Up America: An Insider's View of the Environmental Protection Agency* (Boston: Houghton Mifflin, 1976).

27. Ibid.

28. Kraft, *Environmental Policy and Politics*.

29. Rosemary O'Leary, *Environmental*

Change: Federal Courts and the EPA
(Philadelphia: Temple University Press,
1993).

30. U.S. Environmental Protection
Agency, *History Office—EPA Timeline.*
http://www.epa.gov/history/timeline/
index.htm (4/25/01).

31. Kraft, *Environmental Policy and Politics.*

32. U.S. Environmental Protection
Agency, *About EPA—Organizational
Structure.*
wysiwyg://6/http://www.epa.gov/
epahome/organization.htm (4/25/01).

33. Kraft, *Environmental Policy and Politics.*

34. *Environment.* www.fedstats.gov
(4/25/01).

35. U.S. Department of Interior, Bureau
of Land Management.
http://www.blm.gov/nhp/index.htm.

36. National Park Service, *The National
Park System Acreage.*
http://www.nps.gov/legacy/acreage.html
(4/25/01).

37. U.S. Geological Survey, *Science, Society,
Solutions: An Introduction to the USGS.*

http://www.usgs.gov/aboutusgs.html
(4/25/01).

38. *Environment.*

39. USDA, *Forest Service.*
http://www.fs.fed.us (4/25/01).

40. *Environment.*

41. National Oceanic and Atmospheric
Administration, *Fisheries.*
http://www.noaa.gov/fisheries.html
(4/25/01).

42. U.S. Department of Energy, *The
Origins of Our Department.*
www.energy.gov/aboutus/history/index.
html (4/25/01).

43. Cornelius M. Kerwin, *Rulemaking:
How Government Agencies Write Law and
Make Policy,* 2d ed. (Washington, DC: CQ
Press, 1999).

44. Peters, *American Public Policy.*

45. Douglas Jehl, "Bush Will Modify Ban
on New Roads in Federal Lands," *New
York Times,* 4 May 2001.
http://www.nytimes.com/2001/05/04/
politics/04fore.html.

10

Nonmonetary Policy Areas

Chapters 4 through 9 outline the major areas of public policy on which the United States spends a good deal of money. Although expenditure of funds is important, not all highly significant policy areas demand large amounts of money, and many areas that the nation considers vital do not make the list of the most costly. The policy areas discussed in this chapter—abortion, stem cell research, gun control, global trade, and immigration—fall into this category.

These policy areas tend to be controversial. One reason is that they reflect deeply felt moral values and ideals. In most cases, they involve fundamental values, including the worth of human life. They deal with such normative questions as "should we" or "ought we" rather than with less emotionally charged questions involving the extent to which resources should be committed. These policy areas also touch one of the most sensitive issues in democratic governance—they ask us to think very carefully about the rights of individuals in a free, but ordered, society.

ABORTION

Abortion is one of the most controversial issues in American public policy today. Decisions about whether it is appropriate for the government to allow abortion provoke deep feelings and concerns. The people who oppose abortion, who are often called **pro-life** advocates, argue that abortion is murder and must not be allowed. Some pro-life advocates would permit abortion under certain circumstances, for instance to save the life of the mother if the continuation of pregnancy would result in her death. Some think abortion is permissible in the case of rape or incest. Other pro-life advocates are totally opposed to abortion regardless of the health of the mother or the cause of the pregnancy.

The other side of the debate is championed by **pro-choice** advocates. Their position is that a woman has an absolute right to control her own body. Like pro-life advocates, pro-choice advocates differ in their approaches to the permissibility of abortion. Some suggest that a woman should always be allowed to end an unwanted pregnancy, regardless of the stage of the pregnancy. Others would put limits on access to abortion, frequently supporting the prohibition of abortion in the later stages of pregnancy.

Abortion has been an issue in America since its founding. Abortion was openly available in early America. In the thirteenth-century an English common law doctrine called "quickening" held that abortions were not criminal until the fetus had shown some sign of independent life. The sign was typically taken to be independent motion, something only the pregnant woman herself could feel and attest to. America followed these common law guidelines during its early history. In the famous 1812 case of *Commonwealth* v. *Bangs,* Massachusetts charged a physician with performing an abortion, and the court dismissed the suit on the grounds that quickening had not yet occurred.[1]

In the mid-1800s the American Medical Association (AMA), which was influenced by a pro-life physician, launched a campaign against abortion, and by 1910 every state had abandoned the absence of quickening as a determining factor in whether abortion was allowable.[2] All the states tried to restrict abortions that were not necessary to save the life of the mother.[3]

Opposition to restrictions on abortion arose slowly. By the 1950s considerable opposition had coalesced. The question of the acceptability of abortion to preserve the mental health of the prospective mother emerged. Planned Parenthood and the New York Academy of Medicine became advocates for the liberalization of abortion laws. By the mid-1960s, with the early growth of the women's movement, abortion restrictions were scrutinized even more. The American Civil Liberties Union (ACLU) and the National Organization for Women (NOW) joined the debate. By the early 1970s, nineteen states had liberalized their abortion laws to some extent. The rest of the states still held abortion illegal, and abortion was severely restricted even where some form of it was legal. Only a handful of states allowed what was commonly called abortion on demand.[4]

In 1961 the Supreme Court heard the case of *Poe* v. *Ullman*, which involved the constitutionality of an 1879 Connecticut law prohibiting even married couples from using birth control. A Connecticut physician challenged the law on behalf of two women who wanted to use contraceptives for health reasons. The physician's attorneys argued that the law invaded the privacy of married couples and thereby violated the due process clause of the Fourteenth Amendment.[5] Although the Court upheld the 1879 law, *Poe* started a wider discussion of whether the Constitution guaranteed a **right to privacy.**

Estelle Griswold opened a birth control clinic in Connecticut in 1961 with the intention of getting arrested for violating the 1879 law. Within a few days she was arrested for providing contraceptives to a married couple. *Griswold* v. *Connecticut* eventually reached the Supreme Court. In 1965 the Court ruled that there was a constitutional right to privacy. Even though the specific issue was birth control, the logic of the *Griswold* ruling was soon applied to abortion.[6]

Roe **v.** *Wade* was a challenge to a Texas law that prohibited abortion other than to save the life of the mother. The Supreme Court heard the case in 1973, and the result was a complete reversal of past law. The Court held that all laws restricting abortion violated the right to privacy—a right inferred from the Fourth, Fifth, and Ninth Amendments and applied to the states through the Fourteenth Amendment—and were thus unconstitutional. In *Roe* the Supreme Court held that the states could not ban abortions in the first three months, or first trimester, of pregnancy; that the states could regulate abortions in the interest of the health of the mother in the second trimester; and that the states could ban abortion in the last three months of pregnancy unless the health of the mother was in danger.[7]

As a consequence of *Roe* pro-life forces began to seek ways to once again restrict access to abortion. State legislatures passed laws restricting abortion with the hope of forcing another Supreme Court decision. When Ronald Reagan, who opposed abortion, was elected president, his administration appointed only people who were against abortion to agency offices, the federal courts, and the Supreme Court. With his appointment of Justice Anthony Kennedy in 1987, there were enough votes for the Supreme Court to move away from its fifteen-year history of protecting a woman's right to abortion. Although the Court eventually preserved the right of abortion, it upheld state laws seeking to regulate abortion that had the effect of making abortions more difficult to get.[8]

Congress responded by calling repeatedly for a constitutional amendment to overturn *Roe*. Such an amendment has not been forthcoming. Congress did, however, deny the use of federal funds, including Medicaid funds, for abortion.[9]

Presidents Reagan, George H. W. Bush, and George W. Bush used executive orders to prohibit funding overseas health organizations that provided information or referral services for abortion. George H. W. Bush instituted the **abortion gag rule,** an executive order instructing the Department of Health and Human Services (HHS) to prohibit health care professionals working in facilities drawing any Title X federal funds from providing patients with information on the availability of abortion. Since Title X primarily provides funds to clinics serving low-income patients, the gag rule effectively eliminated poor women's access to abortion. The Clinton administration rescinded the gag rule.[10]

A number of Supreme Court cases since *Roe,* while not banning the procedure, have effectively put restrictions on abortion. In the 1989 decision in *William Webster* v. *Reproductive Health Services,* the Court upheld a Missouri abortion law that required testing for fetal viability (to determine whether the fetus could live outside the womb) when a woman seeking an abortion was deemed to be twenty weeks pregnant.[11] A Pennsylvania law required women seeking abortion to wait for twenty-four hours, doctors to inform women of alternatives to abortion, and minors to obtain parental consent or the consent of a judge in order to receive abortions. In *Planned Parenthood of Southeastern Pennsylvania* v. *Casey,* the Supreme Court upheld the law arguing that as long as laws do not place "an undue burden" on women seeking abortions, states may regulate the procedure.[12]

In 1997 pro-life forces drew attention to a type of abortion performed during the later stages of pregnancy. Pro-choice forces called this procedure "dilation and extraction," while pro-life forces called it "partial-birth abortion." Pro-life advocates emphasized the procedure's brutality, and pro-choice forces argued that it was used infrequently and only if the health of the mother was clearly at risk. Nevertheless, a new chapter in the abortion debate opened, and Congress passed bills outlawing the procedure in 1996 and 1997. President Bill Clinton vetoed both bills, arguing the need for some form of late-term abortion to prevent the deaths of women who could not carry their pregnancies to term.[13]

The development in 1988 of **RU-486,** a pill that terminates pregnancy without surgical intervention, added another issue to the abortion debate. The Food and Drug Administration approved the drug as safe and effective in September 2000. The pro-life lobby immediately began a boycott of all products of Roussel-Uclaf, the company that manufactured the drug.[14] In addition, pro-life advocates introduced legislation in many states to restrict access to RU-486 or limit the number of physicians who could prescribe the drug. With the election of George W. Bush, Republicans in Congress joined the White House in an effort to further restrict access to abortion. In 2001 House panels began working on proposals to provide penalties to anyone harming a fetus during an attack on a pregnant woman and federal restrictions on access to RU-486.

Dissension over abortion has led to violence. Some extreme pro-life advocates argue that violence in defense of an unborn fetus is a moral obligation. Women's health centers that perform abortions have sustained years of violent attacks. Health care workers who perform abortions or work in facilities that do have been murdered and singled out for other attacks. In 1993 a member of an extreme antiabortion group called Rescue America murdered Dr. David Gunn. In 1994 Dr. John Britton was murdered. In 1995 an antiabortion advocate murdered two receptionists at a family-planning clinic in Massachusetts. Bombings of abortion clinics have been frequent.[15] In the aftermath of the terrorist attack of September 11, 2001, and the associated anthrax scare, abortion clinics received hundreds of letters containing substances that were claimed to be anthrax (all were hoaxes). The debate and civil disorder continue.

STEM CELL RESEARCH

The federal government has a long connection with science in America. Several of the early U.S. leaders, most notably Benjamin Franklin and Thomas Jefferson, were advocates of and active participants in the advance of science.[16] Prior to the Civil War the government sent Lewis and Clark to explore and map the frontier, surveyed the coasts, and established the Army Corp of Engineers, the U.S. Military Academy, and the Smithsonian Institution. During the Civil War the Navy began to use technical advisers and scientists. In recognition of the need for interaction between science and the government, Congress founded the National Academy of Science in 1863.[17]

The interaction of science and government continued to expand during the twentieth century. The National Bureau of Standards was set up in 1901, the Public Health Service in 1912, and the National Advisory Committee for Aeronautics (NACA) in 1915. Scientists participated in the administration and regulation of such legislation as the Pure Food and Drug Act of 1906. The Navy, in its search for better weaponry, asked Thomas Edison to head a naval consulting board charged with researching military applications of chemistry, aeronautics, and explosives. This board was the basis of the Naval Research Laboratory, which was created after World War I. During World War I President Wilson created the National Research Council (NRC) as an offshoot of the National Academy of Sciences to help coordinate science for the war effort. The NRC worked on optics and gas warfare, thus establishing a permanent link between these industries and the federal government.[18] Universities were also brought into the war effort and were involved, along with industry, in research and development sponsored by the government.

The Great Depression and the administration of Franklin D. Roosevelt (FDR) increased government interest in sponsoring scientific research. In 1933 the Presidential Science Advisory Board was founded, in large part to consider solutions to the economic downturn and unemployment among scientists. In 1937 the National Resources Committee embarked on a survey of scientific activity in government, universities, and industry.[19] This study concluded that research and development activities might help bring about economic recovery.

World War II radically changed the relationship of science and government. The early success of the Nazi's technology-based assault on England reaffirmed the military advantage offered by new technologies, and the U.S. government turned to scientists for help with war preparations. The weapons and the institutional structures that emerged from World War II revolutionized the world.[20] Scientists also became dependent on government funding to pay for their research.

The importance of the new arrangement between government and science was underscored by Vannevar Bush.[21] In *Science: The Endless Frontier* he showed the importance of science to national security and the advancement of medicine and argued that scientific research led to innovation and prosperity. Bush called for the establishment of a national organization to channel federal monies into basic research projects. After five years of controversy, the National Science Foundation (NSF) emerged. The creation of the national labs (for example, Sandia, Lawrence Livermore, Brookhaven, and Oak Ridge) further strengthened the link of scientists to the federal government. Scientists at universities grew increasingly dependent on federal funding from the Department of Defense, the Department of Energy, the **National Institutes of Health** (NIH), and the National Science Foundation.

Since the 1930s the biological community has used human fetal tissue as a medium and object of experimentation. Fetal tissue has been used for the production and testing of vaccines, the study of viruses, and the testing of many biological products. Allegations about the improper use of fetal tissue arose in the 1970s, fueled by the legalization of abortion and questions about the use of tissue from aborted fetuses for research. Congress established a National Commission for the Protection of Human Subjects of Biomedical and Behavioral Research in 1974 and instructed it to consider the use of fetal tissue. Federal regulations flowing from the commission's recommendations specified that tissues from dead fetuses should be used in accordance with state or local laws. The NIH mandated that research on tissues from fetuses should not involve any activity on the part of researchers to terminate a pregnancy and forbade payments as inducements to abort a pregnancy.[22]

In the 1980s scientists began experimenting with implanting brain tissue from aborted fetuses into patients with Parkinson's disease. NIH scientists were part of this effort. In 1988 the Department of Health and Human Services (HHS) instructed NIH to temporarily ban the use of any fetal material from induced abortions and to cease funding any research using such material. While NIH wanted to reinstate the research, the secretary of HHS extended the moratorium indefinitely in 1989. When President Clinton came to office, he rescinded the ban. A 1993 NIH Revitalization Act stipulated the terms under which NIH could use fetal tissue. The primary condition was that the use of the material was for "therapeutic" purposes. Transplantation research on Parkinson's disease was covered under this provision, but other research aimed at culturing and growing fetal tissue for experimentation was not.[23] Privately funded research could move in this direction, but federally supported research was prohibited.

Stem cell research is a new, controversial scientific technique. Stem cells have the potential to grow into any type of tissue the body needs to repair itself, and in 1999 and 2000 scientists first isolated them from human embryos and fetuses. This amazing discovery raised the hope of cures for countless diseases, assuming that scientists could learn how to make the cells grow into the types of tissues needed. Many people found the use of human embryos for experimentation troubling.[24] Would this line of research promote abortion to provide researchers with stems cells to study? Should researchers be permitted to clone a human being to provide a never-ending source of stem cells? Should stem cell research even be legal? What role should the government play in promoting this type of research? Since the research could not be performed in the absence of direct government funding, should the government fund research that uses human embryos or fetuses?

Government funding of scientific research has the potential to become controversial, especially when a major government science institution takes a strong stand on an advancement that is a matter of public concern and debate. NIH leadership argued that stem cell research had the potential to revolutionize medicine and improve the quality and length of human life. Opponents argued that a 1995 federal ban on using human embryos for research applied to stem cells. Congress and NIH went to work to fashion a solution.[25] Stem cell research raised the ethical question of when life begins, and like many problems that involve ethical considerations, the issue rapidly became politically charged. Does an embryo have the same status as a human being? Do the few cells that constitute the days-old embryonic material from which stem cells can be extracted constitute human life?

The first stem cells used for research were extracted from embryos that had been created in fertility clinics but were not suitable for implanting into a human womb. Others came from abortions. Because of the ban on using human embryos for publicly funded research, early work on stem cells used private sources of money.[26] But for stem cell research to move on, the vast sums that only the federal government could provide were necessary, and the decision of whether the scientific community should proceed with stem cell research became a political one.

Many antiabortion groups and the Catholic Church oppose the use of embryonic stem cells for research and do not want the government to fund this research. They argue that life begins at conception, no matter how primitively, and that microscopic day-old embryos deserve the same protection as any other human life. These groups also worry about the use of cloned embryonic cells in research. Victims of diseases who hope to benefit from therapies resulting from stem cell research also argue for the value of human life—their own lives. They maintain that the government should think about them before making a funding decision.

Another potential source of human stem cells is cloning those already in possession of scientists. If such a process is possible, it would provide cells for research without involving the ethics of abortion. Of course, cloning human embryo cells itself arouses significant controversy. In March 1997 President Clinton released a Presidential Directive prohibiting the use of federal funds for cloning[27] and a Statement of Administration Policy allowing cloning for the purpose of developing stem cells for laboratory experimentation.

In summer 2002 the White House tried to put the issue to rest with a compromise that will probably satisfy no one for very long. President George W. Bush agreed to allow federal funding for already-existing stem cell lines, or colonies, that can be cultured and grown in laboratories. This compromise decision allows promising research to go forward while avoiding the ethical dilemma associated with such research. Specifically, it allows government-funded research on the sixty-four lines of stem cells already taken from human embryos. No new lines are allowed. According to the NIH, the scientists who developed these stem cell lines have said that they can be cultured and that they have been through more than one population doubling.[28]

The people and groups who staunchly advocate no use of embryonic tissue drawn from induced abortions, such as the Catholic Church, opposed this decision. It is likely that the sixty-four lines will prove to be inadequate for the research that scientists want to do. If this turns out to be the case, the issue of government support for stem cell research will reemerge and along with it the controversy over the use of aborted fetal tissue and cloned material.

GUN CONTROL

Heated debate frequently results from discussion of the **Second Amendment** to the Constitution: "A well regulated militia, being necessary to the security of a free state, the right of the people to keep and bear arms, shall not be infringed." Few issues polarize Americans as much as whether access to guns can be denied, limited, or controlled. There are strong lobbies and vocal interest groups on both sides of the debate.

People who oppose gun control argue that any attempt to control access to guns is prohibited by the Second Amendment. Those who favor controlling guns point to crime statistics. For instance, in 1993, the year with the highest gun toll, 39,595 Americans were killed by guns. Handguns were involved in 71 percent of those deaths. Suicides accounted for 48 percent of gun deaths, homicides for 47 percent, accidents for 4 percent, and police killings for 1 percent. In addition, 104,390 people sought medical attention for gunshot wounds.[29] This is an enormous toll.

Of the advanced industrialized nations, the United States is the only one that allows large numbers of citizens to own guns. The current level of gun ownership is no doubt a legacy of our history. For the first several hundred years of the development of the nation, settlers were primarily agrarian and were moving west. Wild game was an important source of food for them. Unlike Europe, where the common people were not allowed to hunt for game, in America the settlers could roam and hunt freely. Guns also provided safety from animal and Indian attacks.

Their familiarity with rifles explains a certain amount of the colonists' success against the British during the Revolutionary War. As Richard Hofstadter pointed out, the success of armed frontiersmen against well-trained British soldiers became a symbolic part of American culture. Likewise, the winning of the West became part of that culture. The image of the gunfighter legitimized violence, and it later was expanded to include police, FBI agents, private eyes, and even gangsters.[30]

History also explains why the United States adopted the Second Amendment. Americans feared the damage done by the standing armies prevalent in Europe, which often plundered the citizenry at the command of political rulers. Their answer was a militia of armed yeomen.[31] Despite complaints by George Washington and other early American military leaders that the militia was ineffective (especially in comparison to the well-disciplined Continental Army), the myth holds that American freedom was won by the armed yeoman militia.[32]

Drawing their strength from the Second Amendment, vocal opponents of gun control frequently operate on the "foot-in-the-door" theory that suggests that any and all attempts to regulate arms must be resisted with full force because minimal regulation will quickly lead to prohibition.[33] The most vocal interest group with this point of view is the **National Rifle Association**

(NRA). Membership dues of its more than 2 million members give the NRA considerable power in funding candidates for political office. Despite their power, however, some highly salient murders and attempted murders of public officials have resulted in a body of federal gun control legislation.

The **Gun Control Act,** which resulted from the assassinations of President John F. Kennedy in 1963 and of the Reverend Dr. Martin Luther King, Jr., and Robert F. Kennedy in 1968, was passed in 1968. It prohibited traffic in guns and ammunition between the states; denied convicted felons, drug addicts, the mentally ill, and minors access to arms; and banned the importation of surplus military firearms. The act was one of the most contentious laws passed by Congress in the post–World War II era, and gun advocates fought against it until the **Firearms Owner's Protection Act of 1986** relaxed some of its provisions.[34]

The **Brady Bill** or Brady Handgun Violence Prevention Act of 1993 was a result of the attempted assassination of President Reagan in 1981. The president and three others were wounded, among them James S. Brady, the president's press secretary. His wife worked diligently for passage of the law. Despite strong opposition from the NRA and others, the bill eventually won the support of Congress. The Brady Act requires a waiting period for the purchase of a gun until an instant check system to identify known criminals is developed. President Clinton signed the law in 1993 and also signed a **ban on assault weapons** that was part of the **Violent Crime Control Act of 1994**.[35] Like other measures to control guns, this ban was controversial, and pro-gun forces including the NRA vigorously lobbied against it.

In 1997 a sixteen-year-old student in Pearl, Mississippi, killed his mother and then killed nine students at school. In Jonesboro, Arkansas, in 1998 a thirteen-year-old and an eleven-year-old murdered four students and a teacher. At Thurston High School in Oregon a fifteen-year-old murdered his parents and killed another student. In 1999 fifteen people were murdered at Columbine High School in a suburb of Denver. The effect of these massacres was increased demand for gun control. Despite the bitter opposition of the NRA, Congress tightened loopholes in the Brady Bill and made a three-day waiting period mandatory for anyone who attempted to buy a weapon at a gun show. This legislation also required safety devices on handguns and included a ban on importing high-capacity ammunition clips.[36]

One hot-button issue that has yet to be resolved is the movement in some states to pass **concealed-carry laws.** Advocates of such laws argue that crime will be deterred if potential criminals believe that other people could use concealed weapons against them. Opponents decry the return to the "wild West" where people are responsible for their own personal safety rather than being protected by a peaceful civil order. A second controversial issue involves attempts by local governments to sue gun manufacturers for manufacture of "unsafe products." Modeling their suits after tobacco legislation, they argue that the gun manufacturers should be made to reimburse cities for the money spent in dealing with gun violence.[37]

GLOBAL TRADE

Americans are divided over whether **globalization**—worldwide economic integration—is good or bad. Globalization raises a host of ethical questions. If it leads to the sacrifice of jobs at home, what responsibility does the government have to help displaced workers and domestic industries? How can Americans compete with foreign laborers willing to work for much lower wages? Which organizations and institutions have the power to control the behavior of international corporations? Do the developed nations have a moral responsibility to the developing world? Should the government prohibit the importation of goods that were manufactured by child or slave labor? Should the government prohibit the importation of goods that were manufactured by adult workers in conditions that are unacceptable in the United States?

International trade has been expanding since a series of trade agreements known as **GATT,** the **General Agreement on Tariffs and Trade,** were negotiated after World War II and periodically renegotiated thereafter. GATT was based on the belief that free trade benefits all nations. The agreements discouraged national subsidies to industrial sectors in an effort to create a level playing field internationally. GATT envisioned a world free of borders where trade would be free flowing.

Those who favor global economic integration argue that, at least since the publication of Adam Smith's *Wealth of Nations* in 1776, economists have agreed that open markets and free trade are the route to better standards of living for a number of reasons. First, it is more efficient for a nation to specialize in what it does best and to trade for other goods than to produce all needed products. Second, trade makes overall production more efficient, thereby reducing the price of goods and services. Trade enhances product variety, and increased competition raises product quality. Finally, those who promote globalization argue that trade promotes innovation in both products and production processes, from which we all benefit.[38]

GATT was replaced by the **World Trade Organization (WTO)** in 1994. The WTO's mission is to increase the volume and extent of trade among member nations (the United States is a member nation). The WTO does not operate under democratic rules. WTO processes are secret, and representatives to the WTO are not elected in a democratic process by member nations. The WTO has the authority to demand repeal of a member nation's domestic laws if they are believed to interfere illegally with trade. In the case of disputes, corporations have access to the WTO, but individuals do not.[39]

There are also regional free-trade agreements. The **North American Free Trade Agreement (NAFTA)** between the United States, Canada, and Mexico opens the borders to trade. Negotiated under fast-track authority, NAFTA was signed by President Clinton in 1992, but he did not submit it to Congress for ratification until 1993, when he also sent a supplementary environmental agreement. The expansion of NAFTA to all of South America is currently being negotiated by the Bush administration. Europe entered into a free-trade agreement that eventually resulted in the formation of the

European Union (EU), in which member nations use a common currency. The **Association of the South–East Asian Nations (ASEAN)** is yet another free-trade agreement, and there is considerable regional integration in southern and western Africa and among the nations of the Arab League.[40]

Critics of global economic integration think that it may reduce **national sovereignty,** the right of nation-states to control their domestic policies. They point to public policies that were previously under exclusive control of nation-states that are now controlled by international groups or agreements. The WTO and NAFTA require the surrender of some levels of national control in exchange for the benefits of open markets. For instance, subsidies given to the U.S. agricultural sector since the Dust Bowl of the 1920s are called into question under NAFTA and WTO. Two other major concerns are the consequences of global trade for environmental protection and jobs. Opponents of multinational agreements are concerned that environmental protection policies are subject to the agreements. As a result of several trade disputes, the WTO ruled that domestic environmental protections are in violation of free trade. This ruling enraged opponents of economic globalization. Opponents frequently argue that U.S. jobs will be lost as manufacturing companies seek less expensive sources of labor in developing nations. Proponents of global trade counter that these agreements are entered into under democratic processes that include presidential signature and congressional ratification, so they do not constitute a threat to national sovereignty.[41]

Opponents of trade liberalization also argue that it encourages consumerism, increases the speed of consumption of the world's limited natural resources, and works against the creation of sustainable economies focusing on production for local markets. They suggest that increased trade will result in increased transport, causing more energy use and accidents. Critics see the focus on producing commodities for export and consuming imported products as a recipe for world ecological disaster.[42]

Controversies over globalization have provoked conflict. Civil protests have accompanied meetings of WTO and NAFTA, demonstrating that many people find these agreements troublesome. Violent protests by anarchists and other radical groups have attempted to disrupt further worldwide economic integration.[43]

IMMIGRATION

By and large, the United States is a nation of immigrants. In pre–Civil War America agrarian immigrants came mostly from the Protestant nations of western and northern Europe. The forced immigration of enslaved people was mostly from Africa.[44] After the Civil War Catholic and Jewish immigrants came from eastern and southeastern Europe to work in industries. Asian immigrants joined the mix in the late 1800s. The United States had a long-standing need for labor and welcomed the immigrants. About a quarter of a million immigrants arrived between the 1780s and 1820s, with another 6.5 million arriving by the time of the Civil War. From the Civil War to 1880, 5 million more immigrants came to America.

Opposition to immigration gradually increased after the 1820s and escalated by the 1880s. Immigrants were blamed for urban poverty, political corruption, and infectious diseases. A "nativist" movement resulted in laws restricting immigration. The first was the 1888 **Chinese Exclusion Act.** In 1904 the so-called **Gentlemen's Agreement** reduced Japanese immigration. The **1906 Naturalization Act** made the ability to speak English a requirement of citizenship. Restrictions on owning land were imposed on Japanese people in several states. The 1917 Immigration Act imposed further restrictions. Within the United States the Ku Klux Klan, American Coalition, Immigrant Restriction League, and American Protective League of True Americans increased their membership. The **1921 Quota Act** limited the number of immigrants to 3 percent of those of same nationality living in the nation in 1890. The **1924 Quota Act** required immigrants to obtain visas before leaving their homes; its goal was to restrict immigration from places other than northern Europe; an unanticipated consequence was an increase in illegal immigration. The 1940 Alien Registration Act required fingerprinting and registration of new immigrants.[45]

Immigration restrictions were somewhat eased by the **1948 Displaced Persons Act,** which permitted the settlement of displaced persons from World War II. The **1952 Immigration and Nationality Act** reinstated the quota system and alien registration. It included a preference for skilled laborers and relatives of citizens and resident aliens. The 1965 Immigration and Nationality Act abolished the quota system, established numerical limits in order of preference (spouses, parents, children, professionals, skilled workers, refugees), and limited the annual number of immigrants from the Eastern Hemisphere to 170,000 and from the Western Hemisphere to 120,000. As a result, illegal immigration increased, as did public demands to do something about it. The limits also created great backlogs and long waits for immigration. In the 1970s the law was changed to allow 20,000 immigrants from each country in the Western Hemisphere.

In the 1980s the government's attention turned to illegal immigrants, granting **amnesty** and temporary residency to those who had been living in the United States for a long time. To reduce future illegal immigration, employment of undocumented workers was banned, and employers who hired them were penalized. Border patrols were increased. The **Illegal Immigration Reform and Immigrant Responsibility Act of 1996** doubled the number of border patrols, and further restrictions were placed on new immigrants. To sponsor a relative, a family was required to earn 125 percent of the poverty level, and the law permitted states to deny Social Security, food stamps, SSI, and nonemergency Medicaid to illegal immigrants and to deny food stamps, SSI, and Medicaid to legal immigrants. This law created a loud outcry, and Congress was forced to allow benefits to legal immigrants who received green cards— the legal right to live and work in the United States—prior to 1996.[46]

There is considerable debate about whether immigrants are a pool of needed labor or a drain on the economy. Immigrants have a substantial impact on schools, social services, and other infrastructure. Some suggest that immigrants pay more in taxes than they absorb in services, while others believe that the opposite is true. The United States is the only industrialized nation with a growing population. People who are concerned about population growth and its effect on the environment point out that much of this population growth is due to immigration and the high birthrate of recent immigrants.[47] Another controversial issue surrounding immigration is revealed in combination with general shifts in the nation's demographics. The largest growing groups are Asians and Hispanics. It is revealing that in 2001 George W. Bush became the first president to give his weekly presidential radio address in both English and Spanish.

After years of lax immigration enforcement, the terrorist attacks of September 11, 2001, moved immigration control to the top of the government's agenda. All nineteen of the hijackers were foreign-born and were living in the United States on temporary visas or in violation of visa conditions. Six months later, the **Immigration and Naturalization Service (INS)** made headlines when it was reported that the INS approved student visas for two of the hijackers. Congressional outrage at INS inability to monitor immigration for security purposes grew rapidly, and President Bush expressed astonishment at the agency's failure.[48]

For years, prior to September 11, thousands of illegal immigrants had found ways into the country in order to find work. For years local police departments had resisted rounding up illegal aliens and handing them over to the INS for deportation. Since September 11, however, a growing number of police forces are putting resources into just such efforts. Florida became the first state to have its police deputized as INS agents with authority to arrest those overstaying their visas or entering the country illegally.

The INS, which has only 1,947 agents, sees partnerships with local law enforcement as essential.[49] But such partnerships raise civil liberties concerns. Should local law enforcement personnel stop all who appear to be foreign-born and subject them to interrogation? How will attempts to guarantee security within our nation interfere with our deeply cherished liberty, which includes freedom of movement? Should we even try to close our very porous borders so that no illegal immigrants can get through? Can a large country that is designed to be an open society even consider such an idea?[50]

As a result of the fear that there are people within our borders who seek to harm us, innocent Middle Eastern and Muslim immigrants and citizens were targeted for scrutiny. The government made a concerted effort to identify and round up Middle Eastern and Muslim immigrants who were illegally residing in the United States, and the Justice Department used immigration laws to arrest hundreds of Muslim men for visa expirations and to hold them for months as terrorist suspects.[51]

Controversy over immigration is not new. Throughout our history the nation has struggled to absorb the foreign-born into American life and culture. In recent years we reached another peak in the number of immigrants coming to America and concern about the high numbers. Efforts in the 1990s to deny newly arrived immigrants access to social services led to considerable controversy. After the

2001 terrorist attacks attention turned to security and the need to assure the public that immigrants are not a threat to public safety. The tension between maintaining an open society willing to accept the foreign-born and issues of security and equity shows no clear short-term resolution.

SUMMARY

Many important areas of public policy do not make the list of the most expensive. The policy areas discussed in this chapter are examples of policies that have great importance but do not demand resources to the extent that other policy areas do. The policies discussed here are controversial in large part because a stand taken on any of them requires a deep consideration of moral and ethical values. Decisions about use of stem cells and the appropriateness of abortion challenge us to weigh the value of human life and to ask whether we most value a fetus or a woman, a sick person or an embryo. Gun control, global trade, and immigration force us to consider the place of the individual in our society and whether we are willing to restrict individual rights so that other concerns can be addressed. These five areas are examples of the many policy areas that ask us to make such choices.

KEY TERMS

abortion gag rule

amnesty

Association of the South-East Asian Nations (ASEAN)

ban on assault weapons

Brady Bill

Chinese Exclusion Act

concealed-carry laws

Displaced Persons Act (1948)

European Union (EU)

Firearms Owner's Protection Act of 1986

General Agreement on Tariffs and Trade (GATT)

Gentlemen's Agreement

globalization

Gun Control Act

Illegal Immigration Reform and Immigrant Responsibility Act of 1996

Immigration and Nationality Act (1952)

Immigration and Naturalization Service (INS)

international trade

National Institutes of Health

National Rifle Association (NRA)

national sovereignty

Naturalization Act (1906)

North American Free Trade Agreement (NAFTA)

pro-choice

pro-life

Quota Act (1921, 1924)

right to privacy

Roe v. Wade

RU-486

Second Amendment

Violent Crime Control Act of 1994

World Trade Organization (WTO)

WEB SITES

http://www.washingtonpost.com/
wp-srv/onpolitics/elections/debate
This site contains a transcript of the presidential debate between Al Gore and George W. Bush in which they were asked about the then recently approved abortion pill, RU-486. The site has the statements of both candidates on the pill and abortion.

http://escr.nih.gov/
A site of the National Institutes of Health that details the policy on stem cell research as specified by President George W. Bush and lists the locations of laboratories that currently have stem cell lines for research.

http://www.cnn.com/SPECIALS/1998/schools/
CNN's detailed account of school shootings with links to information on gun control legislation in each of the states and several *Time* magazine sources on guns and violence.

http://nra.org/
The National Rifle Association Web site contains an extensive overview of the interest group's position.

http://www.ins.usdoj.gov/graphics/index.htm
The Immigration and Naturalization Service (INS) site has links to a variety of statistics on immigration.

http://www.wto.org/
The site of the World Trade Organization provides current information on trade disputes and about the trade association itself.

DISCUSSION QUESTIONS

1. Given the fact that the Supreme Court maintains that a woman has a constitutional right to an abortion, to what extent should the government support providers of abortion services in their efforts? Does the government support abortion alternatives? Should it?

2. Is it right for the government to fund scientific research that uses fetal tissue if such research could lead to cures for serious diseases? Should it make a difference if the tissue is from induced abortions? Why?

3. Should cities have the right to sue gun manufacturers for the damage caused by gun violence? Why?

4. Under current rules, the WTO can rule that a state or federal environmental law is in violation of international trade agreements and that the United States must pay damages to corporations harmed by such laws. Do you think this compromises national sovereignty? Does it conflict with democracy? Why?

5. Should legal immigrants have the same rights to social service as nonimmigrants? What about illegal immigrants?

WEB QUESTIONS

1. Go to http://www.washingtonpost.com/wp-srv/onpolitics/elections/debate and find the statements on abortion and RU–486 made by President George W. Bush and Al Gore when they were running for office. What were their positions?

2. Go to the NIH site on stem cell research at http://escr.nih.gov/. What terms for use of stem cells were specified by President George W. Bush?

3. At the INS Web site at http://www.ins.usdoj.gov/graphics/index.htm, find out how many immigrants came into the United States last year.

4. At http://www.wto.org/ find out where the WTO is located.

NOTES

1. Lee Epstein and Joseph F. Kobylka, *The Supreme Court and Legal Change* (Chapel Hill, NC: The University of North Carolina Press, 1992).

2. Ibid.

3. Mark A. Graber, *Rethinking Abortion: Equal Choice, the Constitution, and Reproductive Politics* (Princeton, NJ: Princeton University Press, 1996).

4. Epstein and Kobylka, *The Supreme Court and Legal Change.*

5. Ibid.

6. Ibid.

7. Clarke E. Cochran, Lawrence C. Mayer, T. R. Carr, and N. Joseph Cayer, *American Public Policy: An Introduction,* 6th ed. (New York: St. Martin's, 1999).

8. Christopher E. Smith, *Courts, Politics, and the Judicial Process,* 2d ed. (Chicago: Nelson-Hall Publishers, 1997).

9. Bob Packwood, "The Rise and Fall of the Right-to-Life Movement in Congress: Response to the *Roe* Decision, 1973–83," in *Abortion, Medicine, and the Law*, 4th ed., ed. J. Douglas Butler and David F. Walbert (New York: Facts on File, 1992), 629–665.

10. Barbara Hinkson Craig and David M.

O'Brien, *Abortion and American Politics* (Chatham, NJ: Chatham House Publishers, 1993).

11. Laurence H. Tribe, *Abortion: The Clash of Absolutes* (New York: W. W. Norton & Company, 1990).

12. Craig and O'Brien, *Abortion and American Politics.*

13. Cochran et al., *American Public Policy.*

14. Lawrence Lader, *RU 486: The Pill That Could End the Abortion Wars and Why American Women Don't Have It* (Reading, MA: Addison-Wesley Publishing Company, 1991).

15. Cochran et al., *American Public Policy.*

16. A. Hunter Dupree, *Science in the Federal Government: A History of Politics and Activities to 1940* (Cambridge, MA: The Belknap Press of Harvard University Press, 1957).

17. J. Stefan Dupre and Sanford A. Lakoff, *Science and the Nation: Policy and Politics* (Englewood Cliffs, NJ: Prentice-Hall, 1962).

18. Ibid.

19. National Resources Committee, *Research—A National Resource*

(Washington, DC: U.S. Government Printing Office, 1938).

20. Herbert I. Fusfeld, *The Technical Enterprise: Present and Future Patterns* (Cambridge, MA: Ballinger Publishing Company, 1986).

21. Vannevar Bush, *Science: The Endless Frontier. A Report to the President on a Program for Postwar Scientific Research* (Washington, DC: National Science Foundation, 1945).

22. National Bioethics Advisory Commission, *Ethical Issues in Human Stem Cell Research* (Rockville, MD: National Bioethics Advisory Commission, 1999).

23. Ibid.

24. Adriel Bettelheim, "Embryo Research," in *Issues in Social Policy* (Washington, DC: CQ Press, 2000), 61–77.

25. Ibid.

26. Ibid.

27. National Bioethics Advisory Commission, *Ethical Issues in Human Stem Cell Research*.

28. National Institutes of Health, *Update on Existing Human Embryonic Stem Cells,* August 27, 2001. http://www.nih.gov/news/stemcell/ 082701list.htm (3/17/02).

29. Lee Nisbet, "Introduction," in *The Gun Control Debate You Decide,* ed. Lee Nisbet (Amherst, NY: Prometheus Books, 2001), 13–22.

30. Richard Hofstadter, "America as a Gun Culture," in *The Gun Control Debate You Decide,* ed. Lee Nisbet (Amherst, NY: Prometheus Books, 2001), 29–37.

31. Alexander DeConde, *Gun Violence in America: The Struggle for Control* (Boston: Northeastern University Press, 2001).

32. Hofstadter, "America as a Gun Culture."

33. Samuel C. Patterson and Keith R. Eakins, "Congress and Gun Control," in *The Changing Politics of Gun Control,* ed. John M. Bruce and Clyde Wilcox (Lanham, MD: Rowman & Littlefield, 1998), 45–73.

34. Ibid.

35. Ibid.

36. DeConde, *Gun Violence in America.*

37. William J. Vizzard, *Shots in the Dark: The Policy, Politics, and Symbolism of Gun Control* (Lanham, MD: Rowman & Littlefield, 2000).

38. Gary Burtless, Robert Z. Lawrence, Robert E. Litan, and Robert J. Shapiro, *Globaphobia: Confronting Fears About Open Trade* (Washington, DC: Brookings, 1998).

39. Amory Starr, *Naming the Enemy: Anti-corporate Movements Confront Globalization* (London: Zed Books, 2000).

40. Ali M. El-Agraa, *Economic Integration Worldwide* (New York: St. Martin's Press, 1997).

41. Burtless et al., *Globaphobia.*

42. Starr, *Naming the Enemy.*

43. Alice Landau, *Redrawing the Global Economy: Elements of Integration and Fragmentation* (New York: Palgrave, 2001).

44. John Kingdon, *America the Unusual* (New York: St. Martin's Press, 1998).

45. Cochran et al., *American Public Policy.*

46. Ibid.

47. Michael E. Kraft, *Environmental Policy and Politics* (New York: HarperCollins College Publishers, 1996).

48. Eric Schmitt, "Agency Finds itself Under Siege, With Many Responsibilities and Many Critics," *The New York Times,* March 15, 2002. http://www.nytimes.com/2002/03/15/ politics/15INS.html (3/15/02).

49. Susan Scahs, "Long Resistant, Police Now Start Embracing Immigration Enforcement," *The New York Times,* March 15, 2002. http://www.nytimes.com/2002/03/15/ national/15IMMI.html (3/15/02).

50. David Carr, "The Futility of Homeland Defense," *Atlantic Monthly,* January 2002, 53–55.

51. Scahs, "Long Resistant, Police Now Start Embracing Immigration Enforcement."

Index

Note: Page numbers in *italic* refer to illustrations.